PARADOX OF POWER

PARADOX
OF
POWER

THE UNITED STATES IN SOUTHWEST ASIA, 1973-1984

MAYA CHADDA

**FOREWORD BY
AFAF MARSOT**

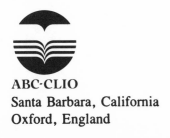

ABC-CLIO
Santa Barbara, California
Oxford, England

© 1986 by Maya Chadda

Cover and book design by Tanya Cullen

Library of Congress Cataloging in Publication Data

Chadda, Maya, 1943-
  Paradox of power.

  Bibliography: p.
  Includes index.
  1. Near East—Foreign relations—United States.
2. United States—Foreign relations—Near East.
3. United States—Foreign relations—1945-
I. Title.
DS63.2.U5C43 1985   327.73056   85-13486
ISBN 0-87436-454-X (alk. paper)
ISBN 0-87436-455-8 (pbk. : alk. paper)

10   9   8   7   6   5   4   3   2   1

ABC-Clio, Inc.
2040 Alameda Padre Serra, Box 4397
Santa Barbara, California 93140-4397

Clio Press Ltd.
55 St. Thomas Street
Oxford OX1, 1JG, England

This book is printed on acid-free paper ∞ .
Manufactured in the United States of America

To Vijay

Contents

Foreword

Aside from Latin America, the Middle East is perhaps the most critical area of interest to U.S. foreign policy. Not only is this because of the region's strategic presence athwart three continents, or the presence of the USSR on its frontiers, but also because of its mineral resources, oil, and its potential for international conflict, which might conceivably lead to a further world war. The area examined in this work does not, however, limit itself to the Middle East proper, but more cogently includes the region of Afghanistan and the Indian subcontinent, which the author rightly perceives as forming one unit, Southwest Asia.

The past few decades have seen the appearance of a number of works dealing with one aspect or another of Middle Eastern events and attempting to explain them in the light of U.S. interests and perceptions, or vice versa. This work, on the other hand, explains how changes in U.S. policy affected the region of Southwest Asia. Studies of U.S. global policies are not new. What is new is the approach used in examining these policies, from 1973 to 1984, and the conclusions reached. In this work the author examines U.S. policies over three administrations and shows how the ideological matrix of these administrations affected foreign policies, as indeed did the domestic determinants present during each presidential era. One can describe this book as a study of the working of a hegemonic power, for it examines the ideologies that guided the world view of one such power, the United States, that rationalized its actions, and that led to its opting for one decision over another. It also examines the domestic events that weighted decisions in the directions of policy finally taken.

The year 1979 was a critical year for U.S. foreign policy. There was a change in Soviet military capabilities and a popular perception within the United States of a decline in U.S. power as the outcome of certain events. That perception later led to the defeat of Carter as president and the installation of a new president with a new style and a different ideology. Previous presidents were confident in U.S. strength, and they pursued a foreign policy that was characterized by diplomacy. The new president saw the United States as operating from a position of weakness and accentuated the military option over the diplomatic. These changes in foreign policy naturally had repercussions in Southwest Asia, as Dr. Chadda ably shows, some of which exacerbated the perception of U.S. decline in the region.

Such perceptions notwithstanding, what clearly comes through in this work is that the author believes that the United States did have consistent objectives in the region and has largely been successful in achieving them, despite the fact that these objectives were often ambiguous, making a perfect record impossible and allowing for occasional setbacks.

Such a notion belies the thesis of a decline of U.S. power in the region. Secondly, it shows how the United States as hegemon has not become reconciled to multipolarity, which it consequently regards as weakness. When the United States seeks to "resolve" that perceived weakness by the option of force or coercion or intimidation, it finds itself enmeshed in a pattern of mistakes in its dealings with the region of Southwest Asia, which reinforces the perception of weakness. The author concludes that the paradox of power is that, even from a position of strength, the United States believes it is weak, opts for the use of force, and finds that the hoped for ends are seldom achieved with that option. The final paradox is that coercion and intimidation are the least successful weapons in the arsenal of the hegemon; to the contrary, it is most successful when it uses the option of diplomacy.

This work is interesting in its novel approach to events and in its well-reasoned argument. It presents events from different viewpoints—local, interregional, and international—which allows the reader to situate events within wide parameters. As a multilevel study it is both original and stimulating, so that, while one may disagree with the author's conclusions or interpretations, one can do no less than accept the merits of the presentation. The conclusion that the use of force does not lead to peace is one that all of us should take to heart.

Afaf Lutfi al-Sayyid Marsot
Professor, Near and Middle Eastern History
University of California, Los Angeles

Preface

The strategic wisdom of the Reagan administration is based on the premise that during the 1970s the United States was in retreat around the globe, while the Soviet Union had aggressively advanced its influence everywhere. A major focus of this new strategic equation was Southwest Asia. "The umbilical cord of the industrialized free world runs through the Straits of Hormuz into the Arabian Gulf and the nations which surround it," said Defense Secretary Caspar Weinberger in March 1981. "That area, Southwest Asia and the Gulf, is and will be the fulcrum of contention for the foreseeable future."

This book takes issue with the "thesis of U.S. decline" as expounded and applied to the events in Southwest Asia during the 1970s and the early 1980s. First, it demonstrates that the setbacks of those years were not a consequence of U.S. military weakness; they were a natural result of political conflicts that were local and indigenous in origin. Second, it questions the merit of policies flowing from these assumptions of U.S. weakness and Soviet strength. While the Reagan administration's "military first" approach might have gained temporary advantages in the region, it has nonetheless failed to build structures of enduring influence, including formal or informal peace agreements. Third, the book points out that, while successive administrations since the 1970s (and perhaps even earlier) have pursued different priorities in Southwest Asia, their policy choices have oscillated between recognizable alternatives. There is a pattern to U.S. mistakes and successes that corresponds to the balance between force and diplomacy in its policies. Last, the book asserts that despite the setbacks suffered in 1979 with the Islamic revolution and the Soviet invasion of Afghanistan, and the life-and-death significance conferred upon the Persian Gulf by Western dependence on Arab oil, the United States remained the prominent external influence in Southwest Asia. It was the United States, and not the Soviet Union, that was more in a position to structure the interactions among the states in the region, and to control the differential payoffs resulting from those interactions. This last position is a more reliable indicator of real U.S. influence in Southwest Asia, and of the gap between perceived and real U.S. strength there.

Another less visible side to the paradox between perception and reality in Southwest Asia is apparent in the dissonance of military power, coercion, and political influence in the region. More often than not the application of coercion has failed to produce the desired results, either for the United States or for the regional powers themselves. The United States' great military strength has proved insufficient to ensure the stability of its allies. At best, it has produced only partial gains—in some cases a temporary respite, in others, a fragile advantage over its adversaries. This became evident in the collapse of the Shah of Iran and in the capitulation of the Gemayel government to Syria, outcomes that the United States had done all it could to avoid. Similarly, military triumph in the 1982 Lebanon war had left Israel weak and internally divided; its economy mortgaged to the U.S. Treasury, and its security dependent upon a massive and steady flow of U.S. arms. Meanwhile, despite a growing desire for peace among the Arab states over the past decade, their arsenals of weapons grew steadily.

There is, then, a curious disjuncture between actions and their results in the politics of Southwest Asia. The concrete manifestations of this disjuncture, as they appeared between 1973 and 1984, form the subject of this book.

One obvious way to bring the means of policy in line with its political ends would be to temper "realism" with a pragmatic concern for justice, and the use of force with active and forceful diplomacy. Exploring the various ways in which this might be accomplished is not, however, the main purpose here. Nevertheless, examination of U.S. policy in Southwest Asia underscores the futility of the "military first" approach to world affairs, and leads to the conclusion that coercion should be used only as a last resort and always in conjunction with active diplomacy that draws attention to the advantage of peaceful alternatives.

I would like to express my appreciation to all those who have supported me in the undertaking of this study. In particular, I would like to thank Halim Barakat of the Center for Contemporary Arab Studies at Georgetown University, Amin Banani of the University of California at

Berkeley, and Amal Rassam of the City University of New York. All three gave freely of their time, and their expertise in several of the larger issues concerning the Arab world and Islam was particularly enlightening. I would also like to thank Steve Shalom, Ralph Buultjens, and Robert Perinbnayagam, all friends as well as colleagues, who were patient but forthright in their comments and criticisms. I owe a special debt of gratitude to Prem Shankar Jha of the *Times of India,* who read through the initial draft and helped me sharpen the focus and arguments. Professor Afaf Marsot similarly provided excellent advice and agreed to write the foreword. Her encouragement and suggestions were immensely valuable. Diane Gurley and Donna McCarthy were prompt and meticulous in their secretarial services, while Michael Pugh patiently edited the manuscript. I am grateful for all their help.

Family acknowledgements come last, but hardly least. My husband Vijay Chadda (who dislikes sentimental tributes) provided a critical mind and a sympathetic ear, even when he would rather have been studying the stock market or listening to Puccini.

List of Abbreviations

AP	Associated Press
ASEAN	Association of Southeast Asian Nations
AWACs	Airborne Warning and Control System
CDM	Coalition of Democratic Majority
CENTO	Central Treaty Organization
CIA	Central Intelligence Agency
CPD	Committee on Present Danger
CSIS	Center for Strategic and International Studies, Georgetown University
CWI	Cold War Internationalists
EEC	European Economic Community
FMS	Foreign Military Sales
FNLA	National Liberation Front of Angola
GCC	Gulf Cooperation Council
GDP	Gross Domestic Product
GNP	Gross National Product
IMF	International Monetary Fund
IRP	Islamic Republican Party (Iran)
KGB	State Security Committee (USSR)
MERIP	Middle East Research and Information Report
MOA	Memorandum of Agreement
MPLA	Popular Movement for the Liberation of Angola
MRD	Movement for the Restoration of Democracy (Pakistan)
NATO	North Atlantic Treaty Organization

NCPAC	National Conservative Political Action Committee
NSC	National Security Council
OPEC	Organization of Petroleum Exporting Countries
PAC	Political Action Committee
PDPA	People's Democratic Party of Afghanistan
PDRY	People's Democratic Republic of Yemen
PFLOAG	Popular Front for the Liberation of the Occupied Arab Gulf
PLO	Palestinian Liberation Organization
PRC	People's Republic of China
PRM 10	Presidential Review Memorandum 10
RDJTF (RDF)	Rapid Deployment Joint Task Force
RHF	Repentance and the Holy Fight
SAC	Strategic Air Command
SALT	Strategic Arms Limitation Talks
SAVAK	Iranian Secret Police
UAE	United Arab Emirates
UN	United Nations
UNITA	National Union for the Total Independence of Angola
USSR	Union of Soviet Socialist Republics
YAR	Yemen Arab Republic

Introduction

The aim of this book is to examine the evolution of U.S. policy in Southwest Asia. While the main focus is on the turn this policy has taken during Reagan's first term in office, the developments of the entire period following the Vietnam War will be examined to bring the changes his administration has made into clearer perspective.

The traumatic experience in Vietnam and the lessons that were drawn from it profoundly affected the conduct of U.S. policy everywhere, including in Southwest Asia. The Cold War ideology and military containment of communism had failed both to protect American interests and to secure democracy in Indochina. These had been, however, the avowed aims. The post-Vietnam years, therefore, saw a partial return to the spirit of accommodation with the Soviet Union and a recognition that the United States would have to exercise restraint in the use of its military power if it wished to secure a peaceful, stable world. These constraints, however, did not last long. In the early 1970s, many individuals in and outside government began to question the validity of the lessons of Vietnam.

They argued that these constraints were leading to an erosion of U.S. power and a consequent increase in turmoil throughout the Third World. What was worse, they argued, the decline of U.S. influence was happening precisely when its principal adversary, the Soviet Union, was attempting to surpass it in military might and political influence. Each of these arguments—the erosion of U.S. power, Soviet expansionism, and growing turmoil as a result of U.S. retrenchment—came to have special relevance for Southwest Asia. Indeed, in the 1970s and early 1980s, this region became the primary testing ground for these arguments.

In fact, the events of 1979—the fundamentalist revolution in Iran, the hostage crisis, and Soviet invasion of Afghanistan—proved critical in laying to rest the constraints and the spirit of accommodation that had characterized the early 1970s. The Vietnam era was finally over. With the new shift in perceptions during the end of the Carter years, the United States seemed to return once again to the Cold War policies of the 1950s. The United States became preoccupied with fears about its weakness in contrast to burgeoning Soviet military strength. The liberal impulses that had occasionally surfaced during the early Carter presidency simply faded from the scene. As the Cold War perspective came to be resurrected, the geographic focus of these anxieties also shifted. In the immediate postwar years, Europe had been the focus of the Cold War; in the 1960s, it was Indochina. In the 1970s and early 1980s, however, the Persian Gulf and the Middle East became the new centers of the new Cold War.

The Region: Southwest Asia and the United States

The region of Southwest Asia is less a geographic than a strategic concept and has only recently found its way into U.S. official statements and literature on strategic and foreign policy. Traditionally, before the 1970s, the entire area was divided into three separate and somewhat autonomous parts: the Middle East, which included Egypt (really in North Africa) and the Fertile Crescent but stopped along the boundaries of Saudi Arabia; the Persian Gulf, which included all the nations around the Gulf waters; and, finally, South Asia, which stretched from Afghanistan to Sri Lanka. Over the past ten years, this same region has come to be redefined in response to the perceived needs of U.S. policy. The concept of Southwest Asia is shaped by two major concerns: U.S. strategic vulnerability and Soviet military threat. Since the perception of these concerns has differed from one administration to another, and even within the same administration from one year to another, the notion of Southwest Asia has accordingly assumed the quality of a kaleidoscope image: Some patterns of regional interaction emerge into sharper focus for a time then become blurred as attention shifts to other locations within the area. A majority agree, however, that the Persian Gulf constitutes the center of the region.

An examination of the current literature shows that as a geographic unit Southwest Asia can include a different set of countries depending on the purpose and nature of the inquiry. For instance, Lawrence

Ziring defines it to include Turkey, while various U.S. official statements have often left Turkey out of their definition and instead focused on the Arab states, Israel, Pakistan, and Afghanistan. This study concentrates on the second definition. It is true that the recent pull of Islam and the heightened anxiety about the entire region have breathed new life into U.S.-Turkey strategic ties, but Ankara has traditionally looked westward to NATO and has avoided getting overly involved in the various conflicts of the region. This is another reason why Turkey is not a part of the discussion here.

Although there are several conflicts that seriously affect the course of politics in Southwest Asia, this study will focus on disputes between the Arab states and Israel, Iran and Iraq, and India and Pakistan. It will also discuss the relevance of the Ethiopia-Somalia dispute, but only insofar as it affected the formulation of U.S. policy. In this perspective, Egypt, India, and the nations in the Horn of Africa also become relevant, although they do not fall within the geographic perimeter of Southwest Asia.

Southwest Asia is extremely divided along religious, ethnic, and political lines. It includes many diverse cultures—Arabic, Judaic, Iranian, and Indo-Pakistani. The geographical continuity is broken by mountain ranges, deserts, and large bodies of water. It is also riven with numerous territorial disputes and more often than not subjected to the personal ambitions of leaders who regard their neighbors as rivals and adversaries instead of potential friends. Nevertheless, for the United States, three common elements have given the region a distinct identity: oil, Islam, and proximity to the Soviet Union.

Evolution of U.S. Policy in Southwest Asia

Confronted with such a vast array of diverse countries, containing over a quarter of the world's population, one may legitimately ask, is there a (single) U.S. policy toward Southwest Asia? There are U.S. policies toward each of the countries included in this region, but is there an overall policy toward the region, into which U.S. relations with each country are dovetailed?

If we look at the evolution of U.S. policy since the 1970s, as this book attempts to do, it becomes apparent that there is an overall policy toward Southwest Asia, and that it is a policy with a wider aim than merely safeguarding the security of Israel and other U.S. allies in the region. It is true that the region enjoyed a relatively low priority in U.S. strategic thinking in the 1960s and early 1970s, when the United States was preoccupied with the Vietnam War. At that time, it could have been said without risk of misrepresentation that the United States had no more than a series of policies relating to each of the countries of the region. Even in relation to the Arab-Israeli dispute, the United States had to adopt a relatively cautious stance and to involve the Soviet Union in the search for a durable peace.

As this book tries to show, three events triggered a change in the U.S. attitude toward Southwest Asia, gave birth to a single policy thrust toward the region, and raised its importance in U.S. policymaking. These were the Bangladesh War and Pakistan's new westward look; Sadat's expulsion of Soviet advisers from Egypt, followed by the Arab-Israeli war; and, lastly, the oil embargo and oil price hike that followed the war. All these occurred in the first three years of the 1970s, and the last two within months of each other.

To begin with, the end of the Vietnam War gave the United States a chance to start reassessing its policies toward other countries and regions of the world. The Bangladesh War pried Pakistan loose from South Asia and compelled it to look for closer ties with the Gulf countries. The expulsion of the Soviet advisers and the shuttle diplomacy that followed the 1973 Arab-Israeli conflict gave the United States an opportunity to establish its preeminence in the Middle East at the expense of the Soviets. But it was the last of these that had the greatest long-term impact. It brought new awareness of the vulnerability of the West to a disruption of oil supplies from the Middle East and the Persian Gulf and made it apparent that the focus of policy in the region would have to be widened from the eastern seaboard of the Mediterranean to cover the entire region from which two-thirds of the world's oil flowed.

The opportunity provided by the Soviet expulsion from Egypt and the fear inspired by the oil embargo brought about a distinct shift in the goals of U.S. policy in Southwest Asia. Whereas previously the United States had been willing to share influence in the region with the Soviet Union in somewhat the same way as it was doing in Europe, from the end of 1973 onwards, its goal became the complete eradication of Soviet influence from the region. Henceforth, the United States would strive to promote peace in the region, but it would be a peace of its own making and one that was in consonance with its global policy aims.

This shift in goals occurred during the last days of President Nixon's administration and continued through the tenure of President Ford. President Carter sought to go back to the earlier policy of seeking stability in the Middle East by involving the Soviet Union actively in the peace-making process. But this effort, which was somewhat ineffectual at best, collapsed under the weight of the series of sharp setbacks to the

U.S. position in Southwest Asia that occurred, once again within weeks of each other, in 1979. These were the taking of the hostages in Iran, the second dramatic hike in oil prices, the short-lived revolt of a Muslim fundamentalist sect in Saudi Arabia, and the Soviet invasion of Afghanistan. In 1980, the United States returned to a posture of confrontation with the USSR, and with this its policy aim once again became the exclusion of Soviet influence from this strategically and economically vital region.

In U.S. popular perceptions, the new Cold War in Southwest Asia began with the Soviet invasion of Afghanistan. In this book it has been argued that this is not so. The shift in U.S. perceptions began six years earlier, with the expulsion of the Soviets from Egypt and the 1973 Arab-Israeli war. However, it began in a low key, because the principal instrument by which the United States sought to achieve its goal was diplomacy and not the threat of use of force. The force-diplomacy mix has varied over the twelve years that form the time-frame of this book. Toward the end of the Kissinger era there had been a small but perceptible shift toward reinforcing U.S. moves with the threat of coercive action. The United States had embarked on a process of building up proxies and arming them heavily. Iran, Saudi Arabia, and of course Israel fell into this category. It had also acquired base facilities in Kenya, Oman, and Egypt to reinforce the position of its proxies. It can even be argued (although that is not the main thrust of this book) that Carter's attempt to reverse the course of U.S. policy failed because it coincided with Soviet aggressive responses to the earlier U.S. moves made during the Nixon-Ford-Kissinger era. These included the creation of bases in Berbera and Aden, the introduction of Cuban troops in Ethiopia and Mozambique, and the invasion of Afghanistan.

However that may be, the distinctive feature of President Reagan's administration is not a shift of policy toward Southwest Asia, but a heavy, unprecedented reliance on force and the threat of force to achieve U.S. goals. It is this that makes Southwest Asia a powder keg. Not only is the superpower relationship exceedingly unstable, inasmuch as at least one of them is seeking the virtual ouster of the other from the region, but also the instrument used to pursue this goal is essentially a military and not a diplomatic one.

In the concluding chapters of this book it is argued that, since the Reagan policy was not intrinsically different from the one pursued by Kissinger, it suffered inherently from the same weaknesses. Whereas the U.S. built proxies in the early 1970s, it is building a network of "strategic alliances" today, with much the same set of countries (the major difference seems to be that Pakistan has replaced Iran as the eastern sheet anchor of the alliances). The success of U.S. policies, therefore, hinges as it did a decade ago on the internal stability of its allies and the degree of convergence of their vital interests with those of the United States. The only difference today, and an important one, is that, thanks to the much greater reliance on military might in pursuing the policy of confrontation with the USSR, the price of failure or miscalculation will be very much higher than it was a decade ago. The U.S. military buildup has been and is being matched by a corresponding Soviet one. The world, and Southwest Asia in particular, is thus being pushed by superpower competition into a more and more unstable equilibrium.

U.S. Policy Objectives and Problems

Closely related to the question of a single policy thrust is yet another question: What does the United States seek to gain in Southwest Asia? In other words, why is the region important to the United States, and what are its objectives there?

U.S. objectives in Southwest Asia are closely related to its global quest, prevention of nuclear war, global containment of the Soviet Union, and advancement of U.S. influence. In Southwest Asia, these objectives resolve into a quest for regional influence, denial of the region to the Soviet Union, access to the region's oil, firm commitment to Israel's security, and protection as well as stability of pro-West states in the region.

The significance of access to the Persian Gulf oil can hardly be overemphasized. For instance, at the time of the embargo, OPEC provided about 58 percent of the non-Communist world's reserves. In the case of the United States alone, between 1950 and 1980, daily consumption tripled, and oil was imported in 1980 at a daily rate thirteen times that of 1950. In 1973, at the time of the embargo, almost half of U.S. energy was provided by petroleum, 37 percent of which was imported from abroad. Six years later, during the fateful year of upheavals in Southwest Asia, oil still supplied almost half of U.S. energy, but the share of imports had risen to 45 percent. The dependency on oil was thus complete.

Nor did it stop here. The rise in oil prices caused a rapid transfer of wealth and an even more dramatic shift in financial power. In 1979, the major oil-producing states, especially Saudi Arabia, controlled a vital resource without which all Western economies could face a collapse. They had accumulated, by the end of 1980, some $300 billion in foreign assets, which went to buy consumer goods, arms, and industrial equipment from the West. With the price of oil increasing by more than 150 percent in 1979–1980 and balance-of-payments deficits dragging the Western economies down, trade with OPEC acquired an added significance.

It became apparent over the first half of 1980 that the skyrocketing oil prices could not be sustained for long. Beginning in 1980, demand slipped, and the industrial economies went into a recession just as new non-OPEC sources of oil supplies became available from Mexico, the North Sea, Canada, and Malaysia. But the glut and the recession are not likely to last forever. What is more, while it is clear that OPEC will not ride as high as it has in the past, the effects of any disruption of oil supplies from it will have incalculable consequences on the Western economies, at least in the foreseeable future.

The region itself lies close to the southern border of the Soviet Union and constitutes a bridge between three continents. This is the second reason why it is perceived as an area of challenge. In military terms, this geographic proximity confers an advantage on Moscow. The Soviet response time to crisis is bound to be quicker than that of the United States. Thus, Moscow can more easily influence the outcome of events in Southwest Asia, merely by changing the readiness status of its border troops. The flying time from southern bases in the Soviet Union to most points in Southwest Asia is not long. What is more, the Soviet Union can use what it is best at, land-based power.

Theoretically, the United States can counter Soviet influence in three ways: first, by pursuing detente, which presupposes mutual restraint and noninterference in each other's preserves; second, by an arrangement with a regionally weighty, middle-sized power to act as a proxy on behalf of the United States; and third, by unilateral intervention and maintenance of visible military presence. Each presupposes a different state of relations with Moscow and a different state of stability or turmoil in the region. The belief that the Soviet Union posed an imminent threat has, however, waxed and waned, based on U.S. perception of Soviet intentions and capabilities. Nor is this all. Soviet intent, power, and strategy have to be appraised in the context of the risk and opportunities that become available in Southwest Asia.

This is the third challenge in the region. Southwest Asia is not only highly unstable, it is intensely politicized. All issues—oil, trade, and arms sales—become inextricably linked to the balance of power among states in the region as well as between their benefactors, the superpowers. The conflicts themselves defy clearcut definition. Some, such as the ones between Iran and Iraq, India and Pakistan, and Somalia and Ethiopia, are regarded as territorial, but that is only a small part of the sum total of their animosities. Differences in their perceptions of each other's intentions and future ambitions also arise out of differences in their internal stability and unity.

Ethnic and religious antipathies further complicate the scene and make compromise difficult. For instance, India resents Pakistan's constant references to the treatment received by Indian Muslims and considers any agreement arrived at with a dictatorship a poor guarantee for the future. Likewise, Pakistan suspects an Indian hand behind the ethnic irredentism of the Baluchis and Sindhis, the two groups that have increasingly agitated for greater autonomy in Pakistan. Ethiopia wants to foil Somalian President Siad Barre's attempts to integrate the disputed Ogadan region within greater Somalia, while Barre is, in turn, deeply concerned over Ethiopia's claim to revolutionary power and its connections with Moscow. The Iran-Iraq conflict is intensely ideological. Iran's appeals to the Shiite population of Iraq are imbued with religious fervor, and its avowed aim to topple Saddam Hussein from the presidency is not an aim within the confines of conventional conflict. The Arab-Israeli conflict combines all the elements—ideological, religious, territorial, and ethnic—that characterize disputes and conflicts in the Middle East. What makes policy formulation with respect to the entire region a real problem is the fact that the outcome of each conflict fundamentally alters the state of equilibrium in the region as a whole, necessitating a political realignment not only among the states within the region, but also between the superpowers locked in deadly competition for influence there.

The problem of maintaining stability of the pro-West states becomes even more difficult in light of the historical forces that have swept through Southwest Asia in the recent past, militant Islam and Arab nationalism. Both combine to a different degree to become at once the cause and the effect of divisions within the region, and both add to the turmoil brought about by the rise in wealth of oil exporters. These in turn have determined the way in which oil wealth is used, whether as a political weapon, as a means of effecting a social transformation, as an asset to investment, as a way to promote ties of interdependency with the West, or simply as a means to buy arms.

Focus and Organization of the Book

Several questions then emerge in regard to the formulation and conduct of U.S. policy in Southwest Asia in the 1970s and early 1980s.

These are

1. On what major premises and rationales did the successive administrations build and implement their policies for the region during this period?
2. What events in Southwest Asia shaped U.S. responses?
3. What was the balance between coercion and diplomacy in the conduct of U.S. policies?
4. How successful were these policies in securing their avowed objectives as well as undisclosed interests?
5. How successful was each administration in building an enduring structure of peace as well as U.S. preeminence?

The book does not take a traditional country study approach but focuses on Southwest Asia as a whole. Nor is it intended to be an exhaustive analysis of every development between 1973 and 1984. Events are selected for their obvious relevance to U.S. policy. Although occasionally Soviet calculations or perceptions of regional states (Israel, Pakistan, Saudi Arabia) have been included, this is not the main focus. Such discussion is meant merely to explain a specific U.S. response more fully.

An implicit conclusion of this book—one that has emerged into clearer focus as it has been written—is that the only way for the United States to obtain a lasting peace in Southwest Asia is through cooperation and power sharing with the Soviet Union. In other words, that the Kissinger and early Reagan policies were wrong, and that President Carter's basic policy thrust was the right one even if his strategy was faulty. One has only to look at other parts of the world to perceive the truth of this. Peace in Europe is still stable and enduring, indeed has withstood all the strains of the new Cold War with ease, precisely because over the three decades that followed the strength-testing in Berlin, both the United States and the USSR have, on balance, refrained from trying to capitalize on destabilizing changes occurring within each other's sphere of influence. This is also true of Southeast Asia, where, since the conclusion of the Vietnam War, both the superpowers have refrained from actively challenging the political orientation (whether pro-U.S. or pro-Soviet) of ASEAN countries. Nor has the Soviet Union intervened in any significant way in Central and Latin America, after the Cuban debacle, except to give limited military and moral support to guerrilla movements in some countries. In contrast, during the 1970s, Southwest Asia became the battleground for intensifying superpower rivalry, including armed clashes among their regional proxies. It is this that gives the book its urgency and relevance. The book is organized as follows.

The Introduction has tried to set out the significance of Southwest Asia and the major themes and problems in formulating U.S. policy for this region. It has viewed this significance and these themes against the background of the major swings of the ideological pendulum in U.S. foreign policy. Chapter 1 discusses the traumatic events of 1978–1979, when Southwest Asia shot to the top of the U.S. policy agenda. These include the second surge in petroleum prices, the revolution in Iran, the incident at Kaaba in Saudi Arabia, and the Soviet invasion of Afghanistan. The next two chapters examine U.S. policy during the Kissinger and Carter years, respectively. The Kissinger years (Chapter 2) are significant because it is to these that one can trace the origins of all the elements that were to later become U.S. policy for Southwest Asia as a whole. In particular, the Bangladesh War of 1971, the Arab-Israeli War of 1973, the oil embargo, and Soviet activities in Africa are examined for their impact on regional balance, as well as U.S. detente policies. Carter rejected the Kissinger approach and forged a different connection between his worldview and the administration's regional calculus. Chapter 3 examines the shifting focus of Carter policies in the context of the new rounds of conflicts and turmoil in the region. The Iran and Afghan episodes are discussed at length for their impact on U.S. perceptions. These perceptions were as much shaped by the shifts in the political climate at home as they were by the numerous crises in the region.

Chapter 4 charts the ascending course of Cold War conservatives and their impact on U.S. perceptions of threats and solutions in Southwest Asia. Globalism, intervention, and preparation for a unilateral response are the three central themes of Reagan's foreign policy. Chapter 5 analyzes their implications for the U.S. regional policies in the 1980s and discusses the directions that the administration in fact pursued upon assuming office. Chapters 6–8 analyze Reagan's policy in action and assess the shifting alignments of states in the region. The Lebanon War of the summer of 1982 tested the efficacy, and exposed the hidden assumptions, of Reagan's policies in Southwest Asia. Similarly, the administration's capacity for flexibility and diplomatic maneuver was tried by the developments in the India-Pakistan and Iran-Iraq disputes through 1984. Chapter 9 examines the long-term prospects for present policies against the background of regional instabilities. It discusses three sources of instabilities: divergence between U.S. interests and regional perceptions; socioeconomic changes; and the sweep of fundamentalist Islam. The Conclusions draw together the major themes and observations discussed and integrate them to develop a perspective for the future course of U.S. policy in Southwest Asia.

1.

U.S. Interests in Danger

The year 1979 proved a fateful one for U.S. policy in Southwest Asia. U.S. influence appeared to be waning everywhere, while Soviet military might had begun to cast a dark and lengthening shadow over the region. Fears about the shifting balance of forces in the region rapidly turned into panic in the United States as crisis after crisis plunged Southwest Asia into turmoil and war. What was extraordinary was the way events triggered by the fall of the Shah of Iran came to a head within a few weeks. The hostage crisis in the first week of November; the turmoil in Saudi Arabia and the attack on the Kaaba at the Grand Mosque in Mecca a mere sixteen days later; the burning of the U.S. embassy in Islamabad in the same week as the incident at the Kaaba; yet another hike in the already high prices of petroleum in the second week of December; and, to cap it all, the Soviet invasion of Afghanistan less than two weeks later—these events shattered the very foundations of previous U.S. policy in the region and all but buried the Carter administration under a mounting crisis of confidence from which it never recovered.

At the end of the year, the balance of power between the two super-powers seemed to have shifted dramatically against the United States. While these fears may have been greatly exaggerated and, indeed, some commentators vigorously argued and warned against such an overreaction, no one could dispute that there had been a major shift in public perceptions in response to the radical changes in the region.

The Soviet intervention in Afghanistan seemed most ominous of all. Whether or not the United States was truly threatened by this remains arguable, but there can be no doubt that by occupying a sovereign, neutral, independent nation, the Soviet Union had violated the most basic premise of the postwar international order. Whatever the Soviet motivation, and there appears to be no agreement on whether this was expansionist or purely defensive, it had set a truly dangerous precedent. It was no longer possible to predict how the Soviet Union would react to similar situations that might arise in other countries of this highly sensitive region. The Soviet invasion did not disturb the United States alone. It sent waves of panic through the other insecure nations of the region and sent them scrambling for countervailing protection from the United States. The Soviet invasion, therefore, not only transformed the superpower relations in the region, but also drastically altered the strategic alignment of the countries in Southwest Asia.

In this chapter, we will confine our discussion to the impact of the events in the year 1979 and their ramifications for the United States and the region, because it is only in this context that the defeat of Carter's visions and the victory of Reagan's become intelligible. This context also explains the extraordinary public concern with foreign policy issues in the 1980 elections and the reason why not only the United States, but also many of the states of Southwest Asia, began to regard themselves as part of a single strategic entity, an interlinked geographic unit that required comprehensive rather than piecemeal solutions to problems.

The Oil Jugular

Maintaining access to Persian Gulf oil has been and remains a principal aim of U.S. policy, but this access was seen as being gravely threatened in the year 1979. Developments in that year alone destroyed all previous predictions about oil supplies and petroleum prices and brought about a situation that had not been expected to arise until after the year 2000. From $12–13 per barrel at the end of 1978, oil prices surged to $24–28 per barrel by the end of 1979 and rose further into the range of $34–37 by mid-1980. From $2 per barrel in 1971, this was an extraordinary leap, but even in that one last year of the decade alone the prices had leaped by almost 150 percent. What made the situation even more intolerable was the growing sense that the political threats to the safety of gulf oil and access to it had suddenly become imminent, although these dangers had not been anticipated for at least another five to ten years.

The price hikes following the Arab-Israeli war of 1973 had been generally accepted as a long-deferred but necessary adjustment in the price of a scarce resource, reflecting its true opportunity cost. Throughout the 1960s and 1970s it was widely acknowledged that oil had been unfairly undervalued. In fact, after the first oil shock in 1973, the years 1974–1978 showed a steady decline in the real price of oil. Between January 1975 and January 1979, prices had crept up gradually from $10.46 a barrel to $13.34 in terms of nominal dollars; however, after correcting for inflation, this rise actually represented a decline of 4 percent in real dollars, while in the stronger currencies such as the Deutschmark, the drop amounted to nearly 18 percent.

Even though this fall had given some relief to the Western economies, beneath the surface calm the situation was rapidly heading toward a crisis. The reasons for this are not difficult to see. First of all, despite measures to rationalize the world oil market and distribution system and Saudi attempts to act as a balancing weight with regard to the oil supply by increasing production in a tight market and cutting down when prices declined, petroleum prices remained highly volatile and subject to political decisions by the Arab states. Second, OPEC members had become alarmed by the rapid disappearance of their petrodollar surpluses as a result of the decline in oil revenues during 1974–1978. By 1978 most of those member nations were becoming concerned about the balance-of-payments deficits against the West and were borrowing heavily from Euromoney markets to keep up the tempo of economic development initiated in 1974–1975. The stage was thus set for some increase in oil prices.

Internal pressures were also gnawing at their economies. Many OPEC members had become uneasy about the social and political consequences of forced industrialization and rapid modernization. Inflation, unsound urbanization, a large influx of foreign labor, the decline of agriculture and traditional industries, and a widening gap between the rich and the poor in their societies were seen as serious threats to the political order. This should have been evident to the United States and should have alerted it to the possible dangers of oil wealth. But until the very end of 1978, Washington paid no attention to the pressures that were gathering force in these countries. No attempts were made to reduce consumption in the West to conserve energy, or to build up emergency reserves. The mad race among Western governments for larger and larger shares of the oil market continued unabated.

President Carter had introduced his energy program in April 1977 based on a pessimistic study of the oil market by the Central Intelligence Agency; but against a background of falling oil prices in real terms, diminishing inflation, and economic recovery, the program failed to gain the support of the public. In fact, the gloomy forebodings of the study were airily dismissed by Carter critics as a mere political ploy. The majority of them argued that another sharp rise in oil prices was highly unlikely, given global economic conditions, and that rising oil production was in fact likely to create a glut in the market.

Even the strike in Iran that stopped the export of oil in November 1978 did not shake these comfortable assumptions. By December 1978, however, the writing was already on the wall for those who were willing to read. In that month, the OPEC countries raised oil prices by 14.5 percent and agreed to spread the increase over the whole of 1979. Although this agreement soon fell apart, the Islamic revolution in Iran at the beginning of 1979 took that country out of the oil market, producing serious shortfalls and tremendous pressures for a further hike in the price of oil. It was estimated that the world market lost about 5.5 million barrels of oil a day and the U.S. market some 500,000 barrels a day. This immediately led to long gas lines and higher gas prices, and dangerously boosted the inflation rate in the United States.

These trends had become visible in the spot market, where oil was sold at about $5 per barrel above the contract prices of early 1979. As the impact of the Iranian crisis began to be felt, there was a further surge in prices. At a meeting in Geneva on 26 and 27 March 1979, OPEC raised prices all at once by 14.5 percent instead of spreading the increase over a period of time as they had earlier agreed. But this was not all. OPEC also agreed to allow each producer to add to its price a market premium that it thought justifiable in the light of its own circumstances. This, as the Saudi oil minister admitted, was "a free for all." According to one analyst, "Two games were being played on the world market. One was 'leap frog,' the oil producers vying with each other in raising prices. The other was 'scramble,' a rough competition among consumers."[1] Such competition had become the order of the day ever since the autumn of 1978. Meanwhile, fearful of shortages of oil for home heating, especially in the Northeast, the Carter administration had offered a subsidy of $5 per barrel for oil imports intended for that use. Thus the American public was sheltered by a subsidy that obscured from view the real reasons behind U.S. oil dependency.

If competition to secure maximum oil prices divided OPEC members, it also drove an uncomfortable wedge between Europe and the United States. Europeans pointed out that between 1973 and 1978 U.S. oil consumption had risen by 1.5 million barrels per day, whereas other industrialized nations had made more determined efforts at conservation. The sheer weight of U.S. consumption and imports neutralized whatever savings the hard-pressed Europeans had made. By mid-June 1979, i.e., within the first five months of that year, oil prices had increased by about 60 percent and on 20 June, despite Saudi attempts at moderation, they had touched $18 for average- and $23 for high-quality crude. The last weeks of the year brought yet another surge in prices. On 22 October, the Shah of Iran was admitted to the United States for medical treatment, and on 4 November, the Iranians took sixty American embassy employees hostage. In response to the Iranian oil embargo, prices hit $45 per barrel in the spot market. Thus, when OPEC met for the third time, on 17 December 1979 at Caracas, the oil market was in total chaos. On 13 December, Saudi Arabia raised its prices by another 33 percent from $18 to $24 per barrel. Angered by Saudi attempts to accommodate Western interests, Libya raised its prices to $30 per barrel. These soon crept up to $34.72 per barrel in the case of Libyan oil and $32 for Mexican crude.

As if the rapid upward hikes in oil prices were not enough, the very character of the oil crisis itself had undergone a dangerous change. It was not just the price of oil that had risen, but its very availability that was threatened. "Hostile" oil now accounted for 30 percent of the supply to the world market. This came from Iran, Iraq, and Algeria, countries that were for one reason or another antagonistic to the United States. Libya and Algeria were distinctly pro-Soviet; Iraq was resentful of U.S. support for Israel; and Iran, once a close U.S. ally, had become virulently hostile. In 1979, 43.4 percent of total oil consumption in the United States was supplied by imports, more than half of which came from Arab OPEC nations. Oil, therefore, emerged as a potent economic weapon that hostile powers could use to bring the United States to its knees.

Collapse of the Shah of Iran

By February 1979, it was clear that Teheran was not only a hostile power that would use its oil weapon against the United States but also a dangerous new source of revolutionary fervor that was likely to threaten the stability of the entire region.

The dramatic events that led to the fall of the Shah of Iran will be discussed in Chapter 3.[2] Before the Shah's departure, the Carter administration had already seen the writing on the wall; even with Washington's attempted support, the Shah's efforts to maneuver within the rapidly changing politics in Teheran had not been sufficient to preserve the monarchy. On 16 January 1979, the Shah left Iran, never to return.

It was now obvious to Carter that the revolution could not be reversed; it was therefore necessary to find a formula that would accommodate the revolution and still preserve governmental stability in Teheran. Several of his advisers had put forward a transitional plan that suggested that the United States should come to terms with the reformist faction of the revolutionary leadership, facilitate Iran's transition to a constitutional monarchy, and persuade the Shah to accept such a plan.[3] Although this option had been available since mid-1978, President Carter had refused to waver in his support of the Shah.

In a last-ditch effort to retain some control over developments in Iran, the Shah had appointed Shahpur Bakhtiar as prime minister of the new provisional government. At that point, the Carter administration accepted the transitional plan, but it was already too late to implement it. First of all, Bakhtiar had very little domestic support.[4] He was also outside the circle of the leaders who were guiding the country through the revolution. Second, he could not reconcile the growing division within the Iranian armed forces—an essential step in returning Iran to some semblance of order.

The division within the armed forces particularly worried Washington since that was the last remaining institution in Iran where the United States could still claim some influence. The administration was extremely anxious to prevent sensitive and sophisticated arms and equipment from falling into the hands of hostile elements. It feared that Soviet-backed leftist forces might gain control of the Shah's formidable arsenal, take advantage of the revolutionary chaos, and force a pro-Soviet regime in Teheran. Only eight months earlier, just such a sequence of events had brought a pro-Moscow leftist government to power in Kabul.

Therefore, President Carter dispatched General Robert Huyser to Iran. Huyser's official mission was to assess the state of morale in the Iranian armed forces and to take steps to ensure the safety of sensitive equipment in their possesion.[5] However, this was not the full extent of his responsibilities. According to William Sullivan, then ambassador to Iran, Huyser's task was to organize a pro-Shah coup with the help of officers loyal to the monarch. Others have contended that Robert Huyser was charged with the mission to prevent such a coup from taking place. Whatever the real nature of his mission, the general could not achieve either of these undisclosed purposes.

On 1 February, Ayatollah Khomeini returned to Iran. His arrival whipped up a wave of revolutionary emotions. There were reports of mass desertions and several mutinies in the armed forces. The Ayatollah denounced the Bakhtiar government, which fell within a week of his arrival in Teheran. On 12 February, Khomeini appointed Mahdi Bazargan, a civilian noted for his religious piety and democratic proclivities, as the new prime minister. Thus far, all of Washington's policy initiatives had come to nought: first it had backed the Shah, and following his collapse it had backed Bakhtiar. Much to Washington's dismay, neither had survived. With Bazargan in power, the Carter administration hoped that Iran and Iran's relationship with the United States could be normalized. Bazargan had been willing, although he had indicated that Iran could never go back to its previous relationship with the United States. There were, however, too many obstacles to normalization.

In the immediate aftermath of the revolution, it was evident that a majority in Iran was overtly hostile to the United States. Washington was therefore cool but very correct in its dealings with Iran. The administration had refrained from any overt show of support for Bazargan out of fear that this might jeopardize his prospects. It was also evident that the majority in the United States did not really understand the nature or scope of the upheaval in Iran. The media and press coverage had been highly distorted, while the unfamiliar ideological mold of the revolution had confounded intelligent comprehension.

There was yet another difficult decision facing President Carter. The Shah had requested admittance to the United States for medical treatment, and there was a growing pressure on the president to grant the request. Washington had apprised the Bazargan government of the Shah's medical problem. Bazargan had warned Carter of possible reactions in Iran but had promised to protect the American embassy.

The Shah was admitted to the United States in October 1979. This let loose in Iran mass protests and large demonstrations against the United States. The Carter decision to admit the Shah was perceived by Iranians as an insult and an act of arrogant defiance on the part of Washington. On 4 November 1979, radical Iranian students broke into the embassy compound and took sixty U.S. personnel as hostages. Hatred for the United States had reached an unprecedented level of virulence in Iran.

Initially, the Carter administration and the Bazargan government thought that, as in the previous takeovers, the U.S. citizens would be quickly released. But this was not to be. Ayatollah Khomeini sanctioned the takeover, dismissed Bazargan, and inaugurated the hostage crisis that was to have the most far-reaching impact on U.S. policy and perceptions. Immediately, the administration declared unilateral economic sanctions against Iran. It froze Iran's foreign assets, suspended all trade, and sent two carrier task forces to patrol the Arabian Sea. However, direct military reprisals against Iran were ruled out for fear that these would endanger the lives of the hostages and perhaps trigger a confrontation with the Soviet Union. By the end of 1979, the pro-Moscow government in neighboring Afghanistan had become very unstable, and the Soviet Union was nervous about U.S. intervention in Iran and possibly in Afghanistan.

With the U.S. presidential elections only a few months away, release of the hostages became the main focus of Carter's foreign policy. The reformist faction in Teheran, this time led by Foreign Minister Sadeq Ghotbzadeh, was also anxious to end the hostage crisis. In fact, serious negotiations for the release of the hostages took place between Iran and the United States. However, Ghotbzadeh was soon under attack from radical religious forces, and the reformists were clearly losing the revolution to these factions. The issue of the hostages had become fully enmeshed in the fierce struggle for political power in Teheran.

This created a terrible dilemma for Carter. There was no stable government or group with whom he could negotiate. His economic sanctions and diplomatic condemnation were having no positive effect and were actually reinforcing the sense of martyrdom in Iran. He could not undertake military measures since that might seal the fate of the hostages. But on the other hand, the president was under enormous pressure from the public and the press to undertake stern action. The ill-fated hostage rescue mission of April 1980 was born under these pressures. It was not surprising, therefore, that its failure would be seen by many in the United States as a humiliating blow to the national pride, and an unmistakable sign of U.S. military decline.

Assault on the Kaaba

It was to be expected that the Iranian revolution would produce a new consciousness among the Shiite community elsewhere in the Persian Gulf, particularly in Saudi Arabia. The first incidents occurred in the summer of 1979, when *mujtahids* (exemplars) of the *Qatif* (villages) in the Saudi kingdom announced that they would perform the Ashura ceremony that had been banned by the Saudi royal family.[6] The Saudi authorities were increasingly concerned about the possibility of Iranian pilgrims, in their religious zeal, subverting the otherwise peaceful *Haj* (pilgrimage) at the holy cities of Mecca and Madina.

Exactly sixteen days after the beginning of the hostage crisis in Iran, the apparently steady and stable Saudi regime was shaken to the core by the attack on the Grand Mosque at Mecca. On 20 November 1979, 700 militants seized and occupied the holy shrine. The Saudis quickly sealed off the Grand Mosque, but it took more than two weeks to kill or capture the last of the fanatical defenders. While the Saudis officially maintained that the group was motivated only by religious extremism, it was suspected that the leaders of the attack had been trained abroad, presumably in South Yemen. The whole incident remained shrouded in mystery, but it was clear that Saudi stability could no longer be taken for granted.

Saudi apprehensions over the events in Iran and in Yemen, its vulnerable southern flank, were evident throughout the year.[7] The border skirmishes between Soviet-backed South Yemen and Saudi-backed North Yemen during February 1979 had set the alarm bells ringing in both Riyadh and Washington.

The U.S. response was swift.[8] Carter promised to speed up the delivery of $390 million in arms including twelve F-SE jets to the YAR. This tended to defuse immediate apprehensions of danger, but the Soviet presence in South Yemen continued to trouble the Saudis. Propelled by these anxieties, the gulf states met on 16 October at Taif to determine ways in which they could collectively ensure the security of the oil routes. A week later, on 25 October, the Soviet Union signed a twenty-year treaty of friendship with the PDRY, consolidating its political and military presence in South Yemen.

The allied Saudi and U.S. interest in these events could hardly remain peripheral. As a chief ally and a major source of oil, Saudi Arabia is one of the most important countries in the region for the United States. The original ultimate quantity of recoverable crude oil within Saudi Arabia has been estimated at 293 billion barrels.[9] Saudi Arabia is also the largest oil exporter in the world. In 1980, Saudi oil accounted for one-fourth of the 14.3 billion barrels traded in world markets. It supplied over 15 percent of the world demand for oil and 7.4 percent of all energy consumed. In 1980, over one-fourth of Western Europe's petroleum consumption depended on Saudi exports. Seven major industrialized countries, including the United States, consumed one-half of the oil requirement in the world, and Saudi Arabia satisfied nearly 17 percent of these countries' oil demands. The United States consumed over 7 percent, France 40 percent, Japan 30 percent, and West Germany close to 20 percent of Saudi oil exports.[10] In addition, Saudi financial resources are enormous. At the end of 1978, its foreign assets were estimated to be worth $60 billion compared to $28 billion for Kuwait, $9.3 billion for the UAE, and $8.6 billion for Iraq.

Tensions in the region did not abate even after the attack on the Grand Mosque was successfully foiled. On 3 December 1979, the Lebanese press reported that although the Saudis had deployed 20,000 troops in the eastern oil region, the demonstrations against the royal family had continued unabated.

Allies Estranged: The United States and Pakistan

While nothing could rival the impact of the events in Iran and Saudi Arabia, throughout 1979 the growing anti-U.S. sentiment in Pakistan was yet another problem for the United States. It should be noted that, over the previous two years, Pakistan had come to bear a heavy share of President Carter's internationalist initiatives: nuclear nonproliferation, restraint on arms sales, and human rights. The assassination of Daoud and the emergence in 1978 of the Marxist-Leninist government of Taraki in Afghanistan had produced genuine fears about the stability of the region, particularly of Pakistan and Iran. The Carter administration therefore attempted to patch up its differences with Pakistan.

Early in 1979, President Carter dispatched Deputy Secretary of State Warren Christopher to Pakistan to formalize a new assistance program. Meanwhile, there was mounting evidence that Pakistan was building installations to acquire nuclear explosive capabilities. Based on a definitive intelligence judgment, Warren Christopher was instructed to obtain reliable assurances from Zia that Pakistan would refrain from developing nuclear weapons. President Zia refused to make any promises. As a result, the assistance program was shelved. According to Thomas Thronton, who was then on the staff of the NSC, "even had the administration been willing to close one eye to Pakistan activities and, say, facilitate sales of advanced military equipment, the Congress would have balked. But the administration was of no mind to undermine its non-proliferation strategy in any event, and the perception of Pakistan's importance had not yet shifted enough to require such a dramatic reversal."[11]

In March 1979, Pakistan withdrew from CENTO, breaking its traditional military link with the United States. Zia had moved steadily toward Islamization of Pakistan and introduced many Islamic laws with punishments that were perceived in the United States as barbaric, including flogging and hanging. The violation of human rights had long been a major irritant in U.S.-Pakistani relationship. Thus Bhutto's hanging in April 1979 only further worsened the strain between the two countries. In the same month, the U.S. Congress applied the Symington-Glenn Amendment to the 1977 National Security Assistance Act and terminated all aid to Pakistan.

Subsequent events contributed further to the downward plunge in U.S.-Pakistani relations during 1979. President Zia once again postponed elections indefinitely, dissolved political parties, banned the press, and jailed a large number of dissidents. Then, on 21 November, mobs in Islamabad attacked the U.S. embassy, killing two U.S. citizens and two Pakistani employees.

Admittedly, the attack was not a result of Islamic extremism as in the case of Iran, but it was obvious that the United States had attained the status of the most unpopular country in Pakistan. A false report from Teheran of U.S. involvement in the attack on the Grand Mosque in Mecca had been believed without question in Pakistan. This led to a virulent antipathy toward the United States and resulted in the attack on the embassy. A slow response by Pakistan's Martial Law Authorities in dispersing the mob was widely seen as a sign that the United States was fast losing its prestige and influence in the world.

All this seemed to change abruptly six days later when the Soviet armed forces invaded Afghanistan. Now a front-line state, Pakistan became a critical element in the Carter administration's Southwest Asia strategy. Sensing the urgency in Washington, Zia dispatched Agha Shahi, then foreign affairs adviser, to the United States. On its part, the administration was anxious to meet Pakistan's immediate needs. However, much to Carter's consternation, Pakistan requested a list of arms far beyond what the administration could reasonably offer. The negotiations were thus bogged down. As a result, when the dangers in Iran, Saudi Arabia, and finally Afghanistan surfaced, the United States found itself without any reliable political base in Pakistan.

Soviet Invasion of Afghanistan

On 27 December 1979, 80,000 Soviet troops equipped with tanks, heavy artillery, and helicopter gunships crossed the Amu Dariya River and took control of Kabul. The event was unprecedented in that it was the first time that the USSR had stepped beyond the cordon sanitaire established at the end of World War II and virtually annexed a sovereign nation. Its previous actions in Hungary in 1956 and Czechoslovakia in 1968, and the subsequent support for the declaration of martial law in Poland, had been mainly disciplinary in nature and had sought to reestablish Moscow's hegemony within its imperium. Afghanistan was, on the other hand, a sovereign state and had never been a part of any alliance. The Soviet move was, therefore, qualitatively different.

The immediate reason for the Soviet invasion can be traced to the April 1978 leftist revolution in Kabul when the Communist party (PDPA), supported by a segment of the army, overthrew the Daoud government and established the Democratic Republic of Afghanistan. Washington was surprised by this turn of events, but refrained from any overt military action.[12] Once a Communist government was in power in Kabul, Moscow moved in full force to strengthen its stranglehold over it. There is little doubt that President Carter viewed the 1978 coup as an adverse development, but did not believe it had changed the strategic balance. The administration was fully aware that, even before the 1978 coup, nonaligned Afghanistan was much closer to the Soviet Union than to the United States.

Lacking real leverage, the Carter administration had to remain content with official warnings and condemnations. In February 1979, however, Adolph Dubs, the U.S. ambassador to Kabul, was kidnapped and subsequently killed. The Carter administration was appalled and decided to cut off all assistance except to projects that benefitted the most underprivileged sections of the Afghan population.[13]

In the following months, the administration's attitude progressively hardened. Harold Saunders, the assistant secretary for Near Eastern and South Asian affairs, stated before the House Committee on Foreign Affairs that the administration had warned Moscow of the dangers of a more direct involvement in Afghanistan.[14] By March 1979, Taraki had been killed and Hafizullah Amin had taken over the reins of control. Amin embarked on a vigorous campaign to speed up the process of socialism and modernization in Afghanistan, and one region after another rose up in fierce rebellion. There is evidence to suggest that Amin was turning out to be too independent for Moscow.

Moscow feared that tribal opposition to the ill-conceived socio-economic measures of the Amin government might overwhelm the latter. In particular, reforms directed against the traditional systems of land ownership and the status of women roused the opposition of the clergy, who joined forces with other anti-Amin elements, including the Parchamis.[15] John Erickson has pieced together an account of events immediately preceding the Soviet invasion. He states that in April–May 1979, the Soviet leadership was convinced that this "situation could not continue on the borders of the Soviet Union—the military drew up its contingency plans and the KGB continued with its political efforts to manipulate the situation." In this attempt, a KGB officer was killed, bringing forcefully home to Moscow that there was no longer any cohesion in Afghanistan and that it was rapidly losing influence in Kabul. According to Erickson, "it was at a relatively late date that the army was given the signal to move in strength."[16]

According to some experts, the Soviet Union was apprehensive of a possible liaison between Amin and the PRC. Others have stressed the impact of fundamentalist Islam on the Soviet Muslim population of the Soviet Central Asia as a compelling factor. The airlift of Soviet troops began on 8 and 9 December, and the invasion was given formal sanction through an "invitation" on the twenty-fourth. Three days later, Amin was overthrown, tried, and executed by the new Karmal government. The Soviet Union claimed it had intervened at the invitation of the legitimately established government, but in fact, Babrak Karmal himself did not arrive in Kabul until the day after Russian troops had crossed the international boundaries into Afghanistan.

Fears in Washington

The year, therefore, ended with Southwest Asia almost unrecognizably different from what it had been a mere twelve months earlier. In December 1978, the Shah of Iran was still on the throne; the Saudi monarchy was unshakably secure; Afghanistan was still a viable buffer state; and the underlying principles of postwar coexistence were still inviolate. Above all, oil prices had been falling steadily for four years in real terms, inflation had moderated, and the economies of the advanced countries were enjoying a mild boom. Now all this had changed, seemingly irreversibly for the worse.

The fall of the Shah was the biggest single setback for the United States in Southwest Asia. It removed the very pivot of America's Gulf policy. The crisis also exposed U.S. inability to understand both the profound social changes and the virulent anti-U.S. revolutionary upsurge that economic development could trigger in a Third World nation. With all its military might, the United States had no measures, diplomatic or political, to cope with the crisis. The new Islamic regime in Teheran had visions of spreading the "true faith" to the rest of the Muslim world and showed a willingness to go to war for that purpose. This was a highly dangerous and destabilizing development from Washington's point of view. Nor was Iran itself very stable. The revolution had triggered separatist movements all along its periphery, making it apparently vulnerable to territorial disintegration. In September 1980, Iraq invaded Iran, further aggravating fears about the political instability in the Persian Gulf. Viewing these developments, Carter's National Security Adviser, Brzezinski, invoked the image of an "arc of crisis" stretching along the shores of the Indian Ocean. He warned that the resulting political chaos could well be filled by elements hostile to the United States.[17]

Although Ayatollah Khomeini seemed to hate godless communism as much as he hated the United States, there seemed no certainty that he would be able to hold the country together. If he failed, it was entirely possible, especially after Afghanistan, that the Soviet Union might carve out another "independent" republic in the region and gain an additional armlock on the world's main reservoir of oil. What is more, Washington feared that, from its military vantage point in Afghanistan, the Soviet Union was in a good position to influence the course of events in Iran and other neighboring countries. In fact, Washington was convinced that the Soviet decision to intervene in Afghanistan was prompted by precisely such calculations. The Baluchis on both sides of the Pakistan-Iran border had been agitating for greater autonomy. When viewed from Washington, the Soviet intervention in Afghanistan, therefore, took on an ominously expansionist significance.

U.S. strategists also pointed out again and again that Soviet troops were now 300 miles from the Arabian Sea and within striking distance of the narrow Straits of Hormuz situated at the mouth of the Persian Gulf, and that there was no military force to oppose Moscow if it decided to cut a corridor across Pakistan toward the warm-water ports of the Arabian Sea. Given the fact that an oil tanker passes through the Straits of Hormuz every twenty minutes, the proximity of the Soviet military was the most alarming development for Washington since the Soviet absorption of Eastern Europe in the late 1940s.

Such a conjunction of events occurring within so short a time span would have been traumatic in any case, but it occurred in an area that by virtue of their dependence on oil was of life-and-death importance to the Western economies. The impact was enhanced by the fact that the U.S. public had already been swinging to the right since 1976. A wave of militaristic nationalism swept over the nation, and demands for immediate action grew strident.

The invasion of Afghanistan finally galvanized the Carter administration into frenetic activity, causing it to move immediately in three parallel courses. The first was to shore up Pakistan; the second, to punish the Russians for violating so blatantly the ground rules of superpower rivalry; and the third, to strengthen U.S. military presence in the region by acquiring bases or military facilities and forging security ties with neighboring countries. Accordingly, Carter suspended grain shipments and the sale of high technology to the Soviet Union. He also postponed the SALT (Strategic Arms Limitations Talks) and ordered the U.S. team to boycott the Moscow Olympics. He reversed earlier policies toward Pakistan, invited Pakistani Foreign Minister Agha Shahi to Washington, and publicly announced an offer of $400 million in military and economic aid to that country.

Carter announced publicly that Brezhnev had lied to him about Soviet intentions in Afghanistan and that he, the president, had now totally changed his views of Soviet intentions. In Carter's view, the

Soviet invasion of Afghanistan was the most serious threat to peace since World War II. He therefore took steps that have since become the cornerstone of U.S. strategy in Southwest Asia and are likely to remain so for the rest of this decade. In his State of the Union Address on 23 January 1980, he announced the creation of a Rapid Deployment Joint Task Force (RDJTF) and warned the Soviets that "an attempt by any outside force to gain control of the Persian Gulf region will be regarded as an assault on the vital interests of the United States of America and such an assault will be repelled by any means necessary, including military force."

As a part of strengthening the U.S. military posture in Southwest Asia, U.S. naval forces in the region were rapidly augmented. The United States ordered replacements for twenty warships that had been sent out during the hostage crisis. Two aircraft carriers and their escorts were dispatched from the West Coast and the Mediterranean to replace the two carriers already in the Arabian Sea. In mid-December 1979, before the Afghan invasion, Pentagon and State Department officials had been exploring the possibilities for greater U.S. use of naval and air facilities in Oman, Somalia, and Kenya; these efforts were greatly stepped up, and these countries responded favorably.

The impact of these events on U.S. public opinion was profound. The headlines that had dominated the news in 1979 had been gravely unsettling to many in the United States. Even before the Soviet intervention, there was widespread anxiety about U.S. standing in the world, its moral authority, its military power, and the political will of its leadership. The U.S. public was outraged by the assassination of the U.S. ambassador in Kabul. That incident, like so many others during the year, seemed to symbolize what many decided was the "impotence" of American power in the face of sometimes subtle, sometimes brutal, but always sinister Soviet expansionism. The Soviet takeover of Afghanistan, combined with the crisis over the hostages, confirmed their worst fears. The year had seen the Shah of Iran and President Somoza of Nicaragua flee into exile, with the United States, as it appeared, helplessly standing by. Both these countries had turned shrilly anti-U.S., if not pro-Soviet. Seen in retrospect, all these seemingly unrelated events began to fall into a distinct and sinister pattern that convinced more and more people that the United States was in geopolitical decline.[18]

But there was more humiliation in store. This came in April 1980, when an attempt to rescue the hostages in a commando-type operation, made familiar by the spectacular success of Israel at the Entebbe airport, failed even before it began. All of this naturally conspired to vindicate the theories put forward by conservative forces in the United States, which had been steadily building up the "Soviet threat" since 1976. Now these charges fell on highly receptive public ears. The tide had been running to the right for some time, and the events of 1979, and particularly those of the last eight weeks, turned it into a millrace.

What gave the rightists' assessment of Soviet intentions its greatest credibility in U.S. eyes was the fear that their ultimate objective was to seize physical control of the oil fields of West Asia. According to CIA estimates of 1977 the Soviet Union was expected to become an oil-importing nation by 1985, and although these estimates have since been drastically revised, at that time the fear of a Soviet move towards West Asia and the Persian Gulf became urgently real. By the end of the year, influential voices in the United States were urging that the threat of Soviet control of the West's oil supply was so grave that the United States would be justified in regarding its commitment to the Middle East on a par with that to NATO. These sentiments were aptly echoed by Egyptian President Sadat when he too declared in 1979 that the Soviet Union was the new world power and had joined the United States in the international "battle for energy." What had brought this situation about? Was the United States genuinely a declining power in Southwest Asia? For an answer, we must turn to U.S. policy over the previous decade.

Notes

1. *The Middle East,* 5th ed. (Washington, DC: Congressional Quarterly, 1981) 92–93. For a detailed discussion see Dankwart Rustow, *Oil and Turmoil: America Faces OPEC and the Middle East* (New York: Norton, 1982).

2. For an account, see Lawrence Ziring, *Iran, Turkey and Afghanistan: A Political Chronology* (New York: Praeger, 1981), 161–189; John Stempel, *Inside the Iranian Revolution* (Bloomington, IN: Indiana University Press, 1981); R. K. Ramzani, *The United States and Iran: The Patterns of Influence* (New York: Praeger, 1982); Nikki Keddie and Eric Hooglund, eds., *The Iranian Revolution and the Islamic Republic* (Washington, DC: Conference Proceedings, Middle East Institute, 1982); William Sullivan, *Mission to Iran* (New York: W. W. Norton, 1981).

3. Ambassador Sullivan had advocated this course of action since mid-1978. See Sullivan, *Mission to Iran.*

4. Bakhtiar was the deputy leader of the National Front. However, after Khomeini had denounced him, the National Front expelled him from their ranks. Similarly, on 11 February a revolutionary militia launched an attack on the Shah's imperial guard. Bakhtiar had to flee the country.

5. For further discussion of the Huyser mission see Sullivan, *Mission to Iran,* 36–37, and Zbigniew Brzezinski, *Power and Principle* (New York; Farrar, Straus, and Giroux, 1983), 354–400.

6. For a succinct account of domestic challenges to the Saudi royal family, see James Buchan, "Secular and Religious Opposition in Saudi Arabia," in *State, Society and Economy in Saudi Arabia,* ed. Tim Niblock (New York: St. Martin's Press, 1982), 117–121.

7. Robert Litwak, *Security in the Persian Gulf, Sources of Inter-State Conflict* (London: International Institute for Strategic Studies; Montclair, NJ: Allanheld, Osmun, & Co., 1981), 86–93.

8. See U.S. Congress, House of Representatives, Committee on Europe and the Middle East, *Proposed Arms Transfers to the Yemen Arab Republic,* Hearing 12 March 1979 (Washington, DC: U.S. Government Printing Office, 1979). The charge that the administration had overreacted and had used the Yemen war to signal its intentions to challenge the Soviet Union is substantiated by Lt. Col. John Ruszkiewicz (Rtd), the just-returned military attache in the YAR, in his testimony before the same committee; see idem, *U.S. Interests in and Policies toward the Persian Gulf,* 1980, Hearings 24 March, 2 April, 5 May, 28 July, and 3 September 1980 (Washington, DC: U.S. Government Printing Office, 1980).

9. Energy Information Administration, Office of Oil and Gas, U.S. Department of Energy, *The Petroleum Resources of the Middle East* (Washington, DC: U.S. Government Printing Office, May 1983), 86.

10. Ibid., 11.

11. Thomas Perry Thronton, "U.S. Policy towards Pakistan," *Asian Survey* 22:10 (October 1982), 967.

12. For a firsthand account of the coup, see Louis Dupree, "Afghanistan Under the Khalq," *Problems of Communism* 28 (July–August 1979), 45–47.

13. *Department of State Bulletin* 79 (April 1979), 50.

14. Testimony of H. Saunders, 26 September 1979, Subcommittee on Asia and Pacific Affairs, House Committee on Foreign Affairs, p. 53.

15. G. S. Bhargava, *South Asian Security after Afghanistan* (Lexington, MA: D. C. Heath & Co., 1983), 37.

16. John Erickson, quoted in ibid., 38.

17. *Time,* 15 January 1979, 18.

18. Henry Kissinger pointed out that America's strategic predominance had so far guaranteed the stability of Southwest Asia. In his view, this situation had changed drastically. He said, "The Soviet march through Africa with Cuban troops, from Angola to Ethiopia, and the Soviet moves through Afghanistan and South Yemen or at least the moves of Soviet clients, altered that perception" (quoted in *Time,* 15 January 1979, 29). See also *The New Republic,* 18 November 1979, 10.

2.

Emerging Axioms of U.S. Policy: The Kissinger Years

Conventional wisdom has it that the dangerous decline of U.S. power in the late 1970s can be traced to the last years of the Vietnam War. The experience of Vietnam had spawned a policy of weakness and an attitude of diffidence that rendered the nation impotent in face of the rising tide of radical nationalism in the Third World and powerless to counter Soviet adventurism. The United States abandoned its great power responsibility, or so the critics claimed.

There is much that is wrong with this assessment, particularly in the context of Southwest Asia. U.S. restraint did not automatically mean Soviet gain, nor was every case of Third World nationalism a result of Soviet machinations. But no one can deny the trauma of Vietnam or its profound impact on the collective psyche of the nation. Indeed, these years are critical because they witnessed the unfolding of a powerful doctrine that set new parameters for U.S. policy in Southwest Asia. In this chapter we will first establish Kissinger's thinking on Southwest Asia in the context of his global design, and then analyze the motivations and reasoning behind the actual course of policy toward the various nations in the region. Finally, we will draw a balance sheet of his achievements and failures and their implications for the U.S. position in Southwest Asia.

Southwest Asia in the Vietnam Perspective

The Nixon-Ford-Kissinger years became significant for several reasons. The domestic consensus behind policy had collapsed, and the

31

foreign policy establishment had become fragmented between different, competing views. As the nation absorbed the lessons of Vietnam, the question of the correct conduct and the just cause for the United States became a matter of intense debate between the hawks and the doves. The latter argued that Vietnam had been a civil war in which the United States had no business interfering and, in any case, could not win; the Communist world was divided and thus a nationalist victory in Vietnam did not necessarily add to the strength of America's ideological enemies. Some in this "centrist" position stressed not so much the short-sightedness of American intervention, but the costs at home: the weakening economy, distorted domestic priorities, and the wounds inflicted on the psyches of young people. On the other hand, the hawks defended the basic decision to intervene and insisted that the United States was fighting for the nation's freedom, and for freedom everywhere. Had not the armed forces been constrained by civilian meddlers, they contended, the United States would have won in Vietnam. The doves rejected this position as militaristic and instead argued that involvement in the civil wars of other nations was hardly the way to protect freedom. What the United States needed above all was to take better care of its own virtue and instead of spreading its armed writ abroad, to work toward promoting its ideals.

A nation bitterly divided on the goals of its national purpose burdened the Nixon administration with an extraordinary intellectual dilemma. It was obvious from the start that the U.S. public would no longer tolerate prolonged involvement in a conflict that was indecisive and not clearly within the parameters of national interest. In fact, in the immediate post-Vietnam era, it was clear that any involvement abroad was likely to produce profound and instant adverse national reaction. How was the administration to demonstrate strength while drawing back from its overcommitment around the globe? The overarching goals of U.S. policy—deterrence, avoidance of armed conflict with the Soviet Union, and world primacy—had not changed. What had changed were the domestic political conditions within which these goals could be achieved. By any measure, this was a difficult task. When seen against the challenges of events in the early 1970s in Southwest Asia, the problem of policy formulation appeared formidable.

Realpolitik Design for Southwest Asia

Kissinger proclaimed that both moralism and blind commitment to anti-Communist ideology had become obsolete as guiding principles for the United States in the world. It was no longer possible or wise to vacillate from isolation to visions of a world utopia. Force had its place in the scheme of things, and so did diplomacy. What was required in the atomic age was a creative blend of the two, unencumbered by passions of either moralism or ideology. The new synthesis was to revolve around one single guideline: national interest that would adhere to the Clausewitzian principle—use of limited force for limited geopolitical ends and use of unlimited (nuclear) force for intimidation and balance only.

In this new global grand design, the "containment with force" of yesteryear was to be replaced by "containment with negotiations," and U.S. primacy was to be ensured by a structure of stability and balance of international power. At the apex of this structure would be the three major adversaries—the United States, the USSR, and the PRC—all locked in a system of mutually deterring relationships, checks and balances, and each possessing a clearly delineated sphere of influence;[1] for instance, the Soviet Union in Eastern Europe and to a lesser extent in South Asia, and the United States in South and Central America. It was hoped that a dampening of rivalry among the three would reduce the tensions around the globe and conflict in the Third World where they exerted direct or indirect influence. For instance, cooperation between China and the USSR would moderate Vietnam's position and allow the United States an honorable retreat.

The triangular relationship was to be based on expanding ties of trade, transfer of technology, and credits. In other words, a whole network of economic and political exchanges would bind the adversaries in a complex web of mutual benefits that could not be abandoned lightly and would, therefore, encourage greater cooperation in managing the Third World. In short, superpower rivalry in the Third World arenas would gradually diminish.

This was the famous notion of the linkage that Kissinger believed would restore flexibility to U.S. diplomacy.[2] If the Third World contest became of secondary importance, if winning or losing there became less critical to superpower influence, and if an "agreement" on broad issues replaced such rivalry, the United States could afford to disengage from some areas of the world without undue damage to its power and prestige.

Under the commanding heights of the tripolar balance, the United States would protect its regional interest, but not all regions were equally important, nor was it necessary to preserve an exact balance in every single arena. Some, such as South Asia and Africa, could be allowed to slide down in importance, while others, particularly West and Southwest Asia, would become the increasing focus of American interest. This had critical implications for the U.S. attitude toward revolution and change in the Third World, a dilemma that it has never been able to resolve satisfactorily. Thus, even while preparing to disengage from some areas considered less important to the United States, Kissinger was careful to warn, "There are changes in the international balance that can threaten our nation's security and have to be resisted however they come about . . . our nation . . . the United States . . . had a duty to defend the security of free peoples if it wanted to preserve its own. . . . We would maintain the world balance of power at all costs . . . there were some changes we would not accept, however disguised the catalyst, even if it appeared as a 'progressive tide.' "[3]

Implicit in this was an affinity almost natural to Kissinger's grand design for right-wing authoritarian regimes. They were meant to play an important role in maintaining a regional balance on behalf of the United States. Radical movements had to be opposed and put down, since such movements were bound to disrupt the triangular order. Some Third World countries could be used as levers to establish regional balance; others were useless. For instance, objectively, Pakistan could not be a factor in global or regional balance, but its good offices could be used to establish contact with China. Just as China was to be a lever against the Soviet Union and U.S.-Chinese ties an insurance against a possible alliance between the two Communist giants, Egypt, in the regional scheme of things, could act as a lever against a united front, whether Arab- or Soviet-inspired. Saudi Arabia, although militarily a nonpower, could act as a counterbalance against the radical Arab states. India, on the other hand, served no strategic purpose in the Kissinger scheme of things. Its nonaligned rhetoric was annoying and its ties with the Soviet Union highly suspect.

This strategy served two other requirements of the post-Vietnam era: reduction in defense spending and withdrawal from military commitment. Both were to have profound effects on the formulation of U.S. policy in Southwest Asia. To begin with, the strategic doctrine governing U.S. interests in the region had to be altered in a way that would now make binding military alliances and U.S. military presence less necessary under the new constraints. The United States adopted three different solutions. First, it began a massive transfer of weapons and equipment to the Persian Gulf nations, including highly advanced and sophisticated arms and equipment. Second, it encouraged certain states in the region to accumulate U.S. armor and play the role of regional surrogates for Washington. Third, it carefully stayed away from military involvement, even in situations that would have brought on a decisive military response in the old days.

In terms of domestic priorities, the new strategy brought on a change in the balance between the military and civilian wings of the government. Gone were the days of blanket approvals of defense budgets. Now, Congress was only willing to sanction money on a piecemeal basis after an item-by-item examination of expenditures. And each request was met with the observation that the Vietnam War was already over. Congressional scrutiny forced the Nixon-Ford administration to substitute more and more machines and technology for men.[4] The new combat strategies relied increasingly on the sophisticated application of technology to warfare and on stockpiling weapons with regional surrogates. Budgetary constraints also led to a leaner force structure, overseas troop reduction, and the closure of bases, mainly in Japan. Logically, it should have also led to greater attention to intertheater mobility—ways of getting centrally located forces mobilized, transported, and deployed overseas. But this aspect of defense planning was ignored, leaving a serious deficiency in the basic infrastructure of the armed forces. This lacuna came to haunt the Carter administration at the end of the decade, when it faced the multiple crises in Iran, Saudi Arabia, and Afghanistan. It also became the springboard for the frantic military spending initiated by President Reagan in 1981.

Shortly after assuming office, Nixon announced a change in U.S. strategic doctrine. Now the United States would plan defense not for a simultaneous prosecution of a "two-and-a-half war" but only for engagement in a "one-and-a-half war." He indicated that under this new doctrine the United States in peacetime would maintain general-purpose forces adequate for simultaneously meeting a major Communist attack in either Europe or Asia, assisting allies against non-Chinese threats in Asia, and contending with contingencies elsewhere. Since military requirements often shape diplomatic actions, reduced U.S. forces had to reflect the selectivity of commitments and greater stress on allied military participation.

The 1969 Guam speech had already spelled out this strategy, later to be known as the Nixon doctrine. Expounding the central thesis of the Guam doctrine, Nixon stated that the United States "will participate in the defense and development of allies and friends, but that America cannot—and will not—conceive all the plans, design all the progress, execute all the decisions and undertake all the defense of the free nations of the world." The United States, Nixon stated in his subsequent report to the Congress, had no intention of abandoning its responsibilities, but at the same time, it had no intention of becoming "the only weight in the scale." The U.S. expected "the nation directly threatened to assume the primary responsibility of providing the manpower for its defenses."[5]

This meant that the United States would not renounce intervention, but that it would intervene only where the danger was present and clear. The process was to be highly selective; stress would be placed on diplomacy and on protecting and promoting U.S. objectives through allies and friends. The U.S. would carefully weigh its interest in each area of the world—South Asia, the Persian Gulf and the Middle East, the Horn of Africa, as well as the nations in the southern cone of Africa—and determine whether specific nations were worth the risk of involvement.

The Bangladesh War

In such a calculus, South Asia, although it contained two major nations, India and Pakistan, came to occupy only a marginal place. In Kissinger's view, none of America's vital interests were at stake in this region.

This was a major departure from earlier U.S. perceptions. In the 1950s, South Asia was regarded as the "heartland of non-Communist mainland Asia" and intimately tied to U.S. national interests, while in the 1960s, it was the "nation's first line of defense."[6] By contrast, during the Nixon administration, the foreign policy bureaucracy had begun to state that the region was entirely marginal to U.S. interests. James Noyes, the deputy assistant secretary of defense, stated, "we believed and continue to believe that no critical U.S. security interests are involved in South Asia." According to Joseph Sisco, the assistant secretary of state, "the subcontinent is very far away. I think our interests are marginal. I think the Nixon doctrine is quite applicable—namely, we ourselves do not want to become involved."[7]

Implicit in this about-turn in policy toward South Asia was the expectation that the United States could trade off South Asia in its priorities with a similar hands-off policy by the USSR in areas such as West Asia, which were of vital importance to the United States. Kissinger's chief aim in South Asia was to safeguard the delicate structure in the subcontinent, where Indian ambitions would remain stymied by Pakistan. The other aim was to protect the new relations with China and to avoid any moves that would endanger the latter's interest in this area.

Kissinger's conceptual design was soon put to the test. In March 1971, political developments in the two wings of Pakistan culminated in a civil war between East and West Pakistan. As the fighting escalated between Pakistani troops and Mukti Bahini—the Bengali freedom force—millions of refugees fled to the adjacent state of West Bengal in India.

The Indian government was forced to carry the enormous burden of providing for nearly ten million refugees. It also came under great domestic pressure to recognize a free government of Bangladesh and to intervene on behalf of the Mukti Bahini. When this intervention took place, on 3 December 1971, Pakistan declared war on India.[8].

President Nixon warned that the United States would not countenance any Indian military moves into Pakistani territory.[9] In an attempt to further deter India, Kissinger visited New Delhi and informed the Indian government that "if China enters the fray—India must not expect any help from the United States."[10] Prime Minister Indira Gandhi was, however, convinced by then that the Nixon administration had no desire to restrain Pakistan and that India had no choice but to intervene. In order to protect itself from possible intervention from China, in August 1971 India signed a treaty of friendship and cooperation with the Soviet Union. The war lasted for two weeks, until the Pakistani army surrendered unconditionally on 16 December 1971. Throughout, the United States and China stood behind Pakistan, while the Soviet Union backed India.[11] The conflict remained confined to India and Pakistan although its outcome profoundly altered the political map of the region. This was to have significant implications for America's interests in the Persian Gulf.

The dismemberment of Pakistan and India's military triumph led everyone to believe that India was the emerging dominant state in the region.[12] It had drawn closer to the Soviet Union while its relations with the United States had settled on a plateau of cool indifference. On its part, Pakistan was forced to reevaluate its policies and perceptions. The loss of Bangladesh and U.S. failure to act on its behalf had been a severe blow to Pakistan's self-esteem. It grew wary of U.S. promises and military alliances and groped desperately for a new identity. In this context, connections with the states in the Persian Gulf, Iran, and Saudi Arabia became increasingly critical. In fact, during the war, Jordan and Libya both transferred U.S.-made F-104 jet fighter-bombers and F-5 jet fighters to Pakistan.[13].

The United States had every reason to encourage Pakistan's westward look. The Bangladesh War had convinced Washington that Pakistan had to be protected from further dismemberment, not only for its own sake, but also for U.S. interests. The Nixon administration feared that in its newfound confidence India might foment trouble and encourage secessionist movements among the Baluchi tribesmen across the India-Pakistan border. Such a dissolution might in fact tempt the Soviet Union to finish what India had begun in 1971. If Iran was threatened, the administration argued, then vital U.S. interests were

also gravely threatened. It was for this reason that the Nixon administration wished to stymie Indian ambitions and promote Pakistan's
growing ties with the states in the Persian Gulf.

There is no doubt, however, that the Nixon policies in South Asia—
the earlier neglect and the later ill-conceived intimidation of India
(Nixon sent a naval task force into the Bay of Bengal hoping to deter
India from intervening in Bangladesh) had weakened the U.S. position
in South Asia. As long as detente lasted and Washington did not fear
Soviet expansionism, such a weakened position gave Washington little
cause for anxiety. The situation could alter if the Soviet Union's intent
and offensive capabilities were to undergo a drastic change. The events
of 1971 and the loss of leverage in South Asia therefore came to haunt
Washington at the end of that decade, when the Soviets invaded Afghanistan and the United States was desperately casting about for firm
allies and understanding friends.

However, what is important to note in the immediate aftermath of
the Bangladesh crisis is that Pakistan had been pried loose from its
traditional South Asian moorings. Pakistan's new westward alignments
progressively strengthened in the 1970s, ending for once and all South
Asia's separate and somewhat autonomous existence in U.S. thinking.
As Undersecretary of State Eugene Rostow stated, "the United States
relied on the security grouping involving Turkey, Iran, Pakistan,
Kuwait, and Saudi Arabia to fill the vacuum left by Britain's withdrawal
from the Gulf."[14]

Alliance of Converging Interests: The U.S., Iran, and Saudi Arabia

This "security grouping" not only tilted the political and strategic
balance against U.S. ideological adversaries in the Persian Gulf, it also
underlined Washington's considerable ability to structure the interaction among the Southwest Asian states. Although the United States
decided to forgo the option of a military presence in the region, its
ability to influence the payoff of such alignments—through offers of
arms and support—ensured that the United States would remain the
prominent power in the region.

The Shah of Iran welcomed the Guam doctrine with enthusiasm.
With the United States deemphasizing its military alliances and the
British withdrawing from the Persian Gulf, Iran got the opportunity to
pursue a more independent course of action in matters that were
becoming increasingly important to the ambitious Shah. First,
Mohammed Reza Pahlavi believed Iran to be the natural heir to the

British role in the region, that is, maintaining stability and a pro-West balance in the Gulf.[15] Second, he wished to promote Iran's influence in the Gulf. For this he needed to assume an increasingly significant role in the Third World, OPEC, the movement of Islamic solidarity, and the nonaligned forums. This new national role conception, if not spawned at least nurtured by the United States, brought Iran into conflict with some of the same radical states that Washington found objectionable, i.e., Syria, Libya, and Iraq.

Inevitably, the new role required a strong Iranian military posture and wide-ranging ability to intervene and defend its interests. For the Shah, the only way to achieve this was to steer a course of policy parallel to that of the United States and act to protect U.S. interests in return for U.S. military and economic assistance. Washington welcomed this view since it lessened the burden entailed in maintaining a high profile in the region. The Shah's offer to play the policeman in the Persian Gulf particularly suited the United States for several reasons. First, despite detente and war, the Arab-Israeli conflict had remained deadlocked. Second, the 1973 war had polarized and radicalized the region, which the Nixon administration believed had benefitted the Soviet Union. Third, the region contained nearly two-thirds of the proved reserves of the world's petroleum, with the Gulf accounting for nearly half of that total. Fourth, the September 1969 coup in Libya and the emergence of the vehemently anti-U.S. Muuammar al-Quaddafi regime there as well as the avowedly radical posture of Algeria under Colonel Boumedienne, underlined the need to secure a countervailing force in the region, a role for which Iran was well suited and more than willing to play. Fifth, the United States was extremely apprehensive about the consequences of British withdrawal from the region in view of the USSR's growing naval presence in the Indian Ocean. In this instance, the lessons of Yemen were too vivid and recent to be ignored. The civil war and revolution there were promptly followed by a growing closeness between Aden and Moscow, in which the former had virtually become a base for Soviet advance activities in the region. And finally, with its ambitious plans for modernization and its burgeoning oil revenue, Iran was both a substantial source of oil and a market for U.S. arms and goods. By 1970–1971, U.S. petroleum production capacity was declining, while consumption and demand for oil were skyrocketing. The United States had no choice but to look abroad for secure and sufficient supplies of oil to keep its economy going. And on his part, the Shah was more than willing to oblige.

Saudi Arabia also became important to the United States for some of the same reasons, but with one difference: Saudi Arabia could not be counted on to exert military weight. It possessed a formidable financial power, however, and was willing to exercise its enormous influence in defense of its own and U.S. interests.[16] Saudi Arabia and the United States in fact shared several objectives in common. The Saudi rulers hated communism and feared radical revolutionary movements as much as the United States feared them. Both desired stability and security in the Arabian Peninsula and the Persian Gulf, and U.S. anxiety to secure an uninterrupted flow of Saudi petroleum was as great as the Saudi desire for U.S. technology and industrial goods. The Nixon administration saw this convergence of interests between it and Saudi Arabia as well as Iran as a way of reducing costs. It pointed out that "there would be fewer overt military interventions, more covert action—fewer troops and bases, but more transfers of arms and investments—to keep America's balance of payment and to make buyers indebted to American banks."[17]

However, as the United States became more and more dependent on the Shah, it was less and less able to refuse Iranian requests for the purchase of U.S. arms. Iran now enjoyed considerable "reverse leverage" with Washington. As Ledeen and Lewis observe, "the Shah could magnify his role on the world stage—something the United States would not only be compelled by erosion of its position in the Mediterranean area to applaud, but to support materially and diplomatically as well."[18]

Iran increasingly intensified its involvement in the region. It extended assistance to Afghanistan, hoping to steer Daoud away from growing dependency on the Soviet Union, and also gave military assistance to Pakistan to put down the Baluchi separatist movement. The Baluchi problem had implications for both Iran and Pakistan. Iran sided with the conservatives of the Arab world, and with Sadat's advent to power in Egypt, Iranian-Egyptian relations markedly improved. By 1974, Iran had extended $1 billion in economic assistance to Egypt.[19] A similar improvement of ties took place between Saudi Arabia and Egypt after Nasser passed from the scene.

Both Saudi Arabia and Iran had actively opposed the Nasserite brand of revolutionary nationalism and Nasser's intervention in the Yemeni civil war—a policy with which the United States had fully concurred. Similarly, in 1971, they extended prompt assistance to the sultan of Oman for his campaign against the guerrillas of the popular front fighting in the Southern Dhofar province of the Sultanate.[20] From December 1973 to the end of 1976, Iranian troops intervened to put down the rebellion. Iran manned the Omani base, and its navy patrolled the Straits of Hormuz. The Soviet-backed rebellion was put down, and the United States had no need to intervene physically. Their joint efforts also went a long way in weaning Sadat away from the Soviet Union. Thus, on several fronts, Iran's policies moved in step with U.S. interests.

The United States reciprocated wherever it could. For instance, it supported the Shah of Iran in his territorial dispute with Iraq. The 1969 seizure of power by the Ba'ath socialists in Iraq had led to an aggravation of hostilities between Iraq and Iran.[21] There were essentially five outstanding problems between the two countries, each with varying significance for U.S. interests in the region. These were the Kurdish disaffection in northern Iraq; the dispute over the Shatt-el-Arab River boundary; the position of Iranian pilgrims and nationals residing in the holy places of Najaf and Kerbela in southern Iraq; Iraq's involvement with the leftist dissidents in Iran; and finally, the rivalry between them for influence in the Persian Gulf.

Of these, the Kurdish problem and the boundary dispute were the most vexing during the early 1970s. The Shah at first secretly and later openly supported the Kurds to struggle against the leftist government in Baghdad. The situation took a turn for the worse when Iraq signed a fifteen-year treaty of friendship and cooperation with the Soviet Union on 9 April 1972. Iraq's main objective in this was to counter the Shah and Iran's growing importance in the region. In response, the United States promptly backed the Shah's clandestine support of the Kurds. Here again, Washington saw its anti-Soviet objectives coinciding with the regional interests of its ally.

The subsequent report of the U.S. House Select Committee on Intelligence clearly revealed that the administration did not want the Kurds to win, nor did it want them to stop fighting. The administration preferred instead that the insurgents simply continue a level of hostility that would sap the military strength of Iraq and keep Iraq's ally, the Soviet Union, off balance.[22] Such an outcome was bound to damage Iraq's ties with Moscow, since Iraq had entered the treaty relationship expressly for this purpose. A similar calculus shaped Reagan's policy a decade later when conflict once again flared up between Iraq and Iran.

The Shah's influence and activities were not confined to the Middle East and the Persian Gulf. During the 1970s, he formed what came to be known as the Safari Club, consisting of Iran, Saudi Arabia, Morocco, Egypt (after the October War), the Ivory Coast, and Senegal.[23] France was the only European partner in this arrangement, but the United States had unofficially endorsed both its objectives and activities. The purpose of the Safari Club was to oppose and prevent the spread of Soviet influence anywhere in the Gulf or northern Africa. Soviet-supported Somalia was one of its early targets. The other was al-Quaddafi of Libya.

Thus, under the Guam doctrine, the United States gained Iran as a chief strategic instrument and Saudi Arabia as a powerful financial ally. Inevitably, the United States came to be increasingly identified not only with the oppressive nature of these regimes, but with the personal power of Sadat, the Shah, and the House of Saud—a situation that was to explode with devastating results at the end of the decade.

In summary, although the British had withdrawn their forces in 1969 and, under the Guam doctrine, America was reluctant to fill that vacuum, the latter had found an alternative strategy to ensure its preeminence. This was the strategy of "twin pillars," in which the United States pledged its arms and its diplomatic support to its allies, Iran and Saudi Arabia, and depended on them to protect and defend American interest in the region.

Prelude to War: Changing Arab Alignments

The five years between the two Arab-Israeli wars fully exposed the way in which Washington came to apply its new global realism to the Middle East. At the time, a majority in the United States believed that another war between Israel and Arab states was likely to benefit the Soviet Union. As in the past, they thought it might expose Arab military weakness and drive them to seek arms and protection from the Soviet Union. Similarly, it was a common perception that a prolonged period of stalemate in the Middle East would also benefit the Soviet Union. On the other hand, past experience indicated that U.S. influence in the region could be enhanced if the United States sponsored new peace initiatives and pledged U.S. prestige to promote their acceptance.

Henry Kissinger's conceptual framework rejected the logic and assumption underlying these perceptions. He reveals in his memoirs that he "challenged the fundamental premise of our diplomacy that the continuing stalemate [in the Arab-Israeli conflict] strengthened the Soviet Union's position." In his view, he goes on to say,

> the opposite was the case, the longer the stalemate continued, the more obvious would it become that the Soviet Union had failed to deliver what the Arabs wanted. As time went on, its Arab clients were bound to conclude that friendship with the Soviet Union was not the key to realizing their aims. Sooner or later, if we kept our nerve, this would force a reassessment of even radical Arab policy. This was my strategy which gradually became our policy from 1969 onward (over the corpses of various State Department peace plans, gunned down by the passions of the partners in the area rather than by me). In 1972 and 1973, the strategy began to succeed.[24]

In line with this new approach, Kissinger strongly opposed the 1969 peace proposals worked out by the State Department and its head, Secretary of State William Rogers.

Kissinger's objections were not wholly a matter of philosophical or policy differences with his opponents; rather they reflected a keen sensitivity to impending shifts in Arab foreign and domestic perceptions. During the five years between the two wars, the Arab world had undergone substantial changes. Nasser had passed from the scene, the Egyptian economy was under tremendous strain, and the Soviet Union was having serious problems with its Arab allies.

The first indication of change came from Egypt when Ali Sabry, a well-known pro-Soviet vice president failed in his bid for power and was initially fired and then jailed by Sadat. It was clear that the Nasser era was over. Under Sadat, Egypt was attempting a drastic reevaluation of its ties with the Soviet Union: The imprisoning of pro-Soviet Sabry occurred three days before William Rogers arrived in Cairo and was widely believed to be a signal to the United States that Sadat wished to improve Egypt's ties with Washington.[25]

The Egyptian press had been urging such a course of action for some time, and influential individuals in Cairo were arguing that the United States would limit its support of Israel if the advantages of better ties with Egypt were to become apparent. In the following months, Sadat purged the government of many individuals known to have been advocates of a pro-Moscow posture. These were disturbing developments for the Soviet Union and perhaps were a reason why they hastened the signing of the Egypt-USSR treaty, which, according to most observers, amounted to no more than a codification of the existing relations between the two nations. For the USSR the treaty was a kind of insurance against U.S. attempts to drive a wedge between Moscow and Cairo, and indeed they had every reason to be worried. The second signal of Egypt's changing attitude came with Saudi King Faisal's visit to Egypt at Sadat's invitation. This marked the beginning of a new entente between the two Arab powers that was to reach a high point during the October 1973 war.[26] The Soviet position had also become somewhat shaky elsewhere in the Middle East. In Iraq, Hardan Al Takriti was ousted, apparently for his role in the failure of the Iraqi troops to aid the PLO in Jordan during the 1970 coup attempt.[27] A far more serious shakeup occurred in Syria, where pro-Russian groups of Ba'athist leaders led by Salah Jedid were ousted by Syrian Defense Minister Hafiz Assad. At the time he was not considered particularly sympathetic to Moscow.[28]

The Soviet position received a further shock when Nimeri ruthlessly cracked down on Communists and dissolved the unions that served as

the "Communists' bases of power" in Sudan.[29] The relations between
Moscow and Khartoum began to deteriorate. The ousting of pro-
Soviet supporters in Egypt, the abortive Communist-supported coup
in Sudan, Egypt's backing of Nimeri, and rapid rapprochement between the United States and China in early 1972 added up to a serious
setback for the Soviet Union.

Apart from the China issue, Egypt's posture was, of course, the most
critical in all these events. The most outstanding problem between
Egypt and the Soviet Union at the time was the extent to which the
Soviet Union was willing to support Sadat in his bid to recover the lands
lost during the 1967 war. The Soviet Union was cool to Sadat's plans and
tried to discourage him from plunging into another war. At first, they
withheld military equipment and supplies and frankly told Sadat not to
seek confrontation, advocating diplomacy instead.[30] However, Sadat
was determined to press on with the preparation for a showdown with
Israel. He was convinced that the humiliation and disgrace of the 1967
defeat had to be reversed and Sinai recovered. Relations between
Egypt and Moscow therefore rapidly deteriorated, leading finally to
the expulsion of thousands of Soviet advisers from Egypt in July 1972.
In the Soviet judgment, another Middle East conflict was certain to
jeopardize detente. Besides, they did not think that the Arabs could
successfully reverse the defeats inflicted by the past three conflicts with
Israel.

While the Soviets were restraining Sadat and unwittingly preparing
for their own expulsion from Egypt, Kissinger had other plans in mind.
What Kissinger hoped for was a reversal of alliances, whereby the
United States would replace the Soviet Union as Egypt's ally. This was
evident from the lack of U.S. diplomatic initiatives since the failure of
the Rogers plan. Kissinger writes at another place in his memoirs, "The
bureaucratic stalemate achieved what I favored as a matter of policy: an
inconclusive course that over time was bound to induce . . . Arab leaders to reconsider the utility of relying on Soviet arms." This strategy of
stalemate also suited the White House agenda of the time, full as it was
with settlement in and withdrawal from Vietnam, cultivation of detente, the SALT negotiations, and overtures to China. According to
Quandt, since 1972 was an election year the administration thought it
wisest to adopt a "low profile on Middle East," where "in absence of any
chance for a negotiated agreement . . . Nixon focused instead on maintaining the military balance in Israel's favor, thereby preventing an
unwelcome outbreak of the fighting and no doubt earning the
gratitude of Israel's many supporters in the U.S.[31]

As Kissinger admitted, the domestic political environment made it necessary that things be kept quiet in the Middle East. Accordingly, he opened secret back-channel talks with Dobrynin, the Soviet ambassador in Washington. The idea was to stymie any Soviet attempts to seek unilateral advantage at the expense of the United States. The talks ensured that Moscow would have an incentive to exercise restraint. During his visit to the Soviet Union, Kissinger discussed privately with Gromyko a basis for a joint U.S.-Soviet approach to a Middle East settlement, but his only purpose in this was "to gain time" and to "give the Soviets an incentive to keep the Middle East calm—a strategy that would only magnify Egyptian restlessness with Soviet policy."[32] Kissinger secured Soviet agreement to a communique that did not in any way weaken Soviet commitment to Egypt, only stressing its desire for peace. But the document had the desired effect of making Sadat very uncertain about Soviet support for the Arab cause. A mere two months later, Sadat expelled the Soviet advisers, which Kissinger claims came to him as a complete surprise. Whether or not this was so, Kissinger had let Sadat know that the Soviet military presence in Egypt prevented Washington from assuming a more vigorous role in settling the Arab-Israeli dispute. In other words, the United States could be persuaded to press Israel for concessions provided Egypt ended its overdependence on Moscow.

The Soviet expulsion from Egypt and setbacks in Sudan meant that the Soviet Union had lost influence in the critically important states in the region. This also meant that the Soviet Union would have to fall back on some other strategy to counter the growing U.S. presence in the area.

In fact, such a shift in Soviet policies soon became apparent. First, Moscow decided to adopt the traditional revolutionary strategy and urged the Arab Communist parties not to merge their identities with nationalist movements; second, it was decided to extend Soviet ties with other states in the region that had so far been neglected. Accordingly, Moscow turned its attention to the nations of North Africa and the Persian Gulf—Algeria, Morocco, and Yemen—and extended for the first time official recognition and assistance to guerrilla movements such as the PFLOAG.[33] In keeping with the second objective, the Soviet Union made important overtures to the conservative governments of the Persian Gulf, Bahrain, Qatar, and the UAE, regimes that the PFLOAG had sworn to overthrow. Although the two lines of its Middle East policy thus contradicted, Moscow was not overly concerned about that.

There were severe limits, however, to the extent to which the Soviet initiatives could succeed in the Persian Gulf. In most places, with the exception of North Yemen, the Soviet attempts bore no fruit. Nevertheless it was clear that Kissinger's stalemate strategy had succeeded only too well and that the Soviet counterstrategy was, in fact, a tacit acknowledgment of America's new gains.

The October Arab-Israeli War

On 6 October, Egyptian forces launched a surprise attack against the Israeli Bar-lev line on the eastern flank on the Suez Canal. Partly because of the Yom Kippur holiday, the Israeli army was caught off guard, and the Egyptians were able to make a breach in the Israeli defense line. After the initial attack, however, the Egyptian advance was slow. Personnel losses on both sides were substantial, but losses in arms and equipment were even greater. Indeed, if the two superpowers had not rushed massive quantities of arms to their respective clients, the war could have ended with perhaps a different balance of loss and gain. The United States immediately airlifted substantial amounts of equipment to Israel. What is remarkable is that U.S. planes were bringing this equipment all the way to Israeli advance bases in the Sinai Peninsula itself, that is, in the theater of war. The Israeli army, having recovered from the initial shock, launched a spectacular counteroffensive and not only recovered the losses, but captured additional territory that was to prove of incalculable consequence in subsequent events.

As Egypt was forced on the defensive, the Soviet Union also began a massive airlift of arms and equipment to the beleaguered Egyptian army. The expulsion of Soviet advisers had strained their relationship earlier, but Moscow had refrained from punishing Egypt for this insult. It continued to maintain cool but correct relations with Egypt and to provide it with limited arms and spare parts. This restraint on the Soviet part may have been due to Moscow's reluctance to see all the bridges burned between itself and its most important Arab partner. Besides, if war were to break out, as it did, Egyptian flirtation with the United States would rapidly come to an end. The Soviet Union thought this could be an opportunity to regain its lost position in Egypt.

From the U.S. point of view, the balance of military power after the war provided an opportunity to secure what it had begun earlier—a reversal in the Egypt-Soviet alliance. Israel had triumphed, but the Arabs had also acquitted themselves with bravery and honor in the war. Nevertheless, the Arab defeat and the loss of Sinai had devastated Egypt and profoundly altered its perceptions. Sadat had made it known he would make peace with Israel if she returned the Sinai. He was also convinced that only the United States could persuade Israel to make concessions. In his view, the military options had been exhausted; trying them had brought only defeat and dishonor to the Arabs. It was therefore time to try diplomacy.[34]

This change in attitude particularly suited the administration, which was anxious to avoid unnecessary confrontation with Moscow and apprehensive about its standing with the Arabs. Every Arab-Israeli war had escalated tensions between the superpowers, and in October 1973, the two had come very close to a direct confrontation. This could not be allowed to happen again. Unequivocal U.S. support for Israel had been one of the main reasons why Moscow had been so successful in spreading its influence among the Arabs. This was not lost on Kissinger. An evenhanded U.S. policy, on the other hand, could reduce Arab dependence on the Russians. It was apparent to him that, given the widespread desire for peace and negotiated settlement, diplomacy was more likely to succeed. There was simply too much at stake—Western dependence on oil and its need for Arab cooperation—to allow Israel to derail U.S. diplomatic efforts.

From these considerations came the strategy for peace—a step-by-step approach from which the Soviet Union was to be excluded. That such a policy would contradict and possibly jeopardize the administration's detente relationship with the Soviet Union did not unduly trouble Henry Kissinger. Nevertheless, the advantages that the United States had gained from the war could not be expected to last indefinitely. It was clear that the administration would have to move on the peace front. An agreement mediated by the United States and endorsed by both sides of the Arab-Israeli conflict could go a long way in securing a peace settlement's relative permanance. At least this is what the administration thought. Apart from excluding the Soviet Union from the peace process, there were two additional conditions on Kissinger's hidden agenda for the Middle East. These were a separation of the Palestinian question from the peace negotiations and a continued division of the Arab world between moderate pro-West and radical Arab states.

To achieve this, Washington first ignored the venue of Geneva for negotiating these agreements, although the Soviet Union insisted that that was the appropriate framework for the peace talks; second, it devised a step-by-step diplomacy of peace so that the moderate Arab elements would remain hopeful about the negotiations and would go along with the idea of keeping Moscow out of the piecemeal bilateral talks.

To some extent, the Kissinger strategy worked. He managed to secure two interim agreements: first, the January 1974 cease-fire and disengagement of Egyptian and Israeli forces in Sinai as well as the May 1974 Syrian and Israeli mutual promise to a cease-fire in the Golan Heights; and, later, a further withdrawal by the Israelis from the strategic Milta and Gidi passes and the Abu Rudeis oil fields in the Sinai. These agreements indicated that both Egypt and Syria could be persuaded to relegate the Palestinian issue to the background when their own territories and national interests were at stake. It was also clear that both would abandon their superpower ally, the Soviet Union, if there were sufficiently attractive inducements to do so. Their willingness to negotiate the agreements outside the Geneva process suggested that their ties with the Soviet Union could be broken. However, this was far more the case with Egypt than with Syria. In President Sadat's view, this was the price Egypt had to pay to achieve peace on its borders and ready access to U.S. arms and investment capital.

From the U.S. point of view, Egypt had been the linchpin of Arab armed resistance; with its neutralization, the position of the Arab states had weakened immeasurably. The United States proceeded quickly to cement this new identity of interests with substantial amounts of military and economic assistance to Egypt. It could not and did not ignore its erstwhile ally, Israel, in this game plan. Israeli concessions and willingness to cooperate with Washington were, in fact, critical to its success. The United States rewarded such cooperations by requesting from Congress $2.2 billion in military assistance for Israel, and by 1975, Israel's arms stockpiles were substantially more than what they had been when the 1973 war broke out.[35] This was the other necessary condition in Kissinger's strategy. He was aware that a strong and well-armed Israel would deter any renewed efforts the Arab states might make to redress the humiliation of their 1973 defeat. An intimidating but cooperative Israel, Kissinger felt, would keep the moderate Arab states at the negotiations. Unfortunately, only Sadat was willing to break away from the traditional Arab positions. His isolation in the Arab world, however, made him vulnerable to Arab anger. It is not perhaps an exaggeration to say that, in choosing this new and untried direction for Egypt, Sadat had sown the seed of his own violent death.

Soon after the cease-fire agreements were concluded, Kissinger's step-by-step diplomacy was in serious jeopardy. At an October 1974 summit meeting (known as the "Palestine Summit") in Rabat, Morocco, the Arab states decided that the PLO would be the "sole legitimate representative of the Palestinian people." The decision cast a dark shadow over further prospects for peace since Israel had refused to negotiate with the PLO and the PLO had refused to recognize Israel's existence. Although Kissinger had tried hard to break the connection between Arab-Israeli talks and the Palestinian problem, a majority of the Arab states were unwilling to endorse such a stratagem. Much to Kissinger's consternation, the Palestinian issue would not stay in the background. In addition, Israel was unwilling to make further concessions, and its cooperation was critical to any progress in the peace talks. Kissinger's shuttle diplomacy thus foundered on Israeli intransigence. In fact, President Ford was so upset at the Israeli stance that he ordered a "reassessment" of U.S. Middle East policy.[36] Seven years later this entire pattern was to repeat itself.

To sum up, Kissinger's policies had partially paid off. The detente and stalemate diplomacy had brought Egypt into the Western orbit and had weakened the Soviet and Arab hand in the Middle East. However, his stratagem brought no decisive movement toward peace and no diminishing of overt animosities. It was not only at Rabat that Kissinger's failures became apparent; the Arab objection to his entire scheme was brought home with devastating impact when the petroleum-producing Arab states took an unprecedented step and declared an oil embargo on the United States and Europe.

The United States and the Arab Oil Embargo

Washington's enormous and continuous involvement on behalf of peace was in no small way propelled by the dramatic demonstration of collective Arab power in 1973. The United States had succeeded in enticing Egypt away but had not succeeded in keeping separate the three strands of American policy: Soviet containment, support of Israel, and ready access to Arab oil. The embargo explicitly linked the last two and thus paved the way to the total breakdown of Kissinger's game plan.

The announcement of the oil embargo and of the first production cuts came on 17 October 1973, when the United States began airlifting military supplies to Israel. The Organization of Arab Petroleum Exporting Countries (OAPEC) began with 5 percent reductions but promised further cutbacks unless Israel agreed to withdraw from the Arab territory occupied in 1967 and to recognize the rights of the Palestinians.

On 20 October, Saudi Arabia reduced its production by 25 percent and completely cut off the United States. By 22 October, most other Arab producers had joined in the cutbacks and the embargo. The world oil market reacted with panic. The prices for premium oil shot up to $20 per barrel, compared to $5 to $12 officially set by OPEC. The impact on Western economies was immediate and devastating. Although estimates varied, the embargo was said to have cost the United States about 2 million barrels of oil a day. A 1974 Federal Energy Administration report estimated that the five-month embargo had cost the United States up to $10 to 20 billion in GNP and had resulted in a loss of 500,000 jobs. Japan and Western Europe were hit even harder since their dependency on imports was far greater than that of the United States. The real economic impact of the embargo has been a matter of considerable controversy; some have claimed that it was not really very effective. No one, however, can deny its political and psychological impact on the United States.[37]

The West was stunned by the display of Arab determination. It also became clear that the convergence between the moderate Arab position and the United States, achieved over the past few years, was far from complete. The Arab states were willing to cooperate with the United States in its anti-Soviet actions, but were not willing to be a mere instrument in the fulfillment of every U.S. objective.

The 1973 war and the embargo proved the severest test yet for the administration's official noninterventionist posture. Nixon raised the spectre of intervention by his characterization of U.S. policy as being "like the policy we followed in 1958 when Lebanon was involved, and also like the policy we followed in 1970 when Jordan was involved." In both those instances, the United States had sent troops but had seen no military action. On 21 November, Kissinger criticized the "Arab shutdown of oil" and threatened countermeasures against OPEC. From then on, the rhetoric of threats and counterthreats escalated. On the very next day, the Saudi foreign minister declared that he would cut production by 80 percent if the West took punitive measures. In fact, he said his country might blow up some of its oil fields if the United States intervened.

During the embargo, the United States kept up its veiled warnings of intervention, and the Arabs countered with threats to blow up the oil fields and installations. Even after the cease-fire agreements in November 1973 and the resumption of oil supplies in March 1974, the press continued to report contingency plans and feasibility studies for a U.S. occupation of Saudi or Kuwait oil fields. Kissinger had warned in December 1974 that in the event of "strangulation" of the industrialized world, the United States would have no choice but to intervene.[38] President Ford endorsed the warning in January 1975. The defense secretary also indicated on 14 January 1975 that the United States would resort to force in an emergency and that, from a military point of view, intervention was a realistic option. In the beginning of 1975, influential journals began to advocate intervention, singling out the coastal regions of Qatar and Kuwait as militarily feasible targets for occupation.[39]

In yet another blueprint published in *Harper's* March issue, Miles Ignotus, according to William Quandt a pseudonym for Edward Luttwak (a celebrated consultant to the Pentagon), drew up a scenario for a rapid deployment strike force by the United States. According to this, the eighty-second Airborne Division would embark on C5 and C141 transports, refuel at Israeli bases, and proceed to drop paratroopers at key Saudi oil fields and airports. Escort would be provided by Phantom fighters "based on Israeli fields or aboard aircraft carriers in the Arabian Sea: The Airborne Division would pave the way for the large marine contingents which would arrive on the scene seventy-two hours later." As to the Arab warnings of fire in the oil fields, the author felt confident that Texan fire fighters were the best in the world and could take care of this problem. He did not think the Soviet Union would seek confrontation. In his words, "Moscow would not risk it." Finally, the Shah of Iran would be asked to "protect" Kuwait and, if necessary, appropriate its oil.[40] In February of that year the *London Times* made public a similar scenario proposed by the U.S. National Security Council, code-named "Dhahran Option Four," to take over the oil field of Ghawar in Saudi Arabia, which contained 40 percent of the world's then-known oil reserves.

By mid-1975, however, the threats began to subside. President Ford announced he would not use force in the event of a new oil embargo. Nevertheless, these events exposed to full view the hidden premises of U.S. policy. These were to be applied again and again throughout subsequent developments in Southwest Asia. First, it was clear that, geographically, the United States could no longer frame its policies for the Middle East separately from that for the Persian Gulf region. The issue of oil and of Palestinian self-determination had become unavoidably interconnected. It was possible, however, to advance U.S. influence over events by a policy that kept the Arab world divided, Israel militarily strong, and peace initiatives alive though moving at a time and pace suited to Washington's larger anti-Soviet purposes.

Second, it was evident that U.S. popular perceptions could no longer be kept insulated from successes and failures in the Middle East. As was evident in various interventionist scenarios, the panic over U.S. dependency on Arab oil had produced a grim reaction in the United States. The embargo had greatly reinforced the ranks of Cold War ideologues and hastened the demise of the detente that had been so carefully crafted by Henry Kissinger. In this context, it is not surprising that the growing Soviet intervention in Angola should affect the public assessment more than was warranted by Angola's overall importance to America's superpower image.

The Impact of Soviet Activities in Africa

The events in Africa, including the civil war in Angola, are outside the scope of this book, but in retrospect they had a substantial impact on the superpower relations in Southwest Asia. The Angolan crisis and Soviet activities in the Horn of Africa had convinced many in the United States that Moscow had entered an era of aggressive expansionism and would ignore any understanding with Washington if it interfered with advancing its own cause. What is more, the embargo had converted many into believing that the Third World was a hostile place and that U.S. ability to control events there had become severely limited.

The Nixon administration's handling of the Angolan crisis had become a matter of fierce controversy in the United States in the mid-1970s. It is not at all clear who first broke the 1972 U.S.-Soviet agreement to limit the competition for influence in the Third World, the Soviet Union or the United States. Some have argued that Soviet support of the MPLA (the radical faction in the Angolan civil war), the airlifting of Cuban troops who acted as a proxy for the Soviets, as well as the ruthless Soviet disregard of international law, clearly indicated that Moscow had jettisoned detente and may in fact never have had any intention of adhering to it. There is, however, equally imposing evidence that it was the United States, through its support of the narrow-based and less popular UNITA faction, that had undermined detente. The Soviet actions were not only a response to what the United States was doing in Angola but also an attempt to hold its own against the PRC's involvement on behalf of UNITA. In addition, there was the South African factor to consider. Pretoria had, with encouragement from the Nixon administration, intervened repeatedly in Angola.[41]

What is more, several experts believe that the loss of influence in the Middle East and exclusion from the agreements between Israel, Egypt, and Syria may have played an important part in the Soviet decision to intensify the ideological struggle in Angola and to score a "win" where it had a clear advantage over the United States.

Whatever the truth in this controversy, there is no doubt that the subsequent damage to American prestige from the unsuccessful confrontation with the Soviet Union in Angola undermined support for

Kissinger's global detente policies.[42] It strengthened the Cold War perceptions among influential circles in and outside the government, eroded support for the SALT process, and set the stage for later shifts in U.S. policies. Those critical of detente brought in further evidence of the growing Soviet presence in Somalia. They pointed out that just across the Gulf of Aqaba lay Saudi Arabia. If the Soviet Union were to gain control of the southern entrance to the Red Sea, it would dominate both the Gulf of Aqaba and the Gulf of Suez and be in a position to bottle up Israel and choke off the Suez Canal. In other words, it would gain command over the shortest oil route from the Persian Gulf to the West.

The years 1975–1976, therefore, saw growing cracks in the tripolar structure that Kissinger had built so carefully. Commitment to negotiated management of U.S. interests in Southwest Asia had thus eroded, but support for a direct military involvement was still weak. The memories of Vietnam were alive, and the disastrous consequences of intervention were still too well etched in the public mind to permit embarking on the interventionist course advocated by the Cold War types in and out of the administration. Their number was, however, rapidly swelling.

The Kissinger Years Assessed

On the whole, the Nixon-Kissinger years achieved significant successes for the United States despite the shocks of Pakistan's defeat and dismemberment, the Arab-Israeli war, and the oil embargo. The United States had managed to preserve a negotiated balance between itself, the Soviet Union, and China. The arms negotiations had resulted in a strategic agreement with the Soviet Union in the early 1970s and had persuaded Moscow to exercise restraint, at least initially, in its support of extremist leaders, although this had strained Soviet ties with Egypt, Sudan, and Libya. The Soviet influence in Southwest Asia was, therefore, effectively contained. Its surrogates were also successfully checkmated. The activities of the Safari Club had neutralized and countered radicalism in the region, while the division within the Arab world between the confrontationist front (Syria, the PLO, Libya, and Iraq) and the pro-U.S. moderate front had produced the opportunity for U.S. mediation.

The second objective of access to the region's oil had been temporarily thwarted. The surging oil prices no doubt shocked the Western economies and highlighted the danger of oil dependency, but the supplies were soon resumed. While the years were characterized by widespread fears of economic strangulation, the antidote was already becoming available. OPEC had to sell its oil, and the oil-rich nations needed weapons, goods, technology, and access to Western financial markets. The Arab economic future and political stability were, therefore, inextricably tied to the health and vitality of the Western economies. This was the undeniable reality, whatever the disagreements on issues, or over the timetable for the resolution of the Arab-Israeli dispute. The greatest problem was in steadying the oil market and ensuring a gradual and predictable increase in the oil prices. In this respect, the Kissinger diplomacy failed, but having absorbed the shock, it nimbly moved to massive arms deals and strategic ties with the oil-producing nations.

At the heart of the dangerous connection between oil politics and war lay the Palestinian problem and a need for an enduring solution to the Arab-Israeli dispute. Here, the Kissinger years must be judged a mixed failure. To begin with, Kissinger failed to grasp the opportunity offered by changing perceptions among the Arabs in the early 1970s. As William Quandt points out, "The period from 1971–1973 . . . seems to have been one of lost opportunities to prevent war and move towards a settlement." The opportunity was created as a result of three factors. First, Egypt, the pivotal state in the Arab-Israeli conflict, had shown clear signs of opting for peace and cooperation along the lines proposed by the United States, provided Israel returned to its 1967 boundaries. Second, in the early 1970s, the PLO and Syria were not the formidable and well-armed force they later became. Third, the Soviet Union was willing to cooperate and had exercised substantial restraint. According to Alexander George, "If one examines the totality of Soviet behavior, not only in the weeks and months immediately preceding the outbreak of the war but also in the several years prior to the war, one sees evidence that Soviet leaders did operate with considerable restraint." In contrast, the author concludes, "U.S. policy in the Middle East during the same years is difficult to reconcile with the injunction [that] both agreed to forego efforts to derive unilateral advantage," an injunction that Nixon and Kissinger had accepted in that document.[43]

In concrete terms, the United States relegated the Palestinian issue to the background, a tactic that was upgraded to the level of a policy ten years later during the Reagan presidency. Henry Kissinger's step-by-step diplomacy ensured the United States primacy as a mediator, but could build no enduring structure of peace. The Sinai agreement and cease-fire negotiations among Israel, Egypt, and Syria brought temporary peace to the region, but also ensured that no permanent agreement could be forthcoming. The U.S. gaining of Egypt as an ally certainly weakened the Arabs politically, militarily, and psychologically, but by the same token it made them uncertain and wary of U.S. mediation and unwilling to participate in U.S.-sponsored binding agreements. In addition, the United States rapidly replenished the loss of Israel's arms and equipment, and thereby ensured its reluctance to make the necessary concession. The linkage of arms to political influence did not work in favor of peace.

The lack of attention to the Palestinian demands, and reluctance to pressure Israel into making concessions to the former, led to an even more devastating result. It was Lebanon that became the next battleground, with the PLO and Syria on one side and Israel on the other. The outcome was most unfortunate. It destroyed the political fabric of that nation, encouraged Israeli territorial ambitions, and made Syria into a power greater than warranted by its traditional place in the region; but worst of all, it solved nothing. The Palestinian problem remained intractable as ever. This paradoxical pattern was to repeat itself over and over again in Southwest Asia.

Although the United States failed in converting its temporary advantage to a more permanent arrangement for peace, it had begun to build a complex fabric of regional ties based on economic and military assistance. The process of enmeshing Southwest Asia—particularly its oil-rich nations, Saudi Arabia and Iran—in this fabric had begun in earnest. Arms sales were reinforced with a tacit understanding (between the United States and the members of the Safari Club) that these arms would be used to support anti-Soviet elements in the region. The salesman had in a way replaced the soldier in U.S. priorities, and coercion had been substituted for diplomacy. Application of force by proxy nations had become the central premise of Kissinger's strategy. There were, however, serious pitfalls in this premise. It did ensure a temporary balance, an uncertain advantage, but it identified the United States too much and too closely with the authoritarian nature and oppressive conduct of the proxy regimes, such as that of the Shah of Iran.

Ensuring a dominant position without intervention was in itself a difficult proposition. It is likely that the Shah's role in rescuing the administration from this dilemma blinded the United States to his oppressive policies; or perhaps the temporary advantage gained in the region was too comforting to allow for worry about the possible domestic reactions to Mohammed Reza Pahlavi. It is also likely that the mechanistic paradigms of Kissinger's *realpolitik* had ultimately underestimated the sweeping force of radical nationalism. Whatever the reason, all three factors combined to create an extraordinary convergence between American interests and the person of the Shah, which led inexorably and inevitably to the disastrous collapse of 1979 and gave birth to the virulent fundamentalism of Khomeini. The perspective of *realpolitik* had failed to cope with the major forces of history in the Third World—revolution, nationalism, and the urge for self-determination.

There is one more element that is critical to the balance sheet of success and failure in assessing the Kissinger years: the impact of his policies on domestic perceptions. Kissinger's ideas of *realpolitik* were much closer to the European tradition than that of the United States and failed to win widespread support. For the anti-Communist activists detente spelled "appeasement," and Soviet triumph in Angola and the Horn of Africa underlined the failures to contain Soviet expansionism. In their eyes, these failures justified a return to the Cold War policies of earlier years. For the liberals, "realism" represented all that was ruthless and cynical in European power politics and alien to the U.S. tradition. For the idealists, detente was too narrowly based, which indeed it was, and for the Cold War types, there was no rational basis for detente at all. At the end of the Kissinger era, there were few converts to the experiment in *realpolitik*. The nation had once again begun to drift away in search of a central theme, a single purpose that would harmoniously combine its ideological traditions and its foreign policy objectives.

At the end of this period, it was clear that access to oil was inextricably tied up with regional conflicts; these conflicts engaged nations that had oil as well as those that did not. But most of all, it was obvious that the nations of Southwest Asia—Iran, Iraq, Saudi Arabia, Egypt, and Pakistan—could no longer conduct their policies in isolation from each other. The rivalries and tensions, as well as alliances between and among these states and their growing importance as new powerful actors on the world stage, required that they be viewed as a single strategic entity. This awareness was beginning to enter U.S. thinking.

Growing Soviet involvement around the perimeter of the Persian Gulf, and its activities in Yemen and the Horn of Africa, underlined its interests in the region as a whole and made U.S. policy makers all the more conscious of the interdependent balance of the various parts that make up Southwest Asia. However, the fact that Moscow had access only to the periphery and not to the center of the region also underlined Moscow's limited and (as the expulsion from Egypt indicated) declining influence. All in all, the United States had emerged in a commanding position in the region at the end of the Kissinger years, but public impatience with the lack of tangible results was beginning to undermine its gains and blow out of proportion Soviet designs on Southwest Asia.

Notes

1. For a general evaluation of Kissinger's global policies, see Roger Morris, *Uncertain Greatness* (New York: Harper & Row, 1977); John Stoessinger, *Kissinger: The Anguish of Power* (New York: Norton, 1976); George Ball, *Diplomacy for a Crowded World* (Boston: Atlantic–Little, Brown: 1976); George Liska, *Beyond Kissinger* (Baltimore: Johns Hopkins University Press, 1975); Richard Falk, *What Is Wrong with Henry Kissinger's Foreign Policy* (Princeton, NJ: Center For International Studies Policy Memorandum no. 59, July 1974).

2. See Warren Nutter, *Kissinger's Grand Design* (Washington, DC: American Enterprise Institute, 1975).

3. Quoted in Ralph Buultjen, *The World of Henry Kissinger* (New York: International Study and Research Institute, 1982), 44.

4. For an excellent analysis of the Nixon Defense Policy, see Yuan-li Wu, *U.S. Policy and Strategic Interests in the Western Pacific* (New York: Grane, Russak & Co., 1975), 13.

5. For a full statement of the Nixon doctrine, see *U.S. Foreign Policy for the 1970's*, I, A report to the Congress by Richard Nixon, President of the United States (Washington, DC: U.S. Government Printing Office, February 1970).

6. Baldev Nayar, *American Geopolitics and India* (New Delhi, India: South Asia Books, 1967), 37.

7. U.S. House of Representatives, Committee on Foreign Affairs, *United States Interests in and Policies towards South Asia,* Hearings before the Subcommittee on the Near East and South Asia, 93rd Congress, 1st session, March 12, 15, 20, and 27, 1973, 80–82.

8. Sudershan Chawla, "South Asia: Security and Stability under Challenge," in *Changing Pattern of Security and Stability in Asia,* eds. Sudershan Chawla and D. R. Sardesai (New York: Praeger, 1980), 156–157.

9. The U.S. launched an action to condemn India in the United Nations. Kissinger told the Washington Special Action Group on 3 December referring to President Nixon, "He wants to tilt in favor of Pakistan" and again on 8 December, "We are not trying to be evenhanded. There can be no doubt what the President wants. The President does not want to be evenhanded." The State Department had disagreed with Nixon's "tilt" policy.

10. Reported in *Time,* 23 August 1971, 7.

11. For an analysis of the Nixon administration's motives behind ordering the aircraft carrier *Enterprise* to the Bay of Bengal see Jack Anderson, *The Anderson Papers* (New York: Random House, 1973), 263.

12. Kissinger stated that the aid was symbolic and necessary to establish a better relationship with India and loosen her total reliance on the Soviet Union. See U.S. House of Representatives, Committee on Appropriations, Foreign

Assistance and Related Agencies Appropriations for 1975, Hearings before Subcommittee on Foreign Operation and Related Agencies, 93rd Congress, 2nd session, 13.

13. *New York Times,* 19 April 1972, 3.

14. Quoted in Shahra Chubin and Sepehr Zabin, *The Foreign Relations of Iran: A Developing State in a Zone of Great Power Conflict* (Berkeley: University of California Press, 1974), 237.

15. Commenting on the Shah's imperial dreams, Michael Ledeen and William Lewis point out that the Shah had served as a mediator in Pakistan-Afghanistan disputes, proposed a loose political federation of Iran, Pakistan, Afghanistan, and Turkey and sought a leadership role in CENTO, "encouraging the notion that he (Reza Pahlavi) should be designated Supreme Commander for CENTO forces." *Debacle: The American Failure in Iran* (New York: Alfred A. Knopf, 1981), 43.

16. See John Duke Anthony, "Aspects of Saudi Arabia's Relations with Other Gulf States," in *State, Society and Economy in Saudi Arabia,* ed. Tim Niblock (New York: St. Martin's Press, 1982), 148–171.

17. Stanley Hoffman, *Primacy of World Order* (New York: McGraw-Hill, 1978), 47.

18. Ledeen and Lewis, *Debacle,* 52.

19. For accounts of the Shah's role in bringing Sadat over into the Western camp, see *MENA,* 10 April 1971; *FBIS Daily Report* (Middle East), 12 April 1971; *al-Ahram* (Cairo), 12 May 1971.

20. George Lenczowski, *The Middle East in World Affairs,* 4th ed. (Ithaca, NY: Cornell University Press, 1980), 684.

21. For a succinct analysis, see Stephen Grummon, *The Iraq-Iran War, The Washington Papers* 10:92 (1982).

22. R. D. McLaurian observes that "Israel, to keep Iraqi forces pinned down within their own country, sent shipments of arms via Iran. This policy was successful in the 1969 Iraq-Iran conflict for example, when major contingents of Iraqi forces were pinned down in Kurdistan." Barzani, the Kurdish leader, had guaranteed the U.S. supply from Kirkuk oil in return for arms, but with the settlement of the dispute between Iran and Iraq at Algiers in 1975, the United States abandoned the Kurds. See R. D. McLaurian, ed., *The Political Role of Minority Groups in the Middle East* (New York: Praeger, 1979), 71.

23. According to Mohamed Heikal, "This remarkable body, the brain child of Comte de Marenches, head of the French Securite' d'Etat et Contre-Espionage (SDECE), was born in 1972, and included the French and Moroccan, as well as three other intelligence services. Its aim was to counter Communist activities in Africa, and more specifically, to protect the heavy investment in Africa of French companies and of banks.... Safari Club's existence was particularly welcomed by Kissinger, who was prevented by Congress from direct intervention. ..." *Autumn of Fury: The Assassination of Sadat* (London: Andre Deutsch, 1983), 70.

24. Henry Kissinger, *White House Years* (Boston: Little, Brown and Co., 1979), 376.

25. Sadat's desire to improve relations with the United States was reinforced further by Chase Manhattan Bank Chairman David Rockefeller's visit and talks

with him at this time. See Raymond Anderson, "Egypt Is Seeking To Win U.S. Favor," *New York Times*, 12 March 1971.

26. See Heikal's analysis in *Autumn of Fury*, 79–80, 85.

27. *New York Times*, 16 October 1970; see also Michael Freed, "Iraq— Growing Realism among Revolutionaries," *New Middle East* 29 (February 1971).

28. J. Gaspard, "Damascus after the Coup," *New Middle East* 28 (January 1971), 9–11.

29. Anthony Sylvester, "Mohammed and Lenin in Revolutionary Sudan," *New Middle East* 34 (July 1971), 26–28.

30. See, for instance, Alvin Rubinstein, *Red Star on Nile* (Princeton, NJ: Princeton University Press, 1977); Jon Glassman, *Arms for the Arabs*, (Baltimore: Johns Hopkins University, 1975); Robert Freedman, *Soviet Policy toward the Middle East since 1970* (New York: Praeger, 1975).

31. William B. Quandt, *Decade of Decisions* (Berkeley: University of California Press, 1977), 129–130.

32. Kissinger, *White House Years*, 1188–1289.

33. Freedman, *Soviet Policy toward the Middle East since 1970*, 67–68.

34. Boutros-Ghali, Egypt's minister for foreign affairs, underlined and justified Sadat's peace initiative in a long article in *Foreign Affairs* 60:4 (Spring 1982), 770–771.

35. *The Middle East*, 5th ed. (Washington, DC: Congressional Quarterly, 1981), 49.

36. Bernard Reich, *The United States and Israel: Influence in the Special Relationship* (New York: Praeger, 1984), 33.

37. *The Middle East*, 5th ed., 91.

38. Interview accorded to *Business Week*, 13 January 1975, 69.

39. This "sabre-rattling" occurred in the context of a leak, confirmed by the Pentagon, that three American divisions were being readied for the Middle East. *New York Times*, 22 January 1975.

40. Miles Ignotus, "Seizing Arab Oil," *Harper's*, March 1975, 45 and note.

41. The National Security Study Memorandum (NSSM) no. 39 laid down the Nixon-Kissinger approach to Southern Africa. See Mohamed A. El-Khawas and Barry Cohen, *The Kissinger Study of Southern Africa* (New York: Lawrence Hill and Co., 1976).

42. John Stockwell, *In Search of Enemies* (New York: Norton, 1979), 67.

43. Alexander George, ed., *Managing U.S.-Soviet Rivalry* (Boulder, CO: Westview Press, 1983), 139. At the first summit meeting in Moscow, in late 1972, Nixon and Brezhnev signed a number of agreements and communiques. The most important of these, achieved after last-minute negotiations at the summit itself, was the SALT treaty limiting strategic arms. The two leaders also signed a more general document, the Basic Principles Agreement (BPA), which constituted a sort of charter defining the basis for the further development of detente. Most importantly, it stated that the superpowers would refrain from taking unilateral advantage in the Third World.

3.

Swing toward Liberal Internationalism: The Carter Years

Three things had become evident by the mid-1970s: first, that Southwest Asia, the region stretching from Turkey to Pakistan through the Persian Gulf and North Africa, required a single, comprehensive policy; second, that U.S. economic well-being and political security depended on its success; and third, that the advantages that had been gained at the close of the Kissinger years were precarious and likely to be lost if the United States did not forge a more permanent arrangement of peace based on a mutuality of interests in Southwest Asia. The Carter years must be judged in the context of these new perceptions. This chapter will trace the evolution of Carter's Southwest Asia policy, its rationale, its contradictions, and also its achievements.

Carter's Global Perspective

President Carter inherited the Kissinger initiatives as well as their consequences: a new regional balance demanding a coherent and integrated response in Southwest Asia; an East-West relationship that was eroding rapidly under the impact of events in Africa; and a restive Congress polarized over issues of Soviet strength and U.S. weakness. On each count, Kissinger's policies had ultimately failed. The measures he adopted for East-West accord had angered a growing number in the Congress, while his attempts to counter the criticism of "weakness" had drawn fire from an equal number in the liberal opposition. As Stanley Hoffman aptly observes, "just as Vietnam had become a symbol of the moral bankruptcy of containment and destroyed the ethical base of the contained crusade, all the disappointments—domestic and

61

internal—of the descending phase of this era came to symbolize the moral deficiency of *realpolitik*."[1] As Carter campaigned for the presidency, the nation was divided over fundamental issues of foreign policy such as the wisdom of detente, the perils of and profits from intervention, and the U.S. approach to revolutionary nationalism in the Third World.

Among the many factions clamoring for attention then, a group of liberal internationalists strongly represented by corporate interests and moderate thinkers known as the Trilateralists came to the forefront.[2] They called for a "redistribution of global resources and a new international order for mutual gain and the aggressive defense of human rights." The latter found particular favor with Jimmy Carter, the Democratic candidate for the presidency in 1976. To the post-Watergate United States, shamed and humiliated by the prolonged public disclosures of moral turpitude in the highest office of the land, themes of morality and rectitude were sweet music. The issues the Trilateralists took up also held a historic appeal for the U.S. public—an open and clean administration, international concord, nonintervention, and support for democracy and human rights throughout the world. In 1977, however, the liberal call for and on behalf of internationalism belonged to a different genre. It rejected the *hubris* that had led to the downfall of both the conservatives who called for U.S. military supremacy and the Wilsonian brand of liberalism that wished to spread U.S. values; instead, it praised moderation, eschewed hegemonic pretensions, and promised to harness U.S. moral energy to the cause of peace and international cooperation. The new platform emphasized the common problems of mankind—world hunger, economic development, and oppression. It also exhorted the nation not to confuse anticommunism with democracy and authoritarianism with stability. President Carter declared that the United States must free itself from the inordinate fear of communism that had in the past clouded its choices and led the nation into war on behalf of oppressive regimes. He also warned against the argument that the defense of capitalism was a defense of democracy, and cited the brutal civil war and the American intervention in Chile as a prime example of this kind of wrongheaded thinking. The Carter program exuded confidence in America's ability to demonstrate rectitude in her conduct abroad and foster democratic forces in the Third World. However, underlying all this was the recognition that America could not shape the world alone. The Wilsonian ideals were still desirable, but the world had changed drastically. It was no longer possible to impose America's ideals from a position of military superiority. In this, the Carter perspective was different from all the previous brands of liberalism in the United

States. The new administration called for a "framework of peace" with which "our own ideals gradually can become a global reality."

The concern for human rights and the economic problems of the Third World was derived from a growing realization that the problems of poverty and peace in the world were inseparable. The survival and health of the Western economies themselves depended on such international cooperation, and although in the past it could be obtained through coercion, in the post-oil-embargo world, this was no longer possible. Similarly, stability in the Third World depended on continued growth and widening political freedom, neither of which were attainable without the cooperation and support of the advanced West. The world had become highly interdependent, where problems of peace called on the ingenuity of engineers and economists, rather than of soldiers and strategic planners. The Trilateralists pointed out that with the whole of the industrialized world in debt to the oil producers, and with the vast increase in the share of their own trade with these and the newly industrialized countries, the old relationships of dominance and dependence had to give way to a more equal partnership, particularly with the oil-rich nations of Southwest Asia. In other words, the United States needed to end the antagonism that had characterized its relations with the Third World, and move its policies more into line with their requirements and perceptions. This, in their and Carter's view, was also the most effective way to counter the problem of growing Soviet influence in the Third World.

While the above perceptions shaped Carter's philosophy, the empirical basis for these views emerged from a study he ordered of Soviet capabilities and intentions, later to be known as Presidential Review Memorandom 10 (PRM 10).[3] This was a major assessment of the global balance, and reflected the administration's initial judgment of Soviet intentions. The study concluded that, at this juncture, the two superpowers stood at parity in weapons, but in comparison with the strength and scope of the U.S. economy, the Soviet Union was destined to remain a weak power, particularly since it was likely to suffer serious shortages of capital and labor, as well as failures in agriculture, in the coming decade. PRM 10 concluded that long-run trends therefore favored the United States, and advocated a more relaxed stance toward the "Soviet threat" and a vigorous pursuit of SALT II. This was, however, totally contrary to the thinking of many influential members of the legislature, the Pentagon, and the CIA.[4]

On the issue of nonintervention, Carter's policies revolved around the achievement of three interrelated objectives. The first and the second were meant to reduce the need for intervention, while the third was intended to ensure the tactical readiness of U.S. forces to intervene if all diplomatic efforts failed. The first of these policies sought to increase America's tolerance of revolutionary nationalism in nonvital areas of the world and the discontinuation of overt and covert operations in support of counterrevolutionary forces. Carter's support to Daoud in Afghanistan, his reoriented policies toward sub-Saharan Africa, and support of the revolutionary front in Nicaragua reflected the new American stance. The rationale behind the attempt to align the United States with the progressive forces of the future and behind nonintervention was the proven instability of repressive regimes. He firmly believed that the reactionary regimes of the Third World belonged to the past and wanted them to liberalize internally, or forgo American support. What is more, many of these regimes violated human rights, an issue on which Carter felt strongly and on which he sought definite commitment from all those who wanted U.S. support on a tactical plane. He believed that popular nationalist regimes would be far better placed to resist pro-Soviet influence. This would make American intervention unnecessary.[5] A corollary to this approach was the extension of diplomatic and economic assistance to regional power centers (i.e., India and Brazil) in lieu of entering into military alliances with unstable and insecure regimes in the Third World. Carter did not, however, extend this liberal vision to nations that he considered vital to American interests, such as Iran, Saudi Arabia, and Indonesia. Carter continued extending military assistance to them, despite the fact that most of these regimes were guilty of violating every principle of human rights. But outside these "sensitive" countries, there was to be a new emphasis on the reduction of arms sales. Carter argued that instead of increasing American military presence abroad, he would harness the influential countries in each region, preferably the progressive ones, to promote regional security.

The third focus of his policy was the security of the Persian Gulf. Carter stressed the need to strengthen American conventional strike forces to give them the capacity for preemptive action to protect the West's trade and oil routes. But he also emphasized the need to hold talks with the Soviet Union for the demilitarization of the Indian Ocean. Unfortunately, this aspect of his policies remained relatively neglected until the upheavals in Afghanistan and Iran in the fateful year of 1979.

In sum, when Carter took office, his administration pledged a departure from earlier policies that were wedded somewhat narrowly to *realpolitik* and the pursuit of a policy of containment. Instead, he promised to initiate an open administration, revive liberal idealism in the United States, tolerate progressive and even revolutionary nationalism, foster and defend human rights, and give greater attention to the growing economic needs of the Third World. All this he promised to do within the framework of growing detente with the Soviet Union. But there were a number of flaws in this strategy. First, Carter had not determined an order of priority about which areas were vital and which could be ignored for the sake of detente, nor had he worked out what the United States would do if the Soviet Union were to score advances in the areas considered vital to U.S. interests. But most of all, he had made no effort to define these issues clearly or to build congressional and public support for their implementation.

In view of this lack of clarity, it is not surprising that Carter's detente policies ran into difficulty from the very beginning.[6] Denied a yardstick by which to judge which areas were vital and which areas were not, the U.S. public and the media continued to perceive every political change in the Third World as a setback for the United States and a potential threat to its security. And faced with the prospect of a loss of public support, Carter was forced time and again to revise his stand, and promise to "hang tough" with the Soviet Union. Thus, in the second phase of his term in office, which began roughly around the end of 1977, President Carter dropped all references to human rights in the Soviet Union. The uneasy negotiation over SALT II continued through 1977 and 1978, but their future appeared to grow increasingly dim as the political situation deteriorated in the Horn of Africa, Iran, and Afghanistan.

Carter's Emerging Regional Priorities

What did the new directions that Carter sought to give U.S. policy imply for Southwest Asia? How did the United States propose to consolidate its position, and safeguard its interests, in the face of intensifying distrust between it and the Soviet Union? Could Israel expect a continued U.S. commitment to its territorial ambitions? Could Iran and Saudi Arabia continue to count on strategic cooperation? And what was Pakistan to expect from an administration that spoke in glowing terms about democratic India?

The Western Rim of Southwest Asia

The Carter administration took office with a commitment to seek a more enduring and encompassing settlement in the Middle East than had been achieved before. Accordingly, Carter announced that the resolution of the Arab-Israeli conflict would receive the highest priority in his administration. He pointed at the changed political perceptions of the states in the region—the Israeli position, Arab moderation, and the deescalation of the civil war in Lebanon—and insisted that the time was ripe for a fresh look at the Middle East and for new initiatives in the region. President Carter, therefore, eschewed several key elements of the Kissinger era, including step-by-step strategy, stalemate diplomacy, and separation of the Palestinian issue from an Arab-Israeli agreement. Instead, he adopted a comprehensive strategy of active participation in which Arab and Israeli interests were more evenly balanced.

The administration argued that all Washington had done so far with its leverage was to establish a cease-fire at a higher level of arms; it had not tackled the basic problems that had caused the wars. President Carter now wanted a policy that directly spoke to the outstanding issues between the Arabs and Israel. In this endeavor, he saw the United States not as merely a mediator but as an integral element in the peace process.[7] To this end the president was willing to bring the full weight of U.S. power, prestige, and resources to bear on the negotiating parties.[8] It was clear that both in substance and procedures President Carter had made a major departure from the approach of his predecessor.

CONCEPTUAL FRAMEWORK

There were five major assumptions in the Carter approach.[9]

1. *Urgency.* Carter believed that the Arab-Israeli conflict was a dangerous threat to U.S. interests in the region, particularly its oil interests, and that a repeat of the 1973 embargo had to be avoided. It was essential, therefore, to begin work immediately on a dialogue for peace in the Middle East.

2. *The U.S. Role.* Washington would be an active participant in reconciling differences and filling the "security assurance" gap if this participation was required.

3. *The Soviet Role.* The Soviet Union was interested in detente and in avoiding confrontation in the region. It was therefore likely to play a positive role, and Washington would encourage Moscow's participation.

4. *Approach to the Arabs.* Washington would promote the role of the moderate Arab states in the process, but it would also deal with the radical Arab regimes and try to bring them into negotiations. Carter believed these states had been forced into playing a negative role because of the past U.S. attempt to divide and isolate them.

5. *Approach to Israel.* Israel had to realize that, while its security was Washington's first interest and Carter would

> continue with military assistance as in the past, Israeli
> notions of timing, tactics, and substance would no longer
> receive the first consideration in Washington.

The connections between President Carter's liberal internationalist thrusts and his Middle East policies are not difficult to identify. First, he had argued that in the past the United States had been overly preoccupied with communism; as a result, it had missed opportunities for peace with the Soviet Union and influence in the Third World, where many regimes professed socialist or leftist nationalism. Since this preoccupation was no longer valid, the president would seek Soviet participation as well as a unified Arab endorsement for his peace proposals. Second, in line with Carter's policy to promote self-determination and human rights in the world, the Palestinians, who had long been denied such rights, were to receive full attention. And third, Carter's aversion to force dictated that all regional parties to the dispute, including their superpower allies, were to be brought into the negotiations. Carter believed that comprehensive accord would protect local regimes from the threat of aggression and diminish the need for U.S. intervention.

Out of this conceptual framework three central elements of the Carter design emerged: first, the meaning and substance of peace had to be redefined; second, territories and borders had to be ensured and firmly defined; and third, the Palestinian role had to be redefined. Defining the substance of peace he envisaged, Carter said,

> that means that over a period of months or years . . . the borders
> between Israel and Syria, Israel and Lebanon, Israel and Jordan,
> Israel and Egypt must be opened up to travel, to tourism, to
> cultural exchange, to trade, so that no matter who the leaders
> might be in those countries the people themselves will have formed
> a mutual understanding and comprehension and a sense of a
> common purpose to avoid the repetitive wars and death that have
> afflicted the region so long.[10]

Carter was thus committed to an accord that went beyond mere nonbelligerency.

The second element concerned territory, withdrawal, and secure borders. Carter did not identify precisely the lines of the future borders between Israel and the Arab states, but believed that Israel would have to withdraw from all occupied territories to the pre-1967 lines, with minor adjustments and modifications to allow for defensible borders.[11]

The Palestinian element assumed increasing significance in the Carter framework. In the past, the United States had either deliberately neglected the Palestinians or emphasized only the humanitarian dimension of the problem. President Carter was the first to officially recognize the legitimacy of the Palestinian demand for a homeland.[12] Although he did not go so far as to endorse an independent state for the Palestinians, he did envisage a Palestinian homeland linked in some way with Jordan.[13] In return the Palestinians had to recognize the Israeli right to exist and refrain from violating Israel's borders or her security.

IMPLEMENTING THE FRAMEWORK

Through 1977 to the end of 1979, President Carter determinedly tried to implement the framework and preserve the directions he had initiated. There were several setbacks and many obstacles, and the eventual shape of the Arab-Israeli agreement at Camp David was not what he had originally envisaged. On the whole, however, his efforts paid off.

As early as Carter's second month in office, Secretary of State Vance had gone to the Middle East to lay the groundwork for the administration's effort. This was followed by a round of exploratory visits by the regional leaders to Washington, in which each expressed his view, and the requisite conditions for peace. For instance, Israeli Prime Minister Rabin sought a statement of support to bolster his image at home and positive responses from Carter on coproduction of F-16 jet aircraft and sale of concussion bombs to Israel. Sadat arrived in Washington on 3 April seeking economic and arms assistance, and stressed the centrality of the Palestinian question. In May, Crown Prince Fahd of Saudi Arabia paid a visit to Carter during which both agreed that "the major effort should continue toward trying to reconvene the Geneva conference in the second half of 1977."[14]

This process received a serious setback in May 1977 when Menachem Begin won the election in Israel.[15] Begin's hard-line view on the Palestinian question and his determination to claim the West Bank and the Gaza were well known. The Carter administration feared that Begin might not play a positive role in the framework outlined by Washington. On his part, Begin was apprehensive about growing "pressure" from Washington.

Through early 1977, several Carter decisions had heightened the Israeli anxieties. For instance, Carter had cancelled the sale of CBU-72 concussion bombs and declared Israeli oil drilling in the Gulf of Suez illegal. The Carter-Begin meeting in July 1977 helped to smooth over some of these differences, but upon Begin's return, the legalization of West Bank settlements once again drove a wedge between Carter and Begin.

The administration continued in its efforts to reconvene the Geneva conference. Vance once again visited several capitals in the Middle East, but his trip was shadowed by Israeli settlement activities in West Bank.

The major problem for the administration was to evolve a formula for Palestinian representation at Geneva that would be acceptable to all. The administration proposed a unified Arab delegation that would include Palestinian representation. Israel agreed to Palestinian representation as long as it did not include the PLO, but the Arab states objected to this Israeli veto.

On 1 October 1977, hoping to influence the pre-Geneva bargaining, the United States and the Soviet Union issued a joint statement stressing the need to achieve a "just and lasting settlement of the Arab-Israeli conflict." The statement made explicit reference to the "legitimate rights of the Palestinian people." Explaining the administration's move to bring Moscow in, Vance said, "If they were prepared to play a constructive role as I believe they were in 1977, then I feel it would be much better to include them, because they could become a spoiler if they are not included."[16]

The joint statement opened floodgates of criticism from many directions. Israel did not like bringing the Soviet Union into the process because the Soviet presence was bound to strengthen the positions of such virulently anti-Israeli elements as Syria and the PLO in the talks. Israel was particularly apprehensive about the references to Palestinian rights and feared that Washington would compromise Israeli interests in its efforts to win favor with the Arab states. President Sadat appeared equally perturbed by the joint statement. He did not think much would come out of the Geneva process. He was extremely suspicious of Soviet intentions and believed that Egypt could no longer afford to postpone peace on its borders with Israel. The Egyptian economy was in serious difficulty, needing immediate attention and a massive infusion of resources.

In an unprecedented move Sadat announced on 9 November 1977 that he would go to Israel to discuss their mutual problems. Begin readily accepted the challenge. Sadat's move undercut the administration's entire conceptual framework. The initiative was now lost to Egypt and Israel while the rest of the Arab states, the Soviet Union, and even the United States were forced to watch from the sidelines. This is not what Carter had anticipated.

In fact, Carter had not anticipated the extent and strength of the adverse reaction to the joint statement. For instance, Congressman John Rhodes, Republican minority leader in the House, wrote in the *New York Times* that "the President succeeded in bringing our foremost adversary back into a position of influence in the Middle East."[17] Brzezinski admits in his memoirs, "we clearly needed the input of the President's domestic advisers, because the foreign policy of a democracy is effective only as long as it is sustained by strong popular support."[18] These words are especially relevant to a consideration of the last two years of the Carter administration. The pro-Israeli lobbies on Capitol Hill had gone to work whipping up opposition to the Soviet inclusion. By October, the president had abandoned all hope for reconvening the Geneva Conference.

Sadat was, however, anxious to have the United States back in the negotiations. The diplomatic activities following Sadat's historic visit began to be narrowed down to reconciliation of two major positions. Begin's autonomy plan envisaged an "administrative autonomy" for the West Bank and Gaza while Israel would remain responsible for defense and security. This meant a degree of freedom for the Palestinians but not self-determination. And Sadat's counterproposal basically reiterated the conditions set out in Resolution 242. On 4 January 1978 Carter met with Sadat at Aswan and devised what came to be known as the Aswan formula, which linked Egypt-Israel agreement to the arrangements for the West Bank and Gaza.[19] Israel had tried to prevent such a linkage. Begin retaliated by continuing the settlement activities and stating that Resolution 242 did not mean withdrawal from the West Bank and Gaza. Their diplomatic maneuvering was soon overshadowed by yet another cycle of the violence that is endemic in the Middle East. After a PLO attack on a busload of tourists on 11 March 1978, Israel invaded southern Lebanon, intending to drive the PLO out of areas bordering on Israel's northern settlements.

Despite the invasion, however, Egypt and Israel continued to negotiate. Finally, in September 1978, after much discord between Carter and Begin, an agreement over two documents was signed by Israel, Egypt, and the United States. These documents were the "Framework for the Conclusion of a Peace Treaty between Egypt and Israel" and the "Framework for Peace in the Middle East." The former was an agreement to conclude a final treaty that would provide for total Israeli withdrawal (in phases) from the Sinai, establish security zones, and bring about a full Egyptian-Israeli peace. The latter, which was more complicated, provided arrangements for negotiating the procedures for the election of a transitional self-governing authority on the West Bank and Gaza, terminating Israeli military presence there, and negotiating the final status of the West Bank and its relation to its neighbors. Jordanians and Palestinians were to be invited to participate in these negotiations.

Israel had signed the accords but feared that the second document would lead to a Palestinian state. Begin therefore continued with the West Bank settlements. The Carter administration saw this as an attempt to undermine the accords, and turn them into a separate peace agreement between Egypt and Israel. Carter threatened Begin with a "reassessment of [the U.S.] entire Middle East policy," just as his predecessor had done in 1975.[20] Not until Carter had paid a presidential visit to Cairo and Jerusalem did the contending parties make sufficient concessions to arrive at an agreement. The formal signature of the peace treaty took place at the White House on 26 March 1979.

A significant number of influential individuals, however, claimed that Carter's policies had greatly weakened U.S. strategic capabilities in the region. They felt that in pressuring Israel and in wooing the Arabs, Carter had not sufficiently acknowledged Israel's traditional role as a reliable ally and great strategic asset of the United States. In one view, Israel had "the best and most advanced facilities in the area, the best trained personnel, and by far the most stable political system." Given U.S. vulnerability in the area, the critics claimed, Carter had compromised a vital U.S. security interest and in fact inadvertently encouraged the Soviet Union to take advantage of the oversight.

Against this criticism it must be pointed out that Carter had displayed rare consistency, fairness, and tenacity in implementing his conceptual framework. He had been set back by Sadat's trip to Israel, but in his justification, for a comprehensive peace the president has been proven right. Had the Camp David negotiation included the PLO and the other Arab states, the later tragedies in Lebanon might have been avoided. In addition, Carter was correct in fearing for Egypt's isolation from the Arab world. Although this has been less dangerous than originally feared, Sadat's assassination and frequent instability in Egypt underline the risks involved in a lonely and separate path to peace.

With the signing of the Camp David agreements, the United States had become a direct partner in peace. The agreements also laid the groundwork for America's enduring influence in shaping the future of Arab-Israeli relations. It is certainly not correct to argue that Camp David had weakened the U.S. strategic position vis-à-vis the Soviet Union. The 1979 revolution in Iran was indeed such a setback, but it would require a great and implausible stretch of imagination to argue that the Islamic revolution was hatched in Moscow or that it has enhanced Soviet influence. Nor was it in any way related to Camp David. Similarly, there is no connection between the U.S. role in Camp David and the Soviet decision to invade Afghanistan. Even if Carter had continued the traditional policy of diplomatic coordination with Israel, that in itself would not have deterred the Soviets from invading Afghanistan.

Nevertheless, the president had been remiss in neglecting to mobilize popular and congressional support for his initiatives. This neglect forced him to abandon the pursuit of the Geneva conference, and to jeopardize most of his policy goals. His global strategy and the philosophical underpinnings of his liberal initiatives came under increasing attack. This shift in political support had become visible as early as mid-1977, when the simmering tensions suddenly gave way to a war between Somalia and Ethiopia over Ogadan.

The Southern Rim of Southwest Asia

The Horn of Africa had been in ferment since the mid-1960s, mainly because of unresolved tribal and territorial disputes. Somalia claimed the region of Ogadan, which was under the actual control of Ethiopia. While Emperor Haile Selassie ruled Ethiopia, it was backed by the United States as a part of the U.S. policy of supporting the three kingdoms of the region, Saudi Arabia and Iran being the other two. At that time, Somalia was supported by the USSR, which had obtained permission to construct a major base at the port of Berbera. Most strategy experts believed that this was an important asset if the USSR wished to influence North Africa and the southern gulf states.

These regional rivalries had larger implications. In 1977, there was a reversal of alliances between the regional contenders and their superpower supporters. Seeking strategic advantage, the USSR switched its support to Ethiopia. Simultaneously, having failed to get Moscow's endorsement for its ambitious plans, Somalia switched its alliance to the West.[21] In July 1977, Somalia invaded the Ogadan region of Ethiopia and made steady gains through the rest of the year.

As the situation worsened, the Soviet Union mounted one of its most spectacular and efficient airlifts, and sent 17,000 Cuban troops to Addis Ababa to help Ethiopia survive and repel Somali aggression. Cuban troops had already intervened in Angola in 1975, but on a scale that bore no comparison with this massive airlift.[22] It was this direct Soviet involvement that rang alarm bells in Washington. The Carter administration came under heavy fire from its conservative critics for its alleged inability to counter Soviet adventurism in North Africa. Carter found himself on the horns of a dilemma. If he came to Somalia's help, it would escalate tensions with Moscow and possibly abort the SALT II negotiations. Carter chose not to risk SALT II. But his growing sensitivity to criticism was apparent from the increasingly strident tone of the statements that now issued from the White House.

At the same time, it was also apparent that the administration remained divided about whether this region was in fact vital to U.S. interests in the Persian Gulf and West Asia. President Carter and some of his advisers believed that Bab-el-Mandeb, at the mouth of the Red Sea, was not really a key transit point of petroleum shipping and could not qualify any longer as a part of the oil jugular of the Western economies, since the oil tankers that had begun to ply the oil routes since the 1960s were too large to pass through the Suez Canal. This greatly reduced the strategic importance of the canal.[23] In this view, the real threat lay at the Straits of Hormuz, which connected the Persian Gulf to the Arabian Sea. Here the Soviet Union or any hostile state could direct a blockade not at the West or even Israel, but at Saudi Arabia. In that event, a blockade of the Bab-el-Mandeb straits would become a serious threat as it would hamper any military support to Jeddah. In 1976 and early 1977, U.S. strategists believed that the United States could rely on the French naval presence in Djibouti to keep it trouble-free. The French could operate from the island of Reunion, while the United States could rely upon the upgraded base at Diego Garcia as a springboard for a naval operation in the Indian Ocean.

On the other hand, the hawks in and out of the administration stressed the dangers of Soviet gains in the region and warned that a U.S. failure to counter them would be misunderstood in the Kremlin as weakness and acceptance of Soviet preeminence in the region.[24] This, they feared, would lead to the radicalization of the littoral states and give the Soviet Union the ability to close the straits of Bab-el-Mandeb, leaving the United States with no option but to respond militarily, at a time of Moscow's choosing, not of its own.

President Carter successfully resisted the advocacy of intervention, but he could not avoid making several concessions to his critics. In early 1978, the administration went on a verbal offensive over the entire range of Cuban and Soviet activities in Africa. Brzezinski warned that SALT was threatened by Soviet-Cuban incursions in the Horn of Africa, and on 16 February 1978, Carter declared that the United States would consider it a serious breach of peace, endangering even worldwide peace, if Cuban-supported Ethiopian troops should invade Somalia.

In a speech at the U.S. Naval Academy in June, President Carter declared, "the Soviet Union can choose either confrontation or cooperation. The U.S. is adequately prepared to meet either choice."[25] The Carter offensive was accompanied by several military measures. The aircraft carrier *Constellation* and a flotilla of escort ships from the Pacific

Fleet was dispatched to the Indian Ocean. Two U.S. AWACS (early radar warning and command planes) were sent from Okinawa to Saudi Arabia to carry out what the administration called "passive surveillance." A squadron of F-15 aircraft was also dispatched to Saudi Arabia, and the U.S. naval presence in the Indian Ocean was greatly reinforced.[26] The administration also stepped up its assistance to Somalia. These measures could not, however, determine the fortunes in the battle being waged on the ground. The Cuban-Soviet backed Ethiopian troops repelled the invading forces and inflicted heavy damage on Somali troops. At the defeat of U.S.-backed Somalia, the interventionists in and out of the administration began to demand immediate action, but President Carter was reluctant to get militarily involved.

The administration had good reasons for not committing U.S. forces to the region. First, given the Soviet airlifts of arms to Ethiopia and promises of more to come, a token U.S. commitment would not have changed the course of the battle. On the other hand, Carter did not think the U.S. public would countenance a large commitment of troops to a region not visibly vital to their interests. The memories of Vietnam were still strong. Third, he believed that arms negotiations with Moscow and agreement on the SALT were more important than winning one superpower contest in the Horn of Africa. Underlying this assessment was the Carter belief that a setback in Somalia was unlikely to threaten areas that were in fact important to the United States, i.e., the Persian Gulf and the Middle East.

Positions of Strength and Weakness

There were indeed sound reasons for this assumption. The U.S. position in Southwest Asia during 1977–1978 was, in fact, enviably strong. In contrast, Soviet influence was on the ebb. A look at the political alignment shows this. For instance, Soviet involvement in the Horn of Africa produced great strains in Iraq's relations with the USSR, because the latter supported Ethiopia. As a result, Iraq began moving more and more toward the West. Although Iraqi-American relations had not yet reached the point where formal diplomatic ties could be resumed, Moscow had every reason to be concerned over Carter's statement, made public on 11 June, that the United States would compete with the Kremlin for influence in Iraq.[27]

Egypt had already moved completely out of the Soviet orbit, while the Saudis had begun playing an active role in weaning Arab capitals away from Moscow's anti-imperialist front. South Yemen, which had been allied very closely to the Soviet Union after the Marxist revolution, was enticed by Saudi offers of aid. Relations between the two were restored in March 1976, and the Saudi cemented the ties by extending Aden $100 million in grants. Similarly, another Soviet ally, Sudan, turned to Egypt and Saudi Arabia after a bloody Communist attempt to overthrow its government. Egypt was persuaded to enter a mutual defense pact in 1976 and to form a joint tripartite organization for close political, military, and economic cooperation among Sudan, Egypt, and Saudi Arabia. With Egypt, Sudan, Somalia, and Saudi Arabia in a tacit anti-Soviet front and Iraq and South Yemen edging away from Moscow, Ethiopia and Syria became its only remaining political allies in the region. And even Syria was bogged down in internecine warfare with the PLO, which had become a reluctant ally of the Soviet Union. Similarly, the activities of the Red Sea Entente had been highly advantageous to the United States. Informally organized, the Red Sea Entente consisted of pro-West, moderate states: Egypt, Iran, Sudan, Somalia, and Saudi Arabia. The main purpose of the entente was to actively oppose the spread of radicalism, whether of the Islamic or revolutionary variety. U.S. collaboration with the entente was, in fact, far wider than was generally acknowledged. This was based mainly on U.S. bilateral security and economic ties with the entente members. For instance, in support of his Camp David initiative and the Red Sea Entente, Carter sold Iran $12 billion worth of arms, including AWACS, in his very first year in office. Early in 1978, he sent Congress a package deal that proposed selling Israel fifteen F-15's in addition to the twenty-five approved previously, plus seventy-five F-16's. To Egypt, he proposed to give fifty F-5E's, costing about $400 million, and to Saudi Arabia, sixty F-15's, costing $2.5 billion in all. A year later, in April 1978, Carter formally revealed a $4.8 billion package of loans and grants, mostly for military equipment, for Egypt and Israel. This was the first time that the United States was willing to sell Egypt sophisticated arms and equipment. Although most of these weapons purchases were financed by Saudi Arabia, it was an indication of the U.S. commitment to Egypt and of the administration's confidence in Egypt's avowedly anti-Soviet posture.

The other countries, Morocco and Pakistan, were also coordinating their efforts with the Red Sea Entente. Entente members maintained close working ties with each other and shared the intelligence they gathered. Although the individual members had differences with Washington over specific issues, on the question of penetration of Soviet influence their interests converged. For instance, in early 1977, President Sadat offered to contribute troops to serve as a "fire-brigade" in Africa, particularly to counter the growing Soviet-Cuban influence south of the Sahara.[28] Similarly, the Shah of Iran feared that the overthrow of Haile Selassie and the rise of revolutionary forces in both

Ethiopia and South Yemen would jeopardize the stability of the states around the Red Sea and the Persian Gulf. He was therefore willing to play the proxy for the United States and support with money and arms the anti-Soviet elements throughout the region.

In fact, the Soviet Union was so alarmed by the activities of the Red Sea Entente that in a major article in *Izvestia* Moscow lashed out at what it believed to be the main culprit. Quoting the French "bourgeois" paper *L'Aurore,* Moscow warned, "Riyadh directly or through other countries is attempting to draw such countries as Somalia and South Yemen into the conservative camp it heads." *Izvestia* further said,

> the heightened interest Riyadh is showing in unification as an intermediary between certain Middle East states should be viewed in this light . . . the furor over the alleged threat to the security of the Red Sea region has not only an anti-Soviet motive, but also objectives of splitting the anti-imperialist unity of the Arab states and diverting their attention from the basic task . . . eliminating the consequences of Israeli aggression.[29]

As far as Moscow was concerned, the Red Sea Entente activities directly threatened Soviet bases at Aden and Berbera, both considered crucial for the operation of Soviet naval forces in the Indian Ocean. It was in fact because of the Shah of Iran's financial and military urging that the Soviet Union was evicted from Berbera and Somalia had turned against Moscow. Although the advantages derived from entente activities were never publicized in Washington, President Carter had good reason to argue against those who claimed that the correlation of forces was tilting against the United States.

Indeed, his assessment of the overall strength of the U.S. position is independently corroborated. In a detailed study of Soviet policy in the Middle East, Robert Freedman concludes that

> the USSR's inability to maintain its position in Somalia had substantial effect on its overall position in the Horn of Africa and the Indian Ocean. Even if the Ethiopian regime ultimately emerged victorious from all of its battles . . . the Soviets had suffered an immediate tactical defeat in the region with the departure of Soviet advisors from both the Sudan and Somalia in the space of six months and the loss of the Soviet bases in Somalia.

He further pointed to the reverses in Yemen and Iraq and observed that whatever success the USSR had in the Ethiopian airlifts, they were adequately countered by the strengthened strategic position of the United States. "Not only did the U.S. unquestionably have the largest and most formidable base in the region on Diego Garcia, but the overall geopolitical balance in the region had shifted against the Soviets."[30]

President Carter could convincingly argue that the Somalian episode was not a significant setback for the United States, but he could hardly characterize the events in 1979 in Iran, Afghanistan, and Pakistan in the same light. As the Islamic revolution swept through Iran and Soviet troops invaded Afghanistan, every single liberal initiative he had espoused simply collapsed. The critics charged that the president had confused the allies of the United States, weakened its partners, and failed to chose wisely between friends and adversaries. We have already discussed this criticism in the context of the Arab-Israeli dispute and shown that Camp David was in fact a major gain for the United States. Were the critics right about Carter's failures in Iran, Pakistan, and Afghanistan? Was Carter handicapped by his emphasis on human rights? Did it encourage the revolutionaries in Teheran? Was Moscow emboldened by Carter's "weakness"? It is to these questions that we now turn.

Crisis in Iran, 1977–1978

The Carter administration, like its predecessors, believed that Iran was firmly under the Shah's control. Carter had visited Teheran at the end of 1977, and praised Iran as an island of stability. It was clear that almost no one in Washington had expected that, within a year and a half, revolution and collapse of the monarchy would totally alter the political map of the Persian Gulf. Throughout 1977 and early 1978, there were indications of growing discontent in Iran, but Washington had minimized their significance. U.S. intelligence assessments had concluded that there was no cause for concern. In their expert view, Iran was not in a revolutionary or even a prerevolutionary situation.[31] They stressed that the Iranian military was loyal to the Shah and that the opposition did not have the power to be more than troublesome. But these assessments were wrong. The protest against the Shah's government began in early 1977 among university students.[32] By autumn it had become clear that these were not the leftist students with whom the SAVAK was familiar, but an altogether different breed of protestors, for their revolts were clearly inspired by religion. In October 1977 there were large demonstrations on behalf of Seyyed Hashami, who had been sentenced to death for involvement in the assassination of other moderate clerics in Isfahan. In the same month, protest spread to the Majlis, the Iranian parliament. Still, at this point no one could have anticipated the events that were to follow. The Shah first attempted to split the opposition by co-opting moderate critics and using force against the extremists, but this strategy did not work.

In early 1978, the Shah reduced state disbursals to the clerics from $80 million to $30 million, hoping to bring them in line, but this had just the contrary effect. Similarly, when new taxes were imposed on the bazzaris, they joined the mullahs, who had already mounted a large protest. In early January, *Elte la' at* published an attack on Khomeini. It was said to be inspired by the Shah. The newspaper article accused Khomeini of reactionary ideas, homosexuality, and ignorance. This, in fact, further consolidated the emerging anti-Shah front of students, bazzaris, and clerics. Violence and strikes spread to many religious centers, bazaars, and universities, culminating in the declaration of martial law in Isfahan in August 1978. Riots broke out in Abadan during mourning ceremonies for 430 persons who had died in a movie theater fire that people insisted had been set by SAVAK. In September, thousands marched through the streets of Abadan and hundreds clashed with and were jailed by the government. The protest now spread to Teheran, and the capital too came under martial law.

It was no longer possible to stem the tide of the revolution that was sweeping through Iran. In October, 40,000 Iranian petroleum workers went on strike, drastically reducing Iran's oil production. By November, the entire country was under martial law. December 1978 was a fateful month. Seventy percent of Iran's petroleum workers stayed off the job in response to Khomeini's call for a strike. The military government failed to restore law and order or establish any balance of control over the revolution. It was at this point that the Shah agreed to a provisional civilian government under his appointee Shahpur Bakhtiar, a member of the opposition National Front. But this did not appease the Islamic leadership. There were massive demonstrations, and the new government also subsequently collapsed. On 16 January, the Shah left Iran, ending once and for all two decades of monarchy and abandoning Teheran to the Islamic revolutionaries.

In retrospect, it is evident that Carter had four basic policy options from which to choose. The first was to offer total support for the Shah. This was Brzezinski's choice. He believed that the Soviet Union had a substantial role in developing the revolution. Based on this, Brzezinski had advocated a pro-Shah military coup during the Shah's last days in Teheran, but by then the military was already in the process of collapse. The second possibility was to help mediate a negotiated compromise involving some reduction in the Shah's power and the formation of a coalition government. Ambassador Sullivan and Secretary of State Vance had favored this alternative. In Chapter 1, we discussed the transitional plan that they had outlined. Third, Carter could oppose the Shah indirectly and perhaps aid in his removal. This was advocated by some in the State Department's Bureau of Human Rights. Fourth, there was the option to avoid a stand and take no action beyond protecting U.S. interests elsewhere in the Persian Gulf.

This last option was never seriously contemplated since to do nothing as a policy alternative is incompatible with the U.S. political climate. The lobby for the third option was the least influential of the four, although the critics have charged that insistence on human rights and lack of support from Carter was the main cause for the Shah's weakening and collapse.[33] In their view, the Carter administration did not understand that, although apparently anti-Communist, Islamic revolutionaries were even more anti-U.S. and therefore potentially an attractive ally for the Soviet Union. Finally, they believed that Carter jeopardized U.S. interests by emphasizing the liberal commitments of imperial power without sufficient regard for its responsibilities.

Carter does admit to having "privately" spoken to the Shah about the need for liberalization during their meeting in 1977, but the Shah was categorical in his reply. "No, there is nothing I can do," he said. "I must enforce the Iranian laws which are designed to combat communism. In any case, the complaints . . . originate among the very troublemakers against whom the laws have been designed. . . . They are really just a tiny minority and have no support among the vast majority of Iranian people."[34] Carter acknowledges that "it soon became obvious that my expression of concern would not change the policies of the Shah." After this, the administration dropped all references to human rights in its policy toward Iran and instead stepped up its support of the Shah. Ambassador Sullivan's account of his last two years in Teheran substantiates this. The Human Rights Bureau had no direct influence on decisions regarding Iran in this crisis period. The "mixed signals" that the Shah saw were most likely the result of routine requests for information regarding human rights that all embassies were required to make by law.

With the power rapidly slipping away from him and the country rising up in revolutionary protest, the Shah faced the classic king's dilemma; he was damned if he acted against popular sentiments and damned if he did not. President Carter faced a parallel problem. Military action would not succeed unless it was large-scale, well planned, and forceful. Even then, there was the danger that the United States could get bogged down in a situation from which it might not be able to withdraw easily. Then the critics would attack him even more vociferously. On the other hand, he could not withdraw American support of the Shah and begin negotiating a coalition government. The critics were already attacking him for not being forceful enough in the support of the Shah. And Mohammad Reza Pahlavi was suspicious that the administration was secretly trying to undermine him.[35] For Carter, it was clearly a no-win situation.

Nor was it possible to rally the Iranian armed forces against the revolution.[36] The Shah had not been able to do it. In fact, advocates of this approach hopelessly underestimated the depth of opposition to the Shah and the long list of popular grievances against him.

First, there was the rapidly growing opposition to the Shah's repressive, authoritarian rule, the brutalities of SAVAK, the rampant corruption of the Shah's family and, above all, the Shah's dependence on the United States. Second, his program of modernization had inflicted a heavy burden on a large segment of the urban and rural population, which had become restive and discontented. Iranian society was fast becoming polarized between a tiny modern segment on the one hand, and the vast majority of the poor on the other. This underclass was to play an important role in the revolution. The Iranian clergy was also unhappy at having lost their lands in the reforms.[37] According to Nikki Keddie, a widely acknowledged expert on Iran, the Shah's industrialization strategy had intimately linked indigenous big business with international capital. While this made available some consumer goods for the urban upper class, the majority of the poor urban class as well as the small entrepreneurs, the bazzaris, suffered heavily from inflation and taxes.[38] The revolution was therefore an expression of mass discontent caused by structural dislocation.

Nicholas Gage's eyewitness account of the revolution fully substantiates the above explanation of the social upheaval in Iran. He writes, "While the religious leaders became the spokesmen of the revolution, they were strongly supported by the bazzaris.... For centuries the wealthy merchants of the bazaar and the mullahs ... have been mutually dependent ... the mullahs were responsible for educating the sons of the bazzaris and in return, the bazzaris financed the clergy."[39] Thus, the revolution was brought about by a wide spectrum of classes who merged together in opposition to oppression and overdependence on the West.

The Shah had come to realize the implications of the protests and demonstrations long before the Carter administration did. In fact, the speed with which the Shah's armed forces became weakened and divided left him with no option but to leave the country. If the Iranian military could not be depended upon, any prolonged U.S. intervention would have inevitably turned into a military occupation. This was a commitment that no administration could make then—or, indeed, can make now.

Nonetheless, the spate of criticism and charges of failure leveled at Carter were driving him closer and closer to the military option. Carter had warned Iran that, if the hostages were punished or executed, he was prepared to launch a direct and immediate military attack on

Iran.[40] "We pored over aerial photographs of oil refineries and many other targets of strategic importance there," Carter says in his memoirs, and "planned how best to carry out our threat to the Iranian leaders of quick punitive action." He made sure that everyone was aware that "we were not bluffing and they knew it." The abortive rescue mission of April 1980 had been the unhappy consequence of this policy.

Pakistan Estranged

Whatever Jimmy Carter felt about the validity of his liberal internationalist policies, Iran had not been the main object of their thrusts. This could not be said of the administration's dealings with Pakistan, a country that constituted the easternmost edge of America's Southwest Asia perimeter.

In Carter's view, close security ties with Pakistan were not critical for the United States. He saw no vital American political or military interest at stake in Pakistan.[41] This became evident in Carter's arms sales policy and in his insistence on nuclear nonproliferation and human rights in Pakistan.

The compromises in Carter's declaratory policies on arms to Iran have already been mentioned. Such compromises could, however, be justified in the case of Iran and Saudi Arabia since there was never any question about their importance to the United States. No such rationale was readily visible in the case of Pakistan, particularly as it was neither a source of oil nor critical to the protection of oil routes and shipping lanes.

In addition, until the end of 1978, the general political situation around Pakistan suggested no cause for alarm. True, the 1978 Saur revolution had altered the calculations there, but Afghanistan was never considered a U.S. responsibility. Kabul was a nonaligned government and, in Washington's eyes, by necessity pro-Soviet. Similarly, as shown earlier, President Carter had no clue about the damaging potential of the revolutionary situation in Iran. In the administration's judgment, the Shah appeared to be in control. What is more, President Carter wished to correct past U.S. mistakes in South Asia. For instance, both the Nixon and the Ford administrations had recognized India as the dominant power after 1971, but had effected no correspondingly appropriate changes in their policies. Although President Nixon had vowed to work through regionally influential states, he had neglected to explore India's potential as a partner in promoting U.S. influence in South Asia. Instead, the entire region was consigned to secondary status. India's pro-Moscow orientation did not overly concern President Carter, first because in 1977 and 1978 he did not believe Moscow to be as expansionist as his critics claimed, and second because the defeat of Mrs. Gandhi (who was known to be pro-Moscow and cool toward the United States) and the advent of Janata rule in New Delhi (which desired closer ties with Washington) had created new opportunities in South Asia. In Pakistan, the civilian government of Zulfikar Bhutto had collapsed and a military coup in July 1977 had ushered in a military dictatorship under Zia-Ul-Huq.

Several writers have hinted at the Carter administration's possible complicity in the overthrow of Mr. Bhutto.[42] They suggest that Washington had developed an intense dislike for Mr. Bhutto and his insistence on making Pakistan a nuclear power. The Carter administration, they claim, might not have discouraged the coup d'etat of 1977. Whatever the truth in these allegations, the Carter administration's ties with Zia began to slide rapidly into bitter and angry confrontations.

Soon after the Martial Law Administration of President Zia was in place, it became clear that President Carter had reappraised the U.S. stake in South Asia and had decided to upgrade India's role in U.S. policy. Deputy Secretary of State Warren Christopher stated in July 1977 in New Delhi that Washington expected India to play a "leading" role in South Asia. As Tahir-Kheli points out, "His statement was . . . seen as conclusive proof that Washington had 'abandoned' Pakistan to the wolves, leading to a sense of isolation that was punctuated by reliance on Chinese friendship and recognition that the future of Pakistan lay with the conservative Arab states who alone could underwrite the costs of Pakistan's independence and security needs."[43] President Carter excluded Pakistan from his itinerary when at the end of 1978 he visited both Iran and India.

The thrust of Carter policies also became evident in his reluctance to sell arms to Pakistan. Early in his administration, President Carter had promised to reduce U.S. arms transfers and declared that he did not wish to make arms trade a major instrument of U.S. foreign policy. The administration claimed that the level and volume of arms sales to individual states were often at variance with their real needs, in addition to the fact that the United States gained no commensurate advantage from such sales. In keeping with this new stance, the Carter administration rejected the Pakistani request for 110 A-7 fighter aircraft. These had been previously offered by Henry Kissinger. The Carter administration argued that its rejection was based on the decision not to introduce sophisticated weapons systems in South Asia.[44] In place of A-7s, the administration was prepared to sell Pakistan A-4s and F-5s.

Pakistan countered the argument by pointing out that India had MIG-23's and was buying Jaguars from Great Britain. These acquisitions were certain to leave Pakistan with no matching air defense. Pakistan therefore rejected the offer as a waste of money, and Washington formally withdrew the offer in June 1977. Pakistan was bitter about being made into an example of Carter's liberal policy initiatives.

Perhaps to return the U.S.-Pakistani ties to some level of amicability, in November 1978 Carter once again offered Pakistan seventy F-5s as a sign of goodwill. The Pakistanis, however, suspected this gesture as a ploy to dissuade them from exercising the nuclear option. The earlier overture, therefore, came to nothing. The administration argued that its offers of arms were commensurate with Pakistan's requirements, while Zia insisted that the proposed arms packages were composed of obsolete and aging weapons systems that could not even begin to meet the Pakistani need.

In line with its nuclear nonproliferation policy, the Carter administration came down hard on various Pakistani efforts to buy or acquire nuclear technology. When Pakistan still refused to forgo its nuclear option and continued to seek nuclear technology and parts abroad, the Congress, at the behest of President Carter, applied the Symington-Glenn Amendment to the International Security Assistance Act of 1977 and terminated all security assistance to Pakistan in April 1979. Pakistan did not see the Carter objections to the Pakistani nuclear program as a bid to prevent the spread of nuclear technology in the world. For Pakistan, Carter's objections were highly suspect since the administration had continued to supply India with U.S. nuclear fuel.

Last but not least, the administration's frequent admonitions on human rights violations irritated Pakistan. Zia had repeatedly postponed elections, banished the political parties, banned the press, and jailed hundreds throughout Pakistan. The indefinite postponement of elections by the martial law authorities in October 1979 was the last straw that broke the back of the U.S.-Pakistani ties. Carter expressed his unhappiness in no uncertain terms.

The Afghan Crisis

This was then the state of the U.S.-Pakistan relations on the eve of the Soviet march into Afghanistan. During 1978 and early 1979, while Carter policies were causing great disappointment in Islamabad, Zia had tried to draw Washington's attention to the events in Afghanistan—the unification of the rival left factions and the Saur revolution. However, President Carter, as we have pointed out earlier, was not overly worried. He was convinced that it was not in the interests of the Soviet Union to destabilize the area.

In this he was obviously wrong. Whether the Afghan invasion was motivated by a desire to control Persian Gulf oil, as a large number of experts claimed at that time, or whether it was merely a defensive operation, it undoubtedly altered the entire political and strategic calculations in the region. President Carter had been highly remiss in not following more closely the course of events in Afghanistan. It is obvious from Carter's account that, although the revolution of April 1978 had installed a Communist government in Kabul, he did not consider Taraki such a hard-line pro-Soviet Communist as some in the U.S. press had characterized him. In any case, the revolution appeared quite genuine.

Indeed, there were good reasons for this supposition.[45] In his early pronouncements, Taraki denied that his regime was Communist. He asserted that his goal was a "national democratic" revolution. Although the first claim was not credible, the second was partly borne out by the regime's moderate programs of social and economic reform. In foreign affairs, the Taraki government appeared keen to adhere to the Afghan policies of the past, i.e., nonalignment. On 6 May 1978, Taraki declared that his government was "trying to maintain friendly relations with the U.S." and added that this would depend on "the amount of economic and political support the revolutionary government received."[46] As to the new government's relations with Moscow, even the *London Times* of 29 May 1978 commented that it may be even more nationalist and independent than the government of Daoud.

Nor was Afghanistan an area of vital importance to the United States. Iran and the Camp David negotiations had Carter's full attention throughout 1978 and early 1979. Therefore, not until May 1979 did he become aware of the dangers of growing Soviet involvement in Kabul. The administration admonished and warned Moscow against intervention, but it was clear that Afghanistan was still almost at the bottom of its priorities. This was not in any way a departure from previous policy, much less an abdication of responsibility, since all postwar administrations had given Afghanistan no more than passing attention. Thus, during the Nixon presidency, the Shah of Iran had been the primary influence in Kabul. He had weaned Daoud away from a pro-Moscow position with offers of $2 billion in aid, a sum far surpassing Soviet pledges to the Afghan seven-year plan (1976–1983).[47] In return, the Shah was allowed to operate a SAVAK station in Kabul to help Daoud root out the "Communists." At Teheran's urging, Daoud even agreed to drop his militant support of the Baluchi and Pushtun tribes and sought a peaceful solution to the border problem with Pakistan.

In other words, both Afghanistan and Pakistan were being increasingly drawn into the Iran-Saudi orbit prior to April 1978. This could only benefit the United States. In fact, Daoud's move toward the West was to culminate in a meeting with Carter in September 1978, but before that could happen he was killed in the confrontation between the government and the newly united Communist party (consisting of both the Parcham and Khalq factions), and Taraki emerged as the new president of Afghanistan.

It is hard to say whether the United States could have prevented this in any way. Subsequent events, the growing turmoil in Afghanistan, and the Soviet invasion of December 1979, have in fact obscured from view the question of why President Carter did not contemplate more drastic measures in 1978. First, the 1978 Saur Revolution took everyone by surprise, including the Soviet Union. A majority at the time believed that the coup had not been a planned, long-awaited Soviet game plan as some were suggesting. Louis Dupree, a leading expert on Afghanistan, stressed the makeshift and haphazard nature of the revolution. Second, there was no public support for U.S. military intervention. The 1978 coup in fact went largely unnoticed. Third, the administration was aware that the Soviets had a special interest in Afghanistan and over the past two decades had developed enormous influence and close links with the Afghan ruling elite. Fourth, since a military confrontation with Moscow over Afghanistan was ruled out, Washington might influence events by providing arms and support for antigovernment Afghan insurgents. But here again, the U.S. hand remained stymied: There was hardly any popular opposition to the Saur Revolution. Mass uprisings and significant rebel activities did not emerge until mid-1979. By that time, the United States was fully occupied with events in Iran. In any event, the Soviet invasion finally put an end to Carter's liberal internationalist convictions.

The Soviet move immediately galvanized the Carter administration into frenetic activity. Carter offered Pakistan a package of $400 million in economic and military assistance and sent his aides to the Congress to canvass for its approval. The A-7 Skyhawk deal was revived, and the Pentagon began to draw up munitions lists for Pakistan. But, at the same time, Carter sought to reassure India that this represented no change in overall U.S. policy toward the South Asian subcontinent. Zia, however, rejected the offer as totally inadequate.

Carter tried to allay Zia's fears by reaffirming the 1959 agreement of cooperation with Pakistan. But Zia insisted on a formal treaty. This, he reasoned, would end once and for all the United States' ambivalence and attempts to balance its moves toward Pakistan against their repercussions in India. The United States remained reluctant for precisely this same reason. On arms also, the two remained very far apart. Pakistan produced a list of weapons that added up to nearly $11 billion. Since the U.S. intention was not to rearm Pakistan so that it would become a formidable military power, but merely to address the immediate threat, no further progress could be made on this question. In any case, it was obvious to all, including Zia, that Carter was fast losing popularity at home and that the hostage crisis, unless resolved soon, could very well cost him the presidency. There was no point in negotiating with a president who was on his way out. Additionally, Zia was gaining wide sympathy and support among the rapidly growing number of hawks and hard-liners both in and out of the administration. He must have felt confident about receiving a favorable hearing at a later point, and he was right.

The Carter Years Assessed

By the end of its term in office, the Carter administration was overwhelmed by charges of indecisiveness, vacillation, and failure, but a closer examination reveals that in Southwest Asia as a whole Carter's performance should be judged as mixed: not wholly a failure, nor wholly a success.

In the Camp David agreement, Carter had established a structure of peace in the region. To that extent he had established a basis for enhanced U.S. presence there. But here the United States was more a mediator and an agent of peace rather than a biased supporter of Israel. The Carter administration had stepped up and strengthened the U.S. strategic infrastructure by building stockpiles of arms in Israel, Egypt, Saudi Arabia, Sudan, Somalia, and, of course, Diego Garcia. As is evident in the activities of the Red Sea Entente, the United States successfully used regional powers to counter Soviet influence and bolster U.S. interests. In this regard, the Carter administration had continued the basic thrusts of the foreign policy implemented during the Nixon-Ford-Kissinger years.

The institutionalization of Egypt's pro-West moderate stance in the Camp David agreements was in fact Carter's major achievement. According to one leading expert, "The new Egyptian orientation has outweighed even the importance of the Iranian revolution, and its benefits have continued beyond Egypt's partial excommunication by those Arab states that oppose the Camp David agreements."

President Carter had refused to be drawn into the crisis in the Horn of Africa, which in any case had only dubious connections with alleged

Soviet designs over Saudi Arabia. This refusal was held up as a grave error of judgment by critics. But in retrospect, the Soviet Union's activities have not enhanced its position there or in Africa. If anything, the cynical flip-flop of commitment in the Horn of Africa has greatly hurt Moscow's standing among its clients in the Arab world.

There is no consensus among critics as to why Carter "failed" in Iran. A major line of criticism focused on Carter's moralistic foreign policy conception and lack of adequate knowledge of Iran. Over the passage of the last few years there has been considerable rethinking on this issue, but at the time, Carter's human rights policies were held to be the major cause for U.S. failures. The advocates of this argument contend that the Shah did not use force because he feared that, if he did, the administration would withdraw support. Against this contention it should be pointed out that Carter could not be held responsible for the Shah's apathy or failures to use force. Indeed, the incident at Jaleh Square in September 1978 shows that force had been used but had failed to intimidate the protestors, who were soon back in the streets. Iranian military officers were also reluctant to confront the revolutionaries. The failure of the Bakhtiar government—which had been one last attempt by the Shah to retain some control—and the division within the armed forces on the question of compromise with the revolutionary leadership, led one to conclude that the military option Carter's critics thought so appropriate was not available before 16 January 1979.

A second line of criticism perceives U.S. "failures" in terms of personality clashes in Washington, tactical mistakes, lack of information, and indecisiveness, but not as a failure to resist the momentum of secular historical forces. To put it simply, in this view, the Iranian revolution was not a genuinely popular movement. Recent research has revealed this indeed to be the case.

The question still remains as to whether President Carter could have done something to better prepare the United States to bear the consequences of the revolution. This issue has two dimensions; the first revolves around developing a better-informed, coherent, firm response, while the second turns on the adequacy of Carter's measures after the hostage crisis. In regard to the first, the assumption that better knowledge about the internal politics, culture, and ideological orientation of a region will automatically enable the United States to make the correct response is indeed debatable. The kind of information that might be available and the sorts of decisions Washington is called upon to make might have very little connection. To "know" that Islamic fundamentalism is a dangerous enemy does not empower a president to stop it. In addition, it must be pointed out that the "information" and "knowledge" the White House receives is often ambiguous and even contradictory.

Many critics often overlook yet another factor that is decisive in the formulation of U.S. policy. This is that U.S. policy goals (moralistic or *realpolitik*) and the U.S. choice of options are conditioned by the balance of political forces within the United States. Even if Carter had been convinced of the soundness of Ambassador Sullivan's advice to open negotiations with Khomeini, while the Shah was still on the throne, such a move was politically impossible. It would have brought angry denunciations from a majority in and out of the administration. The imperatives of political survival often dictate a course of policy that might result in eventual failure, but in the context of politics such a choice is still arguably wise. Indeed the United States is no stranger to this dilemma.

On balance, there was not much President Carter could have done to stem the tide of revolution in Iran. Nor could he have done much after the revolutionaries took U.S. citizens as hostages. It is therefore unfair to accuse Carter of deliberately weakening the position of the United States in the Persian Gulf, or to suggest that such weakening emboldened Moscow to invade Afghanistan.

In fact, it has been pointed out that on the part of Moscow the invasion of Afghanistan was a protective move. After the hostage crisis in November 1979, Moscow was convinced that the United States might be preparing to intervene and might at the same time move against the pro-Soviet regime in Kabul.

As to Afghanistan, U.S. interests there had been only peripheral. On the other hand, Soviet proximity and Soviet policy had given Moscow immense advantages. Carter did not think it appropriate to plunge the United States into an armed confrontation with the Soviets over their activities there. There was very little support for such a move.

In this sense, however, his policies toward Pakistan were somewhat shortsighted. Insofar as India did not serve U.S. strategic interests and Pakistan did, the Carter diplomacy toward Islamabad was unnecessarily heavyhanded. But on the other hand, it is doubtful whether a greater commitment to Pakistan would have deterred the Soviets from invading Afghanistan. It would only have blocked improvement in relations with India.

On balance, the failures of Carter's policies were failures of timing and manner of diplomacy rather than of basic thrust. However, Carter never had the time to carry his thinking to its logical conclusion. The rising clamor for more combative, militaristic measures undermined all that had been proposed. Carter did not fail to balance the responsibility of imperial power with its liberal commitments; he sought to temper the first with the second, and failed mainly because the crises that were beyond his control destroyed the immediate logic of his policies, and the rise of hawkish sentiments undermined their rationale. Carter's greatest failures were not so much conceptual, but political. He failed to convince the U.S. public and preserve intact its support for his global initiatives.

What caused the popular tide to turn against Carter? It is to this we turn in the next chapter.

Notes

1. Stanley Hoffman, *Primacy on World Order* (New York: McGraw-Hill, 1978), 93.

2. For a discussion of the Trilateralist strategy of global interdependence, see Richard Cooper, "A New International Order for Mutual Gain," *Foreign Policy* 26 (Spring 1977); Fred Bergstern, "The Threat from the Third World," *Foreign Policy* 11 (Summer 1973); 2. Zbigniew Brzezinski, "Trilateral Relations in a Global Context," *Trialogue* 7 (Summer 1975).

3. Reported in the *New York Times,* 6 January 1978.

4. The PRM 10 conclusion contradicted the findings of Team B, appointed by President Ford. The team had warned of a continuing Soviet military buildup.

5. For elaboration of these notions, see Tom Farer, "The U.S. and the Third World," *Foreign Affairs* 48 (October 1975).

6. The focus on human rights and Carter's criticism of Soviet treatment of its dissidents angered Moscow. Brezhnev warned Carter not to interfere in the Soviet Union's internal affairs. See *Pravda,* 22 March 1977.

7. Speech of Vice-President Walter F. Mondale to the World Council of Northern California, 17 June 1977.

8. *Department of State Bulletin* 76 (30 May 1977), 547.

9. These are succinctly described by Steven Spiegel, "Does the United States Have Options in the Middle East," *Orbis* 24 (Summer 1980), 399–400.

10. *Weekly Compilation of Presidential Documents,* 13 (Washington, DC: U.S. Government Printing Office, 21 March 1977), 361.

11. The Carter administration argued that Israel could not have both territory and peace. A smaller Israel would ensure Middle East stability, and a stable Middle East would prevent an adverse linkage between oil and Arab-Israeli conflict. See Brzezinski, "Recognizing the Crisis," *Foreign Policy* 5 (Winter 1974–1975), 67.

12. *Weekly Compilation of Presidential Documents* 13 (16 March 1977), 361.

13. *Weekly Compilation of Presidential Documents* 13 (26 September 1977), 1378.

14. Quoted in *Washington Post,* 25 May 1977.

15. Carter hoped that the election of Prime Minister Begin would "not be a step backward" in the achievement of peace. Quoted in *Washington Post,* 22 May 1977.

16. For Vance's interview, see *Washington Times,* 8 June 1983.

17. *New York Times,* 14 October 1977.

18. Brzezinski, *Power and Principle: Memoirs of the National Security Adviser,* 1977–1981 (New York: Farrar, Straus and Giroux, 1983), 73.

19. "President Carter's Statement at Aswan," *Department of State News Release,* 4 January 1978, p. 1.

20. See reports in *Jerusalem Post,* 1 March 1979; *New York Times,* 1 March 1979.

21. See Farer, *War Clouds on the Horn of Africa* (Washington, DC: Carnegie Endowment for International Peace, 1976), Chapter 2; Robert Freedman, *Soviet Policy towards the Middle East since 1970* (New York: Praeger, 1978), 284.

22. *New York Times,* 14 November 1977; also see *Strategic Survey* (London: Institute of Strategic Studies, 1978), 13–14.

23. Scott W. Thomson, "The American-African Nexus in Soviet Strategy," *Horn of Africa* 1 (January–March 1978), 42–46.

24. Shahram Chubin, "U.S. Security Interests in the Persian Gulf," *Daedalus* 109 (Fall 1980), 31–67.

25. President Carter's 7 June 1978 speech at the U.S. Naval Academy is reproduced in its entirety in Congressional Quarterly, *President Carter 1978* (Washington, DC: 1979), 148A–151A.

26. *The Middle East,* 5th ed. (Washington, DC: Congressional Quarterly, 1981), 73.

27. Quoted in *Baltimore Sun,* 12 June 1977.

28. Michael Ledeen and William Lewis, *Debacle: The American Failure in Iran* (New York: Alfred A. Knopf, 1981), 91.

29. *Izvestia,* 16 April 1977. Translated in *Current Digest of Soviet Press* 29:15, 5. See also Vladmir Larin, "Ethiopia: Who Gains from the Tension," *New Times* 19 (1977), 10.

30. Freedman, *The Soviet Policy towards the Middle East since 1970,* 311–312.

31. Jimmy Carter, *Keeping Faith: Memoirs of a President* (New York: Bantam Books, 1982).

32. For the chronology of revolutionary events, see Lawrence Ziring, *Iran, Turkey and Afghanistan: A Political Chronology* (New York: Praeger, 1981), 156–187.

33. See Ledeen and Lewis, *Debacle;* Shirin Tahir-Kheli, "Proxies and Allies: The Case of Iran and Pakistan," *Orbis* 24 (Summer 1980), 333–353.

34. Carter, *Keeping Faith,* 436–437.

35. William Sullivan, *Mission to Iran* (New York: W. W. Norton, 1981), 156–157.

36. Ibid., 239.

37. For political perspectives on the Iranian revolution see *MERIP Report Iran in Revolution,* 75–76 (March–April 1979); *Iran: Imperial Pretensions and Agricultural Dependence,* 71 (October 1978); *Land Reform and Agribusiness in Iran* 43 (December 1975); *Iran: The Economic Contradictions* 69 (July–August 1978). See also Nikki Keddie, "The Iranian Power Structure and Social Change 1800–1969: An Overview," *International Journal of Middle Eastern Studies* 2 (1971), 320.

38. For a succinct discussion of these issues, see Keddie, "Iran: Is 'Modernization' the Message?" *Middle East Review* 11 (Spring 1979).

39. Nicholas Gage, "Iran: Making of a Revolution," *The New York Times Magazine*, 17 December 1978, 134.

40. Carter, *Keeping Faith,* 466.

41. This new stance was underscored by the exclusion of Pakistan from Carter's itinerary during his December 1977 visit to Teheran and New Delhi.

42. Tahir-Kheli, *The United States and Pakistan* 68–69.

43. Ibid., 73.

44. Ibid., 93.

45. G. S. Bhagava, *South Asian Security after Afghanistan* (Lexington, MA: Lexington Books, 1983), 34–36.

46. *The Times* (London), 8 May 1978.

47. Maya Chadda, "Super Power Rivalry in Southwest Asia," *India Quarterly* 37 (October–December 1981), 506.

4.

Domestic Sources of U.S. Policy in Southwest Asia

Jimmy Carter had the misfortune to preside over some of the most traumatic events in postwar U.S. foreign policy. Not only was the United States in retreat everywhere, or so growing numbers of citizens thought, but his policies were held directly responsible for this state of affairs. In fact, no president since Johnson had endured, as Carter did, the fierce attacks on his administration from both the right and the left of the political spectrum. The right attacked him for mismanaging the economy and for remaining complacent in the face of an obviously dangerous Soviet drive for global hegemony, while the left castigated him for not doing enough to reshape the main thrusts of post-Vietnam U.S. policy, for selectively and only conveniently applying human rights, and for underwriting repressive and undemocratic regimes in the Third World, notably in Iran and Saudi Arabia. This peculiar dilemma of the Carter presidency cannot be understood except in terms of the two competing worldviews that have traditionally shaped U.S. policy, what Daniel Yergin calls the Riga axiom and the Yalta axiom.[1]

These are the two principal perspectives from which U.S. conduct in the world is usually judged and criticized. The main difference between the two lies in their views about the Soviet Union and about what each defines as the strategies and intentions of the men in the Kremlin.

Those who subscribe to the Riga doctrine believe that the Soviet Union is an international revolutionary state committed to unrelenting ideological warfare and powered by a Messianic drive for world domination. The Yalta doctrine, on the other hand, admits to the competition between the two superpowers but argues that Moscow should be viewed as a traditional great power attempting to expand its reach within the existing international system, but mainly through defensive rather than offensive strategy. The corollary to the Riga doctrine is that Soviet leaders are not amenable to reason and cannot be relied upon to abide by agreed-upon rules of international conduct. The Yalta axiom, on the other hand, assumes that competition between the two great powers is manageable and that Soviet actions reflect more Moscow's sense of inferiority than its aggressive designs.

President Carter, for his part, followed neither the Yalta nor the Riga axiom in shaping policies. Carter and his "trilateral" minded advisers contended that the post-Vietnam world had changed and that the assumptions that had guided U.S. policies in the past no longer applied.[2] They believed that all events could not and ought not be interpreted in terms of U.S.-Soviet relations. This was why President Carter emphasized the centrality of North-South dialogue and sought to uncouple SALT from negotiations with the Soviet Union over their mutual interests in the Third World. Unfortunately, these diverse parts of his policies did not add up to a coherent, integrated whole. Therefore, although he was right in perceiving the need for a new international order, and in a dim way his policies did indeed reflect this, at best their purpose and their connections to national interests remained unclear.[3] Carter could neither deflect nor resist the growing demands for accelerated defense spending and for hanging tough with the Soviet Union. He had no option but to reverse his policies in midcourse, and it was equally clear that such a reversal would cost him the presidency.

Yet, as shown earlier, until the events in Iran and Afghanistan occurred, the U.S. position on the whole and influence in the Middle East and the Persian Gulf were enviably strong. The Camp David agreements had brought Egypt, the linchpin of the Arab bloc, firmly on the side of the United States. Massive arms sales and agreements for strategic collaboration with Israel and Egypt had immensely strengthened the U.S. presence throughout the Middle East. Displeased with Soviet activities in the Horn of Africa, Iraq was moving away from Moscow. Saudi persuasiveness and financial assistance had succeeded in opening up doors even in staunchly pro-Moscow South Yemen. In Iran, the Shah appeared to be firmly in control. (As detailed in the last chapter, no one seriously thought that the Shah would lose his grip in Iran.) Sudan had signed a mutual defense pact with Egypt, and the combined efforts of Riyadh, Cairo, and Teheran were successfully winning friends for Washington in the Persian Gulf, North Africa, and Southwest Asia.

What, then, caused Carter to totally reverse his policies on all major issues—the Soviet Union, the Third World, and the value of coercion in the conduct of U.S. policy? Why did he withdraw the SALT from being ratified in Congress and order the creation of the Rapid Deployment Force, committing the United States to a military response in Southwest Asia? Why were earlier achievements in the region totally ignored while the nation so single-mindedly focused on the Soviet threat? To be sure, the succession of setbacks in 1979 was dangerous enough, but these cannot fully explain Carter's total reversals on all fronts, nor can they explain why even before 1979 events came to be increasingly seen as U.S. retrenchment and Soviet advance. This view permeated the consciousness of the nation to the point where the United States was believed to be in full decline everywhere while the Soviet Union was seen to be on an offensive throughout the world.

By 1978, the United States was welded together in its fear of growing Soviet military strength and Moscow's unrelenting drive to gain control over the strategic areas of the Persian Gulf. These fears were reinforced by the weakening of the U.S. economy; inflation, declining productivity, and rising deficits had become chronic problems. The critics of the Carter administration, particularly those of the New Right, had found two targets for attack: the decline in U.S. power abroad, and the weakening of the economy at home. They insisted that the decline in the economy was a result of the expansionist welfare state, and the strategic weakness a direct consequence of shrinking military expenditures. In their view, the welfare state had undermined the creative, innovative, and enterprising spirit of the United States, while weakening in the U.S. military posture had caused the nation to seek appeasement. What the country needed was strong leadership and a firm resolve, but Jimmy Carter, the critics claimed, was not the man to provide either.

The Riga Axiom versus the Yalta Axiom

Both major perspectives on U.S. policy, whether as defined by the Yalta axiom or the Riga, agreed that the world had indeed changed in ways that required a thorough reassessment of the dangers and opportunities abroad, but they differed on what these dangers were and what would constitute an effective solution. The controversy revolved around four key issues, each of which had a clear and direct implication for U.S. policy in Southwest Asia. The first concerned the capabilities and intentions of the Soviet Union and the appropriate response to Soviet actions. The second focused on the uses of U.S. military power, especially in the Persian Gulf and generally in the Third World. The third and related concern was the dangers to the United States of instability in the Third World and its causes, and the fourth addressed the nature of U.S. economic interests in the Persian Gulf and ways to protect them.

The advocates of the Riga axiom, or what Holsti and Rosenau call the Cold War internationalists, believed that post-Vietnam U.S. policy had become defunct because it had ignored the most fundamental factor that must underwrite U.S. national interests, i.e., its strategic military strength.[4] This folly was further compounded by both the Nixon and the Carter administrations through their failure to understand the true nature of Soviet communism and the significance of its military build-up, which had been both massive and steady since the mid-1950s. According to early estimates cited by the Cold War internationalists, the Soviet Union was spending $12 billion or thereabouts on defense since 1976.[5] This represented a cumulative increase of more than 40 to 70 percent over that in the 1960s.

By the fall of 1979, the proponents of Cold War internationalism were insisting that the dollar value of Soviet military expenditure exceeded U.S. military spending by 25 to 50 percent.[6] "It is quite evident," they declared, "that strategic parity is slipping away from the United States and that the Soviets can be expected to achieve meaning-ful strategic superiority probably by 1982 and most certainly by 1985, unless we take the most urgent steps to reverse current trends." According to their estimate, the Warsaw Pact enjoyed a more than 50 percent edge in nuclear warheads and the continuing buildup of SS-20s gave the Soviets a decided advantage in the European theater.[7] What is more, in 1979, the Soviet forces numbered 1.6 million men, 80 percent more than what the United States could claim, giving them an immense lead in both the conventional and strategic military balance. These advantages were further reinforced by "asymmetries of geogra-phy, which placed the most critical theaters (the Persian Gulf in particu-lar) close by Russia and far from the United States."[8] These analysts insisted that the combined strengths of the Soviet forces enabled Mos-cow to project its power abroad and shape politics in the Third World to suit its purpose. It is interesting to note that the early Reagan assess-ment echoed precisely similar concerns. The Reagan defense depart-ment declared that "the USSR is gaining increased access to military facilities and is supporting proxy conflicts in Africa, Southwest Asia, Southeast Asia, and the Western hemisphere."[9]

To the advocates of the Riga axiom, the Soviet Union had acquired nuclear superiority over U.S. land-based missiles, which posed an incalculable threat for the United States as well as for the world because, in their view, the Soviets could launch a surprise attack, destroy 90 percent of U.S. Minuteman missiles, and threaten the free world. Even if the United States retaliated with the thousands of nuclear warheads remaining on its submarines and bombers and reduced Soviet cities to a rubble, the Soviet Union could still fire back with the missiles they had not used and kill at least 100 million more in the United States. Facing such a choice, the president would be forced to abstain from retaliation and give in to the Soviet leaders. Even if the attack never came, the Cold Warriors insisted that a president, fearing Minuteman vulnerability, would never have the nerve to test this. In other words, the Soviet military buildup and U.S. neglect had made the United States vulnerable to Soviet blackmail.[10]

The Cold War internationalists (CWI) further argued that even if the purpose of the Soviet military buildup may not be to precipitate such a confrontation as just outlined, it undeniably conferred important political advantages on the Kremlin. In fact, those who adhered to this view claimed that this had been a long-held Soviet ambition. Since the postwar revolution in Soviet doctrine, its strategy was first to create a counterweight to U.S. nuclear capabilities; second, to achieve a progressive rollback of U.S. extended deterrence over its global strong points and commitments (Japan, NATO, and the Middle East), creating thereby a way to successfully carry out a low-risk Soviet political military offensive on a matching scale (Angola, the Horn of Africa, and Afghanistan); and third, to build a "paralyzing counterdeterrent or a strategic nuclear posture so formidable as to prohibit even a desperate lashing out by the United States in its retreat before advancing socialism. This is why, the CWI argued, the Soviet Union had built up their strategic forces and sought to divide the NATO by talk of detente and by concentrating great effort on its war-fighting posture."[11] In the view of the CWI, the U.S. position in the 1980s in the Persian Gulf resembled the Soviet position at the time of the Cuban missile crisis in 1962, when the Soviet Union had to retreat, but this is not likely to be the case in a future confrontation.

That the Soviet Union was aware of U.S. vulnerability was evident from its success in establishing air and naval bases ringing the globe, the CWI pointed out. These are "located at choice points which stake out some of the most strategic real estate in the world. These extend across Southern Asia from Vladivostok to Cam Ranh Bay and westward to the Horn of Africa and in the Caribbean, eastward from Cuba to Grenada—with naval infrastructure in the South Atlantic on the western coast of Africa."[12]

On the Soviet resolve, the CWI observed that "the Soviets may not be bright enough to feed themselves, but they have not forgotten what war is all about, nor do they fail to comprehend, as we seem to, what is needed to project air power and naval power on a global basis." To suggest that this extension of its military power was merely for defensive purposes showed nothing but a total lack of understanding, the CWI claimed, and a blind refusal to recognize in the Soviet Union the profile of a classic military power. If the invasion of Afghanistan, the CWI argued, was to be construed as merely defensive, the Soviets would "quite obviously leave no country in a state of safety, except possibly New Zealand."[13]

In the CWI view, the acquisition of conventional fighting and long-range airlift capabilities by the Soviet Union was clearly meant to challenge the U.S. strategic position in Southwest Asia and the Persian Gulf. The Soviet purpose was to acquire a degree of preponderance that would keep regional powers in line with the Soviet Union.

A series of events in the recent past had indicated that the Soviet Union, far from tiring of its responsibilities as a leader of communism, had in fact entered a new phase in which orthodox Marxist-Leninists were to be supported over governments and regimes that espoused a nationalistic socialist posture. Moscow's new-gained confidence in its military power was outlined in the Brezhnev doctrine, which committed the Kremlin to the defense of new revolutions in the soft areas of the Third World. The Persian Gulf and the Middle East were just such areas and offered ready opportunities for Soviet penetration.[14] The CWI pointed out that this was evident from the establishment of slavishly pro-Soviet governments in South Yemen and Ethiopia in 1975, and Afghanistan in 1979. Each was strategically located in relation to the rich oil fields and oil supply routes from the region. Afghanistan in itself was not important to the Soviet Union, but it was a hotbed of disputes among tribes that spilled over into both Iran and Pakistan. The Baluch and Pushtun irredentism offered Moscow a priceless opportunity to undermine the U.S. position with its CENTO allies, Iran and Pakistan. Under the most optimistic scenario, the CWI pointed out, pressure from Afghanistan and India would lead to a breakup of Pakistan, paving the way for the emergence of a pro-Soviet client state in Baluchistan and direct naval access to the Persian Gulf and the Indian Ocean.

In order to gain these strategic advantages, the Soviet Union did not hesitate to have Daoud assassinated or to promote a Communist takeover in Kabul. According to the CWI the 1978 Soviet involvement in South Yemen similarly led to the purge of government opposition and establishment of a pronouncedly more pro-Moscow regime in Aden. When some resistance developed later in the person of Selim Rubai Ali, he was executed in a strange sequence of events that began with the assassination of North Yemeni President Ghashami. At the time, 5,500 Soviet, Cuban, and East German advisers were stationed in that country. Moscow also tried to overthrow Siad Barre and was behind the attempted, but failed, coup in Iraq in the spring of 1978.[15] In each case, the existing government's pro-West moves had precipitated the attempts. The Soviet moves were not, therefore, accidental, nor were they simply opportunistic, the CWI declared. These gains, in fact, had the potential to become cumulative and self-reinforcing. The CWI contended that the network of Soviet military facilities in Yemen, North Africa, and Afghanistan was likely to become a springboard for future Soviet expansion.

Western access to Persian Gulf oil was, therefore, clearly threatened, since the Soviet Union also coveted the oil, both in order to deny it to the West and to supplement its own declining production. Viewed in conjunction with the weak and unstable conditions of the Gulf powers and their inclination to use the "oil weapon," the growing Soviet pressure clearly endangered the United States in the region. By undermining the U.S. position in Southwest Asia and the Gulf, the Soviet Union in effect threatens U.S. position in Europe and, for that matter, everywhere.

The Cold War internationalists argued that the United States had no way to counter and offset Soviet advantages in the region. The first priority, therefore, had to be to close the gap between U.S. and Soviet strategic forces and to make U.S. land-based nuclear missiles invulnerable. Secondly, there was no real substitute for a strong U.S. presence in the Persian Gulf and Southwest Asia. Past attempts to build regional security arrangements or find proxies to protect U.S. interests had failed and were certain to fail in the future. Thirdly, U.S. conventional forces and military doctrine had to be strengthened. The Rapid Deployment Force (RDF) envisaged in the Carter doctrine was not adequate to stem the tide of Soviet advance if the occasion so demanded.[16] What had been proposed by Carter was essentially a trip-wire force. Therefore, the United States must first enlarge and strengthen the RDF and establish strategic ties with states in the region, and then secure bases for prepositioning equipment and supplies to rapidly counter a Soviet offensive or domestic instability that might threaten U.S. interests. Since, with the exception of Egypt, most of the Arab nations had refused the United States the use of their territory for bases, the United States had little choice but to depend on Egypt and

Israel for strategic collaboration. This is why the United States, they said, must consolidate the gains of the Camp David agreements and forget about settling the Palestinian problem for the time being.

Not all Cold War internationalists subscribed to the last condition but many highly influential members of the Reagan entourage advocated that the United States should make Israel the centerpiece of its Middle East strategy. Others perceived collaboration with the Arab states to be a better alternative, particularly in view of the oil, but no one disputed that Israel's security was central to U.S. interests in the region. As we will see later, the Reagan administration was confronted with these two conflicting advocacies during the Lebanon war in the summer of 1982, but managed to resolve these tensions by following both policies simultaneously. In the Middle East environment of 1980, this proved to be highly successful, at least in the beginning. Aided and abetted by the pro-Israel lobby, the CWI continued to stress the reliability of Israel over the Arabs. In fact, the idea of refusing accommodation both to the Soviets and to their surrogates in Afghanistan, Ethiopia, the PLO, and Syria was particularly appealing to them.

To sum up, this view called for a mass strengthening of U.S. defense; the rollback and containment of Soviet advances all along the Soviet heartland; unabashed but not injudicious use of force as an instrument of U.S. policy; and the reversal of anti-U.S. trends in the Third World through security assistance and economic and diplomatic offensives. In the CWI view, the soldier and his role had been neglected for too long by U.S. policymakers in favor of the diplomats. It was time the balance was tilted in favor of the former or else, they warned, the future would be lost to the Russians forever.

Those who opposed this view and argued in favor of the Yalta axiom rejected both the analysis and the solution proposed by the Cold War internationalists. Their main criticisms took the following line of argument:

1. Soviet policy was not a deliberate, planned, and masterly march toward world domination. More plausibly, it was a relentless attempt at achieving equality with the United States, an effort to gain equal power to shape the world and to be consulted in the settlement of disputes, and an attempt to break the U.S. monopoly of control of the high seas. All evidence suggested that the Soviets meant to achieve and exercise the power to intervene if the occasion arose (as the United States had done for the past three decades), but that they were not bent on some relentless search for world domination.[17]

2. Although the Soviet Union would skillfully exploit opportunities, it was mainly a cautious power. The argument that upheavals in Angola, Mozambique, the Horn of Africa, South Yemen, Afghanistan, and Vietnam somehow represented a preconceived Soviet blueprint for control over strategic areas was simply untrue, because these were essentially disparate events resulting from diverse reasons that had little initial connection with Moscow. Of the above, the leftist nationalism in Mozambique, Ethiopia, South Yemen, and Vietnam had genuinely indigenous origins. What is more, in most instances, the pro-Soviet elements profited from Western mistakes, defeats, or as in the case of Afghanistan, indifference.

3. Despite the steady buildup, the Soviet advance in strategic and conventional forces was in no position to overwhelm the West, which still retained a clear superiority in all but land-based missiles. And even here, the nightmarish scenario of Soviet surprise strikes was totally baseless. First of all, the estimates of Soviet defense expenditures were highly exaggerated.[18] Admiral Gene La Roque and David Johnson of the Center for Defense Information pointed out that dollar estimates of Soviet defense will almost always be high because such calculations assume that Soviet soldiers are paid at U.S. pay scales and the cost of their weapons and equipment are also based on estimates of how much it would cost to produce those items in the United States, where inflation, labor, and other such costs are high. The same arguments were advanced by Arthur Macy Cox in the *New York Review of Books* about fears of Minuteman vulnerability. These were based on assumptions of technical accuracy that were simply not obtainable at this time.[19] If the Soviet Union were indeed to launch an attack on U.S. Minutemen, it would have to be totally sure that its missiles would hit the targets after their flight of many thousands of miles. In principle, this should happen, but both sides knew the gap between theory and practice. Most experts agree that a sure hit is impossible to predict in advance. Gravitational quirks, unexpected winds, and varying densities of the air could disrupt the intended ballistic path. This meant that the Soviet Union

had to be ready to absorb a massive U.S. retaliation in a
Soviet first-strike scenario. No one doubted that, despite
all the inaccuracies of their missiles, both had sufficient
nuclear warheads to destroy each other almost
completely. But this could hardly be the objective of
Soviet leadership. The "Soviet first-strike" scenario
assumed that the Soviet Union would not only hit the
targets, but that the Soviet leaders were sure that they
could get away with little or no damage. Thus, alleged
Soviet superiority or ability to blackmail the United
States was nothing but a fantasy.[20].

4. The United States was not militarily weaker. The Soviet
Union had merely acquired parity in some realms. In any
case, U.S. preponderance could not have been expected
to last forever. Nor was the loss of preponderance
entirely a Soviet doing. The resurgence of Europe and
the rise of economic nationalism among Third World
countries, for instance the OPEC nations, had made the
world multicentered. To impose a bipolarity of vision
could only result in distorting reality. The United States
had to learn to live with this as it had to learn to manage
its relationship with a competitor that had achieved near
parity in armed strength.

The recent setbacks in Africa and Southwest Asia were said to be U.S.
defeats, but in every instance, proponents of the Yalta axiom argued,
the setback was due not to lack of material power but to a deficiency in
political analysis—a failure to anticipate events and judge the force of
nationalism. U.S. strategic superiority could not prevent the humiliation in Vietnam, nor could the United States bring all its firepower to
bear on Iran to force the release of the U.S. hostages. Superiority in
arms did not necessarily add up to an advantage in regional balance of
power. Nor was it wise to ignore regional situations in favor of global
advantages.[21] U.S. policy in Angola under Nixon was a disaster because
it endorsed and promoted a link between UNITA and South Africa in
order to rout the FNLA, which initially had a very limited fighting
capacity. This turned most of black Africa against the United States and
brought Soviet-Cuban forces into the region. Intervention only made
sense if the United States was not engaged in propping up an unpopular, corrupt, or weak regime in the Third World. At best, these efforts
turned out to be only "quick fixes." The long-term problem of stability
in the Third World could not be solved by intervention.

These analysts also argued that Soviet involvement in Africa and elsewhere did not stem from any strategic reversal between the United States and the USSR, nor could the United States do anything about the Soviet efforts to enhance their own capabilities. Strengthening U.S. capabilities in itself was not sufficient to deter the Soviet Union from intervening if Moscow was presented with an opportunity. Such an opportunity could be a result of realignment of internal politics within a country, or it might be an outcome of regional conflict. The proponents of the Yalta doctrine argued that if the Soviet Union was quick to seize such opportunities, then one had to remember that the U.S. record in this regard was not without blemish.

In their view, the CWI underestimated and deliberately ignored the immense advantages the United States already enjoyed. To begin with, the U.S. economy was immeasurably more powerful than the Soviet; and second, the United States played a key role in the open international economy, wielding great influence over many nations in the world. By comparison, the Soviet system suffered from inefficiency, agricultural shortages, a bloated bureaucracy, and a backward technology. Politically also, the conflict with China and the turmoil in Eastern Europe (Poland) was a constant source of anxiety for the USSR. Nor was it successful for long in retaining the allegiance of Third World nations. Its expulsion from Egypt, Sudan, Somalia, and Mali, and its growing problems with Iraq, India, and even Syria as well as the total failure to make any headway in Iran, all suggested that local nationalists were as capable of ousting the Soviets as they were of betraying the good faith of the West. While the CWI were obsessed with the services Cuba provided Moscow, they overlooked the cooperation the United States had received from Egypt, Saudi Arabia, Iran under the Shah, and even from South Africa, not to mention Britain and France, its NATO allies.

Besides, there were serious obstacles to projecting Soviet power. For instance, much had been made of the Soviet occupation of Afghanistan as a springboard for the invasion of the Persian Gulf nations, notably Iran and Saudi Arabia. But it was not at all clear if this was the Soviet intent. First, the Soviet invasion of Afghanistan had been a defensive action motivated by a need to shore up a fledgling pro-Soviet revolutionary regime. A step-by-step chronology of the Afghan episode revealed no premeditated Soviet grand plan to threaten the Gulf. The Soviet Union had been opportunistic, but it was also reacting to being ousted from the Middle East. Fear of Islamic fundamentalism spilling over Soviet borders was yet another motivating factor in the Soviet invasion. To ignore the circumstances that led to it and to focus on the act alone was a willful attempt to distort reality in the interest of self-justification.[22] Second, military experts point out that, despite improvement, the "current Soviet force projection capabilities represent, at best, only a rudimentary potential to project into and to sustain power in distant crisis areas, particularly when opposed by an adversary."[23] In any case, the best invasion route into Iran was through the north, and here too, the Zagros Mountains and the difficult terrain were likely to offer a formidable barrier to any invading force.[24] The Soviet Union had, therefore, to be prepared to make a major commitment if it meant to threaten the oil fields. It could hardly be a low-risk adventure. Thus the imminent threat to Persian Gulf oil was more imaginary than real. A more plausible scenario for many Gulf littoral states was an Iran-type internal upheaval. But in this case, military solutions would simply not work.

It is obvious from the foregoing that although both the hawks and doves agreed that the post-1962 Soviet military buildup had carried superpower competition onto a different plane, the two drew diametrically opposite conclusions with regard to the appropriate U.S. response.

Ascendancy of the Riga Axiom

Opposite perceptions about the Soviet Union were not simply ad hoc views gathered and produced by a single event, nor were they a result of specific actions by Moscow. Rather, they were part of a larger whole, a Weltanschauung in which each competing ideology served as a filter through which perceptions about the Soviet Union passed and acquired specific meaning. Thus, the CWI ignored evidence that did not fit into their overall belief, and instead focused on events that reinforced their assertions. In other words, particular Soviet actions on the world stage did not in themselves amount to a "threat" but had to be perceived as such. This was true of liberal internationalists as well.

By the end of 1978, the advocates of accommodation had dwindled to a minority, and the nation seemed to single-mindedly focus on the Soviet threat. There were several reasons why this happened. First, since the Second World War, there had been a distinct shift in international politics from bipolarity to multipolarity, which allowed greater freedom to other nation-actors to pursue their national destiny, often at the expense of former great powers—i.e., the United States or the USSR. For instance, since the mid-1970s several revolutions had brought nationalistically minded independent governments to power in Africa, Central America, and Southwest Asia. The breakup of the

Portuguese empire had brought left-leaning regimes to power in Angola, Mozambique, and Guinea Bissau. Similarly, a revolutionary command council had toppled Haile Selassie in 1974 and ushered in a regime that was sympathetic to Moscow and espoused socialist ideology. In Central America, indigenous guerrilla movements in Nicaragua, Guatemala, and El Salvador were directed against U.S.-backed military juntas and military dictators. The anti-Shah revolution in Iran was almost by definition against the United States. In the circumstances, it was understandable that the United States should feel it was losing control over events. However, it is important to bear in mind that not all events were instigated by the Soviet Union, nor did they benefit Moscow in every instance. The setback to the United States, although undeniable, was not on account of Soviet advances. This was not its only or even the main reason. Nor was it from a U.S. lack of will to act. Instead it was a reflection of a growing autonomy of other political actors on the world stage.

Fear of growing resource vulnerability was the other reason why the United States felt insecure and anxious about its position. The formation of OPEC and the successful exercise of the "oil weapon" raised the frightening possibility of other nations in the Third World following suit with regard to other strategically important resources and minerals. And this the United States feared could produce serious problems, particularly when its economic dominance over the Western alliance was rapidly eroding. In 1950, the U.S. GNP accounted for 50 percent of the total world GNP, but in 1980 the figure had sunk to about 30 percent. With tough competition from Germany and Japan and the loss of markets to those two, the United States was definitely on the defensive in international markets. The economic resurgence in Europe and Japan had generated tensions and differences between the United States and its allies on policies toward the Soviet Union, the Arab-Israeli conflict, and even over the handling of the Afghan crisis.

Added to all of the above was the increased power and strengthened strategic capacity of the Soviet military forces, which could be neither ignored nor dismissed as insignificant. And although acquisition of new weapons by the Soviet Union may arguably have no aggressive purpose, it was certainly a cause for concern. All three developments—anxiety about resource vulnerability, relative loss of power compared to other nation actors, and Soviet military strength—combined to produce a profound sense of insecurity and fear about the future of the United States. The geographic focus of this anxiety was inevitably the Persian Gulf, since that is where Western access to vital resources could arguably be threatened, and where the

Soviet Union enjoyed the advantage of proximity. Fears about the vulnerability of Southwest Asia and a Soviet grand design were therefore a part of a larger, more general sense of anxiety that gripped the United States in the 1970s and not, as some have proposed, a result of any single sequence of events.

What were the domestic implications of this perceived weakness of the U.S. position? For an answer, we should turn to the rise of conservativism in the United States. Under the pressure of a host of New Right groups, diverse anxieties were welded into a single national platform for the 1980s. The major opposition working against the liberal internationalists was generally of two varieties. On the one hand, there were the old conservatives, organized into right-wing anti-Soviet groups such as the American Security Council, which included some retired military officers and ambassadors; the Emergency Coalition Against Unilateral Disarmament, whose constituents included the American Conservative Union, Young Americans for Freedom, and the Committee for the Survival of a Free Congress; the National Strategic Information Center, a pro-military lobby; and the Center for Strategic and International Studies, a research institute at Georgetown University. These were joined by two relatively new groups made up chiefly of old-time liberals, anti-Communist trade unionists, some intellectuals, and dissident conservative democrats. The group that called itself the Coalition of Democratic Majority, which had been formed in opposition to McGovern's presidential nomination in 1972, also did not favor Carter's brand of populist internationalism. The second new group was the Committee on Present Danger, formed in 1976. The committee was supported by intellectuals and conservative critics such as Norman Podhoretz and Richard Pipes. To this, one must add the corporate lobbies for defense contracts as well as a group of Jewish organizations collectively recognized as the Israeli lobby. On domestic issues, the new right-wing religious groups, such as the Moral Majority and the National Committee for Conservative Action, joined forces with the above and together constituted a formidable opposition to the liberal internationalists and detente-minded administration of President Carter.

The resurgence of Cold War militancy can be largely attributed to the efforts of these groups.

Cultural Malaise and the Breakdown of Authority

In the late 1970s there was a growing feeling that the United States faced a breakdown of the international order from which it would emerge the loser and that this in turn was the result of its economic decline. No one could really dispute the decline. It was evident in double-digit inflation, gaping budget deficits, a fluctuating dollar value, the growing noncompetitiveness of major industries, and declining productivity. However, one could certainly argue about the cause of the decline and its contribution to the alleged weakening of U.S. global power, particularly the proposition that this weakening was a consequence of the rising Soviet threat.

What the economic disarray did was to provide the neoconservatives with issues and a public receptive to their particular theory of the "American decline." It also provided them with an opportunity to vastly widen the popular base of Cold War ideology. The reasoning they offered centered around two basic themes: social instability and political impotence. The analysis they presented focused on the weakening of the national will. The causes they offered stressed the "subversive influence" of the "new class" that espoused anti-American values and made undue demands on the political structure that the latter could neither avoid nor fulfill. This, they believed, led to the overload and breakdown of government and the undermining of its legitimacy as well as its authority. They claimed that this sapped the will of the elite and made the United States vulnerable to threats from within and without.

The initial warning of the impending crisis was sounded in the 1970s by Daniel Bell in an article published in *Encounter* entitled "Unstable America." The conditions of plenty in the late 1960s had prompted Bell to call for an end of the ideology of the 1960s; the *Encounter* article, on the other hand, was suffused with concern over the setting in of instability. He was soon joined by Irving Kristol (now the editor of *Public Interest,* a conservative journal), and other well-known figures in the academic world including Nathan Glazer, Robert Nisbet, and Aaron Wildavsky.[25] All repeatedly expressed alarm over declining social stability and the growing fragility of social and political institutions in the United States.

In an important study entitled *Neo-conservatives,* Peter Steinfels identifies the basic beliefs of members of this group. They were hostile to the "Great Society" programs and paid considerable respect to the forces of the market as well as to traditional values and institutions such as religion and the family. These beliefs made much of the "high culture" of Western civilization and showed a bitter dislike of the "counterculture." They were also intensely opposed to communism and the course of the Soviet Union.[26]

The neo-conservatives claimed that the weakening of the national will had reached crisis proportions and was linked to the rise of what they called the "adversary culture." Lionel Trilling had used this term to describe the "subversive intention" of modern writings—the opposition to bourgeois values, the need to affirm the sense of self over social constraints. The neo-conservatives believed that the "adversary culture" had rapidly gained ground in the West and had become the ruling spirit of an entire "new class" in the 1960s. This new class was the university-government-media combine, or, mostly those with higher education, cosmopolitanism, and theoretical training. According to Steinfels, the neo-conservative's "new class" is half an analytical concept, half a political device, but above all, the new class is a "convenient" way to label whomever the neo-conservatives don't like. These are "affluent professionals, secular in their values and tastes and initiatives, indifferent to or hostile to the family, equipped with post-graduate degrees and economic security and cultural power." Steinfels argued that the neo-conservative thesis about the emergence of such a class was not necessarily wrong, but that its explanatory power was based on how widespread and how powerful it was believed to be, and on both these points, the neo-conservative judgments are largely speculative and personal—and, in Steinfel's own judgment, patently wrong. The belief in both the nature and pervasiveness of the new class, however, charged their "sense of crisis, their fears for social security and their militancy."

The neo-conservatives also argued that government and political institutions were in a state of crisis because of the excessive demands on their capacity. The *Trilateral Report* of 1975 joined the neo-conservatives in this concern. It argued that the "democratic surge" in the late fifties and early sixties had led to a substantial increase in governmental activities. While this fulfilled some of the demands of the liberal left, it unfortunately destroyed the one condition that is imperative for true liberty: a delicate balance between public and private responsibilities. As a consequence, the U.S. was in the grasp of a "distemper of democracy" which could only be relieved by scaling down government and going slow on demands for equity and political participation. This represented the preoccupation of Samuel Huntington (later to become part of the Carter inner circle), Aaron Wildavsky (who warned about the increasing weakness of the presidency), Nathan Glazer, and James Wilson. They all saw free society threatened by consequences of allegedly unrestrained political pressures. Although Carter had based his position on Trilateralist thinking and rejected the arguments made by the neo-conservatives, these two perspectives had much in common. They were concerned about the crisis of authority in society, overextension of government control, and the need to recapture America's leadership of the international economy. In any case, by 1978 neo-conservative themes were increasingly echoed in Carter's statements, sometimes, it appeared, even against his better judgment.

The notion of "overload" is linked in neo-conservative thinking to the decline in "necessary" defense expenditures and the rise of the "unnecessary" welfare state. The "overload" was, they argued, caused by naive liberalism, the exhausting demands of an "underclass" that stubbornly resisted integration into the mainstream of America, and ever-increasing demands for real and immediate equality. Although there was no consensus on which of the three causes explained the breakdown of governmental institutions, in neo-conservative thinking the real threat lay in the opportunity and issues they provided for the "new class" to capture power.

In the face of this crisis, neo-conservatives urged that authority must be reasserted and the government protected. This could be done by retaining only the programs that forestalled and defused social tensions. The rest had to be phased out. In their view, the excesses of the welfare state had created the current problem, and so there was no choice but to retreat from such overcommitment to social and economic equality. Decisions regarding the allocation of resources and investment, they insisted, were the legitimate concerns of the market. Governmental interference not only overloaded political institutions but also undermined the effectiveness of the most efficient agents of economic decision making, i.e., business and the corporate world. Moreover, such interference only gave greater power to the "new class," which invariably capitalized on the problems of the "underclass" to extend its domain. This kept public attention and energies focused on the wrong issues. The problems of the underclass were largely insoluble, but the demand for economic equality had destroyed the delicate balance between the public and private domain, which the neo-conservatives perceived as critical for the preservation of economic vitality and political freedom. The United States had to be freed from the influence of the counterculture, they argued, and returned to the moral and cultural values that constituted its fundamental strengths—the restoration of family, private initiative, the work ethic, and greater respect for law and government. These were not just the neo-conservative remedies for the restoration of national stability. The same panaceas, they argued, had to be applied to the international order—in short a stable, unified society at home and an assertive U.S. policy abroad. But both needed discipline and a strong allegiance to the nation. This, they knew, could be obtained by emphasizing the Communist threat to the United States and the Third World and by rejecting liberal values in the United States.

This was the continuous thread running through much of neo-conservative thinking, whether on domestic problems or international instability. The U.S. "failure of nerve" in face of the Soviet peril paralleled the alarm over governmental failures in face of the relentless demands for welfare benefits. In the first case, Soviet totalitarians were the main enemies, while in the second, the "new class" was the villain. It was therefore not coincidental that many members of the "new class" were also seen as "appeasers" and "apologists" for the Soviet Union who had to be ousted from power. It is this crusading spirit, however ill conceived, that charged the neo-conservative with a sense of mission for the 1980s. Their analysis of the domestic causes of the "failure of institutions" was matched by similar and equally vigorous attempts to inform the nation about the implications of growing Soviet military power and its consequences for international posture of the United States in the world, but particularly in Southwest Asia and the Persian Gulf.

To sum up, the neo-conservatives' logic was as follows: The decline of the United States was caused by the wrong-headed policies of the "Great Society" and unjustifiable faith in detente. Both had failed. The nation already faced a dark period of danger and immediate peril. The Soviets were surging ahead with their global ambitions and their military buildup, while the "appeasers," practicing the politics of weakness, were busy handing them every opportunity to do so. Nowhere was the U.S. decline more evident than in Southwest Asia, a region offering ready and ample proof of growing Soviet ascendancy. As one CWI publication put it, "over the past ten years, a series of events have occurred which have made it more difficult for the United States and Western powers to project military forces into the Persian Gulf. The reasons for this have to do with the growth of Soviet power projection and the growth of the military capabilities of local states [Syria, Iraq]. . . . A third, more negative reason has to do with the decline of United States and allied . . . military presence."[27] This argument went on to state that the United States could do little if the Soviets decide to invade Pakistan or intervene in the Persian Gulf. U.S. impotence was complete. What the author suggested was that the United States had to reassess its strategic concepts and the relationship between its interests in the Persian Gulf and NATO, particularly its southern flank. "The first innovation should be that the Western alliance must 'redraw' the maps of its strategic theaters to indicate growing linkage between them." The world was one, the peril was indivisible, and so the response had to be global. To conclude in the words of Geoffrey Kemp, "Geopolitically, this means that the artificial distinction between

NATO's boundaries—which end at the border and the Tropic of Cancer—and the Middle East must for purposes of wartime contingencies be removed."[28] Armed with these arguments, the conservatives had no difficulty in translating the slightest setbacks to the U.S. position in Southwest Asia into a major advance by the Soviet Union. These arguments had the added virtue of being simple and seductively logical. They reduced complex forces in the world to one or two simple propositions. For citizens bewildered and anxious about the succession of crises during 1979, global politics suddenly became intelligible and the solution to their problems deceptively easy.

Sources of Neo-Conservative Influence

The New Right had launched a thoroughgoing ideological attack on the entire philosophy and practice of the policies of the 1960s. For them, it was a "philosophy of weakness."[29] By 1976, they had achieved considerable national unity and had begun enjoying the center stage in the national debate, but their efforts in fact go back well before that.

The 1973 oil embargo had enabled the conservatives to forge a link between the oil crisis and the Soviet threat. Still, in 1975, their assessment of the likely Soviet reaction in the event of a U.S. takeover of Persian Gulf oil remained largely optimistic. In a January 1975 issue of *Commentary*, Robert Tucker argued in favor of such intervention and thought it was technically entirely feasible. He wrote that the oil embargo was a turning point in history and must be responded to by "employing extraordinary means" to break the power of the cartel (OPEC) politically and economically. Soon there followed another piece in the March issue of *Harper's* attributed to Edward Luttwak, a highly influential voice in military circles and one of the principal proponents of the Riga axiom. He too advocated an unhesitating use of military force should the Arabs interrupt the flow of oil, and predicted that the Soviet Union would not move to counter this. Robert Tucker had also argued that the seizure of Arab oil fields would "markedly improve Israel's position" and had added that it would be both useless and insincere to deny the present linkage between the oil crisis and the steady erosion of Israel's position in U.S. strategy. He pointed out that, in the volatile Middle East, Israel was the only reliable and effective U.S. ally if the purpose was to deny the Soviet influence in the region, and hence Carter's pro-Arab position made little political sense. Such was the response of the Jewish intellectuals to the U.S. predicament. They advocated strategic collaboration with Israel, separation of Egypt

from the rest of the Arabs, and a deemphasis of the Palestinian problem.[30] They sought to focus popular anger on the Arabs and hoped
that some or perhaps all of these objectives could be accomplished. In
any case, they were convinced that such a strategy would strengthen the
U.S. position in dealing with the Arabs and the Soviet Union. Given the
above calculations, it became automatically necessary to harp on the
worst-case scenario and appeal to both the fear and pride of the U.S.
public, the two elements that are critical to the mobilization of
nationalistic sentiments. Throughout the late 1970s there was no
dearth of reports and articles in the media, as well as academic journals,
attempting to do precisely this. However, in 1975, as one general
observed, "the no-more Vietnam" dictum was still powerful.[31]

Nonetheless, the controversy over the seizure of oil remained very
much in the public eye, channeling popular anger against the Arabs
while portraying U.S. helplessness against price-gouging by greedy
Arabs. Ironically, this was happening when in fact oil prices had
stabilized and even declined somewhat in real terms. The repeated
harping on the oil problem in the U.S. press invoked a great many
apprehensions in the Arab world. For instance, the *Arab Report*
claimed, the "United States National Security Council has completed a
detailed review of top-secret Department of Defense Plan to invade
Saudi Arabian oil fields in the event of another Middle East war." The
plan code was named operation "Dhahran Option Four." The *New York
Times* concurred that such blueprints, once a matter of mere party talk,
had begun to be taken seriously in Washington circles. According to
Walter Goodman, if the operation were swift and successful, "polls
would show overwhelming support for the action," and "we should see
a flowering of friendship for the Israelis who would then . . . be our
main allies in the area."[32]

In August 1975, John Collins and Clyde Mark presented a feasibility
study entitled *Oil Fields as Military Objectives* and concluded that such a
seizure would not be without serious problems.[33] Although the United
States could defeat the armed forces of a given OPEC state, the element
of surprise could not be achieved. In other words, the Arabs could
deliberately blow up their facilities, which would defeat the very purpose of the action. The significance of the report lay in the fact that,
although it doubted the efficacy of intervention, it had not questioned
the wisdom of using force to obtain resources that did not belong to the
United States in the first place. This much, therefore, had been accomplished. As the oil urgency vanished, President Ford declared that the
United States had no intentions of taking over Arab oil. In the popular
mind, the oil threat was, however, properly linked to the decline of the
U.S. economy and international prestige.

While Carter was careful not to unduly anger the Arabs, a pro-Israeli and anti-Arab mood predominated in Congress. U.S. strategic weakness in the Persian Gulf began to receive inordinate attention. For instance, a frequently cited Brookings study of U.S. intervention between 1946 and 1975 concluded that there were benefits to be derived from discrete and limited use of armed forces when they complemented diplomatic postures.[34] One by one, therefore, the restraints of the post-Vietnam era were being shed by the U.S. intellectual establishment. The study drew attention to this and observed that "as the Vietnam War faded from the nation's consciousness and as other recent blows—Watergate, the 1974–75 recession—likewise receded, voices urging a more active United States role in world affairs are being heard more clearly."[35]

Above all, the issue of detente engaged the Cold War internationalists' attention most. SALT II became their principal target. In his introduction to a collection of essays on problems of national security, W. Scott Thomson wrote that as the belief that force was an outmoded instrument in the discourse of nations spread in the post-Vietnam America, "a most extraordinary gathering of some of the nation's senior strategists was held at Strategic Air Command (SAC) headquarters in Omaha in the blistering cold of December 1975. It was the first time that so diverse and wide-ranging a group of experts had gathered at so high a level of secrecy to assess what most of them in their individual arenas were coming to see as worrying trends in the balance of forces." Apparently, the decision to launch a campaign against the "detente mentality" was made at that time, because the themes that were sounded at the conference have since become stock arguments of the CWI. The first systematic platform of the new campaign was laid out in a book entitled *Defending America* (1977). In this, Paul Nitze warned that the Soviet Union was fast acquiring a "theoretical war-winning capability," while Fred Ikle, who later became the undersecretary of defense policy in the Reagan administration, discussed the ways in which crisis mentality could be provoked to obtain increases in defense spending. In a sequel to *Defending America,* the CWI published a volume entitled *National Security in the 80's.* In this, Albert Wohlstetter warned the nation about the alarming decline in U.S. defense spending and its dangerous consequences for the nation. He claimed that, since the early 1960s, the United States had systematically underestimated Soviet increases in their offensive forces. Since the CIA undertakes to collect such estimates, Wohlstetter's study was not unlike the findings of Team B, which had rejected earlier estimates and asserted that the USSR had embarked on a massive buildup in order to gain a dangerous edge in strategic and conventional forces. Team B included Paul Nitze and Richard Pipes; both later came to be leading members of the Committee on Present Danger (CPD). At about the time Wohlstetter's article appeared, Pipes led a study of Soviet strategy in Europe sponsored by the Stanford Research Institute. Pipes was highly critical of detente as a one-sided phenomenon and argued that it dovetailed with the Soviet strategy of trying to detach Western Europe from the United States. In keeping with the theme of "loss of nerve," Ray Cline at the CSIS wrote a *World Power Assessment* stressing the factor of "will" as the key to the strategic equation and attacking detente for its role in eroding the will of the West.

After being eased out of the Nixon administration, James Schlesinger spoke directly to the theme of weakening national will. He wrote, "world-wide stability is being eroded through the retrenchment of American policy and power." "This growing instability," he argued, "reflects visible factors such as the deterioration in the military balance, but also, perhaps more immediately, such invisible factors as the altered psychological stance of the United States, a nation apparently withdrawing from the burdens of leadership and power."[36] He and others who shared his views expressed deep worry over the loss of confidence, "faltering American purpose," and U.S. "impotence."

What was remarkable about the resurgence of the Cold War ideology in the 1970s was that the argument it presented for the first time linked the Soviet menace directly to U.S. control over resources, and these two in turn to the decline of U.S. power in ways that could be seen and felt in the daily lives of every citizen. Also, the threat was no longer confined to Europe, but had shifted decisively to the unstable region of Southwest Asia and the Persian Gulf and had taken Europe along with it. The choice between a pro-Arab as opposed to a pro-Israeli policy and its implications for countering the Soviet menace, as well as maintaining continued supplies of oil, all now came to be intimately linked with the domestic pocketbook issue and the daily discomforts of inflation, unemployment, and long gas lines. But this was not all. These issues were in their turn linked to the choices between the welfare state of the past and the alternative of a return to market policies and restraint on governmental intervention. The latter was the course usually advocated by the New Right.

The most systematic attempt to reverse the Trilateralist, detente policies of Carter was, however, launched in November 1976 by the highly influential Committee on Present Danger (many of whose members had participated in the 1975 SAC conference). In its opening press announcements, the committee warned the nation of a "Soviet drive for dominance" based upon an unparalleled military buildup and suggested that the United States needed not only to take a tough stance toward the Soviet Union, but also to counter the Soviet menace with a rapid buildup of its own. The committee included such well-known personalities as Paul Nitze, head of the State Department's policy planning division during the Truman administration, a member of Nixon's SALT delegation (from which he had resigned in protest) and, more importantly, the coauthor of NSC-68, the secret paper in early 1950s that advocated a shift from political to military containment of the Soviet Union. He was joined by Eugene Rostow, Dean Rusk, and David Packard, names that had been in and out of the government for the past thirty years. Commenting on the illustrious membership and support of the committee, Alan Wolfe pointed out that

> they in turn spoke for a broad-based coalition of 141 persons ranging from *Commentary's* editor, Norman Podhoretz, to erstwhile Presidential hopeful John Connally. Among the committee's founders were ten labor leaders; also listed were numerous literary and academic figures, among them Nobel Prize winners Saul Bellow, Eugene Winger, and W. F. Libby. A platoon of retired military commanders was led by Kennedy's adviser, General Maxwell Taylor, and Nixon's Chief of Naval Operations, Admiral Elmo Zumwalt. And as one might expect, a whole host of Cold War architects and long-time Presidential national security advisors, including Leon Keyserling, Gordon Gray, Charles Burton Marshall, Arthur Dean and Douglas Dillon. . . ."[37]

As the *Washington Post* commented, "The new NIE, plus the Pipes Report, plus the encouragement given to pessimists or 'worst-case' theorists on Soviet intentions inside the government [was] regarded as a high barrier for the Carter administration to overcome and to carry out its own broader objectives for U.S.-Soviet arms control."[38]

When the Soviet Union rejected Carter's first somewhat hastily gathered proposals for arms control in March 1977, the CPD seized on the Soviet rejection and issued a paper entitled "What Is the Soviet Union Up To?" The question was rhetorical. Its answer could be none other than world conquest. Similarly, the CPD fiercely campaigned against the appointment of Paul Warnke as the chief delegate to SALT. The opposition was led by an ad hoc group called the Emergency Coalition against Unilateral Disarmament with headquarters in the office of the CPD. Daniel Graham, a member of Team B, was its chairman. Alan Wolfe comments on this and adds, "it was a shock to run down the list of the officers and steering committee of the Emergency Coalition and discover the new bedfellows of the CDM," an organization that Norman Podhoretz proudly proclaimed to be the home of the "Cold War liberals." The steering committee was laden with such representatives of the ultra-right as James D. Roberts, executive director of the Republican National Committee, and Howard Phillips, national director of the Conservative Caucus. The latter was the main connection with the rapidly emerging right grassroots organizations that had singled out progressive liberals for defeat in the congressional and senatorial elections of 1980. Paul Weyrich, director of the Committee for Survival of a Free Congress, was yet another member of the steering committee. He was a key member of the new right "network" consisting of Richard Vigaurie, Howard Phillips, and Terry Dolan. Dolan reported that NCPAC had poured $1.7 million into the presidential race and $1.2 million into six key Senate races and made direct contributions of $250,000 to 112 other candidates in the 1980 elections.[39] Four of the six targeted senators lost, and 58 of the candidates it directly supported won. In fact, throughout 1978 and 1979 the Political Action Committees (PACs) took a very aggressive stance. The business PACs contributed a total of $30 million to the House and Senate elections. They gave to conservatives in both the parties, but always the objective was to secure a business-oriented, defense-conscious Congress in Washington.

While the Cold War internationalists were busy fusing their position with the rising phalanx of right-wing organizations, fortunately for them, the international situation had begun to deteriorate. By the end of 1978, the U.S. position in Iran was once again raising the spectre of oil shortages, although Saudi Arabia had stepped up its own production to make up the shortfall. But the demands from the right were becoming strident, and even liberal Democrats who had vociferously opposed intervention in Vietnam were forced on the defensive. Senators Church and Javits, both staunch advocates of nonintervention during the 1960s, began moving the Senate Foreign Relations Committee toward a hawkish stance. The Carter administration responded similarly. In a speech at the Foreign Policy Association, Brzezinski evoked an "arc of crisis—along the shores of the Indian Ocean." He warned that the resulting turmoil was bound to benefit the Soviet Union. The old domino theory was now in full sway. Testifying before the Senate Energy and Natural Resources Committee on 17 January, James Schlesinger sounded an alarm over the "encirclement of OPEC" and stated that the balance of power in the Persian Gulf region had changed and that the United States "will have to take steps to shore up the nations around the Gulf."[40]

In February 1979, Defense Secretary Harold Brown went on the record, saying, "We will take any action that is appropriate, including military force, if the oil supplies were threatened and the Soviet Union tried to fish in troubled waters."[41] In the Senate, the SALT treaty was running into trouble. Senators Sam Nunn of Georgia, Alan Cranston of California, and Senate Majority Leader Birch Bayh refused to vote for the treaty unless the administration substantially increased defense spending.

In the midst of this debate on the level of defense spending, the opposition suddenly "discovered" 2,000 to 3,000 Soviet combat troops stationed in Cuba. The administration played the episode down and countered it by pointing out that the Soviet brigade had only about forty tanks and no airlift or sealift capabilities that would enable them to attack a Latin American country. What is more, the force had been in Cuba with U.S. knowledge since the mid-1970s, but this was hardly the issue. The Cuban brigade provided a dramatic opportunity for the hard-liners and the hawks inside and outside the administration. To them, it was a serious breach of understanding between the two super-powers and a clear case of Soviet perfidy. But even more important, it demonstrated the unremitting Soviet ambition for political gain, even with the use of military force when necessary. The president's 1 October speech to the nation did not appease the hawks. Senator Baker raised once again the spectre of a faltering national will, while an entire issue of *Business Week* in March 1979 was devoted to these concerns and entitled "The Decline of United States Power." The Cuban crisis dissi-pated as rapidly as it had appeared on the scene, but the damage was done. Larry Keegan and Daniel Yankelovich wrote in the 1980 annual issue of *Foreign Affairs,* "Intelligence photographs and official pro-nouncement about the limited significance of the force did little to allay public concern that the Soviets were having their way with little regard for any United States response."

The seizure of the U.S. Embassy staff in Teheran in November 1979, on top of events in Angola and Cuba, had therefore the most far-reaching impact on U.S. public opinion. It produced profound an-guish and frustration with an administration that for all practical purposes seemed paralyzed in face of such national humiliation. Many advocated military measures. National pride was deeply hurt, and all the arguments of "declining America" suddenly acquired concrete meaning. According to a public poll taken after the seizure of the U.S. Embassy in Teheran, a decisive 65 percent of the public agreed that the taking of the hostages and the U.S. government's handling of the situation had "decreased United States prestige abroad."[42]

If the Cold War alarmists needed final proof of all they had been saying since the mid-1970s, it was provided by the Soviet invasion of Afghanistan. Paul Nitze, the leading spokesman for the Riga doctrine, stated, "the thrust into Afghanistan advances the Soviet base structure by 50 miles so as to outflank Iran and bear directly on the Arabian Sea." This, Nitze insisted, was a move to militarily and politically dominate the Persian Gulf. He claimed the Soviet aim was to politically separate NATO Europe from the United States and that control over the Persian Gulf oil was likely to give them the necessary advantage to do so. It would also enable the Soviet Union to dominate Pakistan and other Southeast Asian countries by encircling China in partnership with India.[43] Similar warnings were published in the *Strategic Survey* of 1980–1981. The air bases in Afghanistan being occupied by the Soviet Union "not only placed much of the Persian Gulf region within range of Soviet tactical aircraft, but shortened the air route to more distant Soviet clients, such as South Yemen or Ethiopia. In a crisis, they also would give the USSR a route to the Arabian Sea which would only involve overflying the poorly defended Baluchistan area of Pakistan." Numerous articles and reports in the media and popular journals followed suit. Beginning on 21 September 1981, the *New York Times* published a series of seven articles entitled "Defense: Is the United States Prepared?" The impact on public opinion was electric. President Carter went on record saying Brezhnev had lied to him and that the Soviet invasion constituted the "greatest single threat to the world since World War II." There were now no more doubts about the Soviet Union's intentions or its unreliability as a partner in global cooperation. The administration had completely surrendered its position to neo-conservative reasoning. The pronouncement of the Carter doctrine not only confirmed this, but brought the Riga axiom to dead center of U.S. foreign policy.

Afghanistan coalesced divergent views and public anxieties into a single concrete focus on Soviet aggression, and proved catalytic in producing the belligerent stance on the part of the Carter administration. The nation was ready, as it had not been for many years, to "pull together and do what must be done," to reassert U.S. military and diplomatic power. But the matters did not stop here. Over and above the anxiety over strategic weakness came an endless variety of economic bad news, confirming changes for the worse in the standing of the United States in world affairs. Serious trade imbalances, deficits and rising unemployment, inflation and frequent decline in the value of the dollar, and the crisis in steel, auto, and other basic industries—all reinforced in one way or another the belief that the United States was in retreat. In the public mind, domestic economic problems were increasingly tied to international development, and together the two coalesced into a firm belief among more than 50 percent of the public that the nation had grown weaker and was "behind the Soviet Union in terms of military strength."

By 1980 the number had reached a peak of 84 percent. In their *Foreign Affairs* article, Yankelovich and Keegan wrote,

> On our analysis of survey data, the American public holds strong and clear ideas about how the nation can regain control over its foreign policy and vindicate the country's honor. The actions encouraged by the new public mind include a tougher stance in dealing with the Soviet Union; adding muscle to our defense capabilities; showing a willingness to aid our allies with military force if necessary in the event of Soviet aggression; brushing aside the moral squeamishness that diminished the usefulness of the CIA; employing trade as a legitimate weapon in support of our national interests; and in general, acting more forcefully against our enemies and on behalf of our friends.[44]

This then was the mandate for the new president of the 1980s. It was not, therefore, accidental that 32 of the 182 members of the Committee of Present Danger entered the Reagan administration in positions dealing with matters of national security and arms negotiations with the Soviet Union. The CPD and other Cold War internationalists had done their work well and united the nation decisively in support of the Riga axiom.

Notes

1. The former is named after the Latvian city from which U.S. diplomats watched the Soviet Union in the 1920s and concluded that it represented a threat that must be checked if the "free world" was to be preserved. The Yalta axiom is named after the famous postwar conference among Churchill, Stalin, and Roosevelt that opened the era of goodwill and negotiated agreements with the USSR. It should be noted that here Yergin's concepts are used strictly for heuristic purposes. U.S. policy is not impervious to public opinion as Yergin suggests. Nor is the Soviet policy merely reactive as *Shattered Peace* implies. The Riga and Yalta axioms are, however, useful concepts in capturing the ideological dynamics of U.S. policy and its connections with domestic politics in the United States. Daniel Yergin, *Shattered Peace* (Boston: Houghton Mifflin Co., 1978), 17–88.

2. The 1977 Trilateral report, *Collaboration with Communist Countries in Managing Global Problems*, talks about widening cooperation with the Soviet Union and winding down the arms race (Chihiro Hosaya, Henry Owen, Andrew Shonfield, *Trilateral Paper* 13, 1977). For the Trilateral global strategy see *Toward a Renovated International System* by Richard Cooper, Karl Kaiser, Masataka Kosaka, The Trilateral Commission: *Triangle Paper* 14, 1977.

3. Lawrence H. Sharp, "Jimmy Carter and the Trilateralists' Presidential Roots," in *Trilateralism,* ed. Holly Skalar (Boston: South End Press, 1980), 208–209.

4. See Ole Holsti and James Rosenau, "Vietnam, Consensus and the Belief Systems of American Leaders," *World Politics* 32 (October 1979); "Public Opinion and Soviet Foreign Policy: Competing Belief Systems in the Policy-Making Process," *Naval War College Review* (July–August 1979). Also see Michael Mandelbaum and William Schneider, "The New Internationalisms: Public Opinion and American Foreign Policy," in *Eagle Entangled,* ed. Kenneth Oye, Donald Rothchild, and Robert Leiber (New York: Longman, 1979).

5. *The Soviet Military Buildup and U.S. Defense Spending* (Washington, DC: Brookings Institute, 1977), 7.

6. Elmo Zumwalt, "Heritage of Weakness: An Assessment of the 1970's," *National Security in the 1980's: From Weakness to Strength* (San Francisco: Institute of Contemporary Studies, 1980), 19.

7. Ibid., 19–20.

8. Ibid., 30.

9. U.S. Department of Defense, *Soviet Military Power* (Washington, DC: October 1981). Reproduced in its entirety by the Institute for Defense Studies and Analysis, New Delhi, *Strategic Digest* (April–May 1982), 230.

10. James Fallows quotes from his interview with Paul Nitze, a leading member of the CWI. Cited in "Muscle-Bound Superpower: The State of America's Defense," in *At Issue,* 3d ed., ed. Steven Spiegel (New York: St. Martin's Press, 1981), 346.

11. A. G. B. Metcalf, "Which Windows of Vulnerability?" *Strategic Review* 10 (Spring 1982), 5–10.

12. Ibid., 9.

13. Edward Luttwak, "Why We Need More Waste, Fraud and Mismanagement in the Pentagon," *Commentary* 73:2 (February 1982), 17.

14. Frances Fukuyama, "A New Soviet Strategy," in *At Issue,* 39–53. Also see Paul Nitze, "Strategy for the 80's," in the same volume, 315–316; Richard Pipes, "Soviet Global Strategy," *Commentary* (April 1980), 31–39; Henry Rowen, "The Threatened Jugular," in *National Security in the 1980's,* 275–295.

15. Fukuyama, "A New Soviet Strategy," 47.

16. Kenneth Edelman quoted from the Carter interview after the 1980 State of the Union Address. Carter admitted, "I don't think it would be accurate for me to claim that . . . we . . . have enough military strength and enough military presence there to defend the region . . ." in "Revitalizing Alliances," in *National Security in the 1980's,* 305.

17. Stanley Hoffman, "Muscle and Brains," in *At Issue,* 233.

18. See Fred Kaplan, *Dubious Specter: A Skeptical Look at the Soviet Nuclear Threat* (Washington, DC: Institute of Policy Studies, 1980), and "NATO and the Soviet Scare," *Inquiry,* 12 June 1978, 16–20; Representative Les Aspin, "What Are the Soviets Up To?" *International Security* (Summer 1978), 30–52; Arthur Macy-Cox, "The Truth about Soviet Arms Spending," *New York Review of Books,* 6 November 1980, 21–24; George Kennen, "The Soviet Threat: How Real?"

Inquiry, 17 March 1980, 15–18; Franklyn Holzman, "Dollars or Rubles: The C.I.A.'s Military Estimates," *Bulletin of the Atomic Scientists* (June 1980), 23–27.

19. Macy-Cox, "The Truth about Soviet Arms Spending."

20. Fallows, *At Issue,* 346.

21. Henry Binen, "Perspectives on Soviet Intervention in Africa," *Political Science Quarterly* 95:1 (Spring 1980), 30–31.

22. Selig Harrison, "Dateline Afghanistan," *Foreign Policy* 41 (Winter 1980–1981).

23. James McConnell, "Doctrine and Capabilities," in *Soviet Naval Diplomacy,* ed. Bradford Dismukes and James McConnell (New York: Pergamon Press, 1979), 6–7.

24. Keith Dunn, *Soviet Constraints in South West Asia: A Military Analysis,* Strategic Studies Institute, U.S. Army War College, 7 December 1981.

25. Nathan Glazer, "The Limits of Social Policy," *Commentary* 60 (September 1971); Aaron Wildovsky, "Government and People," *Commentary* 62 (August 1973); Robert Nisbet, "Where Do We Go From Here?" in *Income Redistribution,* ed. Colin Campbell (Washington, DC: American Enterprise Institute, 1977). Also, in the same volume, see Irving Kristol, "Thoughts on Equality and Egalitarianism."

26. Peter Steinfels, *Neo-Conservatives: The Men Who Are Changing America's Politics* (New York: Simon and Schuster, 1979).

27. Geoffrey Kemp, "Defense Innovation and Geopolitics: From Persian Gulf to Outerspace," in *National Security in the 1980's,* 71.

28. Ibid., 72.

29. James Schlesinger, "A Testing Time for America," *Fortune* 106 (February 1976), 76.

30. This position is argued most persuasively by Robert Tucker in various articles in *Commentary* and in *The Purpose of American Power* (New York: Praeger, 1981).

31. *New York Times,* 10 January 1975.

32. Walter Goodman, "Fair Game," *New Leader,* 17 March 1975, 15.

33. John Collins and Clyde Mark, *Oil Fields as Military Objectives: A Feasibility Study,* U.S. Congress, Committee on Internal Relations, August 1975.

34. Barry Blechman and Stephen Kaplan, *Force without War: U.S. Armed Forces as a Political Instrument* (Washington, DC: Brookings Institute, 1978), 553.

35. Ibid.

36. Schlesinger, "A Testing Time for America," 76.

37. Alan Wolfe, "Resurgent Cold War Ideology: The Case of the Committee on Present Danger," *Capitalism and the State: U.S. Latin American Relations,* (Stanford, CA: Stanford University Press, 1979), 41.

38. Murry Marder, "Carter To Inherit Intense Dispute on Soviet Intentions," *Washington Post,* 2 January 1977.

39. *Newsweek,* 24 November 1980.

40. *Mideast Observer,* 15 January 1979, 3; *Wall Street Journal,* 18 January 1979.

41. TV remarks of 24 February 1980 by Harold Brown reported in *Middle East International*, 14 March 1980.

42. *Time,* 14 May 1980.

43. Nitze, in *At Issue,* 315.

44. Daniel Yankelovich and Larry Keegan, "Assertive America," *Foreign Affairs,* No. 3 (Annual 1980), 705.

5.

Reagan's Assessment of Threats and Strategy in Southwest Asia

The Reagan victory in the 1980 elections was a clear indication that the period of national self-doubt characteristic of the post-Vietnam era was over. The nation had subscribed to the premises of the Riga axiom and was ready to move on. The major overarching theme of the Reagan administration was the growing Soviet threat and declining U.S. strength. Its main preoccupation was therefore to recast U.S. strategy and strengthen the military to meet this threat.

It is often argued that in order to unify the conservative coalition and obtain congressional support for the defense program, the administration needed to harp on the "Soviet threat" and label the 1980s as the period of peril. Whether or not this is true, its defense program and policies were real enough. During the first term in office, President Reagan's global and regional policies went into effect: Defense expenditures were stepped up; a new central command for Southwest Asia was created; strategic collaboration with regional powers was initiated; and visible U.S. presence in and around the Persian Gulf became a routine exercise for the armed forces. These programs were a measure of the administration's concerns about the loss of U.S. power and the extent to which Southwest Asia was critical in recovering it.

What were the purpose, the rationale, and the instruments of Reagan's policy in Southwest Asia, and how did this policy fit into the administration's overall perspective on Soviet power?

Was the Reagan administration anxious about merely recovering the losses of the Carter presidency, or was it intent on establishing unchallenged American hegemony? The next few chapters will discuss these issues. This chapter examines the overall intellectual design of President Reagan's strategy, and Chapters 6–8 will analyze its implementation in response to events and actions in Southwest Asia. Accordingly, in this chapter, we will focus on (1) the Reagan assessment of Soviet capabilities and intent; (2) the major themes of Reagan's foreign policy; (3) the translation of these themes into actual strategy for Southwest Asia; (4) the regional threat assessment; (5) the choice of instruments and purpose; and (6) the implications of this new strategic thrust in this part of the world.

Perception of Soviet Military Power

President Reagan and his advisers proclaimed that the relentless Soviet military buildup over the entire past decade represented the single most dangerous threat to world peace, although, as many knowledgeable scholars had pointed out, this claim was highly debatable if not patently false. What did the administration mean?

In its first comprehensive statement, entitled "Soviet Military Power," the Defense Department contended that Moscow was spending "12 to 14 percent of its annual gross national product on defense, 70 percent more than the United States spent in 1979, and there were no signs of a de-emphasis of a military program."[1] As a result, both the political and military balance had shifted in favor of Moscow. This was as true in strategic nuclear arms, Reagan claimed, as it was in conventional warfare. The growing accuracy of Soviet strategic ground-based missiles had given Moscow the capability to "take out" U.S. Minuteman II land-based missiles. In Reagan parlance, this was the "window of vulnerability" that gave the Soviet Union a clear advantage, while it rendered ineffective the entire U.S. strategy of "massive retaliation." The United States could only counter a Soviet first strike with unacceptable damage to its own national substance. Clearly, the Soviets were in a position to blackmail the United States.

If the Soviets had attained threatening power in missile forces, their buildup in conventional forces was even more formidable. The Defense Department proclaimed, "as a superpower with global ambitions, the USSR and its expansionist efforts abroad are targeted at spreading and solidifying the USSR's political, economic, and military influence and drawing nations into its orbit.... The USSR's enhanced confidence in its capabilities to project power through a variety of military and non-military means has widened Soviet options." As the Reagan administration saw it, Soviet ability to project military power had become "a key factor underlying its increased activities in Africa, the

Middle East, Asia, and Latin America." The use of force as an instrument of Soviet policy had evolved from military assistance alone in 1950 to "extensive use of proxies in advisory position and combat operation." In 1980, the Kremlin had not hesitated to apply large-scale military force in Afghanistan.[2]

In Reagan's view, the Soviet power projection was not episodic military reactions to regional or world crises. "Rather, it was a continuously applied means of foreign policy activity," in other words, a Soviet grand plan for world domination. The administration pointed out that, besides military force,

> the Soviets project power and influence through the employment of a mixture of less visible . . . elements, including KGB, diplomats and traditional state-to-state activities, military advisers and aid, treaties and legal ties, support for terrorists and pro-Soviet guerrilla groups, economic aid, cultural, media and educational diplomacy, and use of . . . propaganda, blackmail and forgery. The coordinated use of those tools allowed Moscow to develop what the administration called an "infrastructure of influence in a target country.

The main Soviet objective was to terminate Western and Chinese influence in the Third World and to gain a "strategic foothold to promote the accession to power of radical, anti-Western regimes." Although the Soviets were anxious to portray themselves as the vanguard of world national liberation movements, the real objective was to promote world instability and develop viable oil and strategic minerals by means of "denial strategy," through physical disruption, market manipulation, or domination of oil-producing or neighboring states.[3] Reagan's advisers believed the Soviets understood the nature of Western dependence on imports of vital strategic materials from Africa and the Middle East. "By undermining Western ties with the oil and raw materials producers and exacerbating differences in the Western alliance over policies towards the region, the Soviets sought to erode both the economic health and political cohesion of the West." Obviously, the Soviets had singled out Southwest Asia and the Middle East as targets for extending their power.

These Soviet aims were evident in the fact that, over the past twenty-five years, they had extended $50 billion in military aid to fifty-four non-Communist nations, 85 percent of which went to the Middle East and countries along the Indian Ocean littoral. The Soviets sold $37 billion of arms to the Third World, but again, 70 percent of this was sold to four major Arab clients. The Soviets had also stationed large numbers of advisers in Algeria, Libya, Angola, Ethiopia, Iraq,

Syria, and South Yemen. The concentration of Soviet attention on
North Africa and the Middle East was no accident; in the administration's view, it clearly underlined the Kremlin strategy, i.e., to achieve
countercontrol over Western access to these regions and to dominate
the "oil Jugular" at as many choke-points within the region as it could.
For this purpose, the administration claimed, the Soviets had used
large numbers of Cuban and East German proxy forces. While covert
KGB operations penetrated and destabilized a target country, proxy
forces secured the military objectives, and the rest of the infrastructure
was rapidly implemented to consolidate and shore up the newly
created client state.

For this purpose, the Soviet Union had created seven divisions of
mobile airborne and special-purpose units well suited for rapid introduction in places far from the Soviet homeland. In the Defense Department's view, "the Soviets could move, under optimum conditions,
major elements of an airborne division into a country such as Syria in
three to five days," which was considerably quicker than anything the
United States could achieve. What is more, "utilizing its substantial
geographic advantages, . . . the USSR could attack vital regions such as
Iran and the Persian Gulf with massive ground and air forces staging
directly from the Soviet homeland and secure contiguous areas." The
only thing that was likely to stop them, the administration argued, was
"the USSR's assessment of the Western response." The other key element was the Soviet Union's ability to forcefully project its power and
intimidate Third World nations.[4] Its rapidly expanding navy had
through the 1970s attained an impressive capacity to span the globe.

In Reagan's view, the Soviet menace was, however, primarily military
and only secondarily ideological and political. The Soviet economy was
perceived to be faltering and beset with formidable problems of low
productivity and chronic agricultural failures, inefficiency, and declining morale. There were also tensions and stresses within the Soviet
system and a growing dependency on capital goods, technology, and
credits from the West. A corollary of this assessment was what Reagan
believed to be an imminent shortfall of energy resources within the
Soviet Union. In 1977, the CIA had predicted that Soviet oil production would peak shortly, followed by a steady decline.[5] As a result, the
Soviet Union would become a net oil importer by the mid-1980s.
Although these estimates were subsequently revised (and, in fact, disputed) even within the administration, the argument that the Soviets
would step up pressure on the oil-rich Persian Gulf region continued in
full force in the Reagan assessment of the Soviet threat.

In the administration's view, the Soviet Union's economic vulnerability did not, however, mean that it ceased to be a formidable adversary.[6] In fact, this economic weakness made the Soviet Union particularly desperate to alter the "correlation of political forces in its favor," with force if necessary, and now, the administration claimed with ominous frequency, it had demonstrated that it had the military means to do so.

Major Themes of Reagan's Policies

The detente policies of both Nixon and Carter had to some extent disconnected regional competition for influence from rivalry for global power. In Reagan's view, this was a misguided approach. For this administration, the global growth of Soviet power and its relentless drive had destroyed what distinction one could draw between competition for regional as opposed to global advantages. Soviet regional advances made them increasingly bold in seeking regional predominance. This assessment produced three guiding themes for Reagan's policy.

Globalism

Since Soviet regional policy, particularly in Southwest Asia, was clearly an integral part of its global objectives, the United States could do no less than to evolve a counterstrategy in which improving its regional influence would subserve more directly and clearly its own global objectives. In other words, the weakness or strength of the U.S. posture in Southwest Asia would be assessed in light of its global interests and so would the choice of its methods and instruments. This required a reordering of priorities; that is, abandoning Carter's regionalism in favor of greater coherence between the two levels of U.S. policies. This remained the principal theme of Reagan's first term.

Unilateralism

The globalist perspective naturally meant mobilizing all U.S. assets to achieve this coherence: its international economic strength, the global reach of its military, and, most important, its major allies. This meant convincing its allies of the correctness of the Reagan perspective and persuading them to contribute to the effort. U.S. alliance diplomacy, whether in Europe or in the Middle East, had to dovetail with its global objectives. However, alliance relationships are more often than not reciprocal. If there are major differences between allied and U.S. perspectives, the United States must work for a compromise. However, the Reagan approach to this problem was quite different.

The European allies had serious doubts about the U.S. assessment of the Soviet threat and the proposed measures to contain it. As a result, they rejected Reagan's view of Soviet intentions in Europe and the objectives of Soviet policies in the Persian Gulf and the Middle East. Controversy over arms control and nuclear strategy reflected the first, while differences over Afghanistan and the Arab-Israeli dispute exposed the second. How to mobilize allied resources and support without allowing the allies to dilute the anti-Soviet thrust of U.S. policy was, therefore, a major concern for Reagan. The administration tried to cope with this problem by developing a two-track policy with one overriding objective. On the one hand, it strengthened the NATO alliance and exhorted Western-bloc nations to contribute to Soviet "containment" by spending more on defense, restricting trade credits and loans to the Soviets, and barring altogether the transfer of high-level technology, particularly any that may have dual uses (civilian and defense purposes). It also pressed the Europeans to adopt a Persian Gulf strategy and stressed the importance of preserving access to the region's oil. On the other hand, it tried to live without allied support, that is, to develop a capacity for a unilateral intervention.

This meant evolving a strategy that would give the United States the capacity to defend the Persian Gulf and the Middle East—or, for that matter, any region of the globe—alone if necessary. Reagan's hefty defense budgets reflected this, as did his choice of weapons such as the MX and the proposed 15-carrier, 600-ship navy. Many in and out of the administration opposed this and pointed out that the United States would not have to spend such amounts on defense if it based American strategy on coalition defense and incorporated within its calculations allied military strength. But the administration refused to make a clear-cut choice.[7] Instead, it tried to keep available both those options for the future. The growing opposition to the increased budgets, however, underlined the need to protect its defense-minded constituency both at home and abroad, that is, the conservative domestic coalition in the United States and the pro-Reagan, generally right-wing governments abroad.

Interventionism

The third guiding theme of Reagan's policy flows directly from the above. The supporting domestic groups may find themselves up against formidable opposition unless policies show results. It is this need that partly explains the new mix between force and diplomacy in Reagan's policy. There is, however, a decidedly greater emphasis on force. The creation of the RDJTF (Rapid Deployment Joint Task Force), the planned expansion of the navy, the revitalization of the special forces meant for counterinsurgency operations—all under-lined the shift toward coercive instruments. On the other hand, eco-nomic and developmental issues, subsumed under the North-South dialogue, receded into the background. The Third World, particularly West and Southwest Asia and North Africa, were singled out for special attention. Use of force for preventive purposes was more acceptable and more often to be put into practice during the Reagan presidency. The United States also encouraged anti-Soviet elements and coun-terinsurgency forces to pin the Soviets down in as many spots (in Africa, the Middle East, and Southwest Asia) as possible.

These three themes added up to a major change in U.S. foreign policy. Indeed, it buried successfully the fear and guilt of the Vietnam era. Although all three themes were the ruling axioms of U.S. actions in the world in the 1950s, they are immensely more dangerous in the context of the 1980s because the Soviet Union is no longer the inferior power it was then. Whether or not the Soviet Union is what Reagan claims it to be, that is, an expansionist state with designs of world conquest, it is certainly a formidable foe with ample ability to checkmate its adversary.

Reagan's Themes Translated into Policy

The administration concluded that the intellectual basis of U.S. de-fense and foreign policy had been rendered obsolete by global devel-opments that called for a new conceptual framework and a new set of strategic imperatives. The administration, therefore, proposed to abandon many of the key elements of U.S. policies of the recent past. To begin with, the United States had to jettison the notion of maintaining a military balance and parity of strength with the Soviet Union since such a balance had already been destroyed by the Soviet military buildup and, instead, focus its energies on neutralizing the Soviet lead. Rearm-ing the United States, and not arms control, was, therefore, the first priority of the administration.

Accordingly, during Reagan's first three years in office, his defense budget topped Carter's last year's budget by 52 percent. The original budget and the five-year defense plan submitted to Congress for fiscal 1985 called for $305 billion in budget authority for the initial year, rising to $446 billion in fiscal 1989. This last figure, according to a Brookings Institute study estimate, "would be 73 percent higher than the $258.2 billion appropriated by the Congress for the military fiscal year 1984."[8] Detente as a basis of East-West negotiation was rejected. The Reagan team argued that if any negotiations were to take place at all, they would come only after U.S. defenses were properly secured and only on terms that would give Moscow no opportunity to "cheat, lie or hoodwink" the world while gaining military advantages over the United States. Obviously, this meant that Reagan would propose a thorough overhaul and strengthening of U.S. defenses to match those of the USSR, and postpone all serious negotiations until such time as all the weapons and defense systems were in place.

Secretary of Defense Casper Weinberger declared on 4 March 1981 that the administration would do everything necessary to "significantly and quickly strengthen our ability to respond to the Soviet threat at all levels of conflict in all areas of the world vital to our national interest."[9] Throughout the first term of the Reagan administration, there was no letup in these intentions.

There are two major, related dimensions of U.S. defense policy, strategic defense and conventional defense. The first is clearly outside the scope of this book. Nevertheless, it should be noted that, in the politics of East-West relations, arms negotiations—or their absence— determine the context of superpower competition in different parts of the world. Reagan's proposed defense budgets and weapons procurement program were responsible for the steady deterioration in the U.S. ties with the Soviet Union. Although this new strategic posture was not directly relevant to the balance in Southwest Asia, it did affect the overall political climate within which policy for this region was formulated. This was particularly significant because the administration had insisted on merging its global concerns with its assessments of threats in Southwest Asia.

Nor can one ignore the fact that the objectives that guided the administration in its nuclear strategy also guided it in formulating policy for Southwest Asia. For instance, the Defense Department proposed the deployment of the MX missiles, the Trident II, and the B-1 bombers to ensure the invulnerability of the U.S. triad, its land-, sea-, and air-based missiles. The MX was meant to close the "window of vulnerability" in U.S. land-based missiles. It was a new intercontinental ballistic missile that was larger, more expensive, more powerful, and more accurate than anything in the U.S. arsenal and, most important, would give the United States a decisive first-strike ability against the Soviet Union. In other words, the administration proposed a weapon on the argument that the United States was weak, but the weapon they proposed gave it the ability to preempt and gain a clear and early advantage in conflict.

Similarly, the first *Defense Guidance Plan* presented by the Pentagon in May 1982 ordered the U.S. armed forces to prepare for a protracted war in one or more theaters simultaneously, and to ready the forces to "prevail" over the Soviet Union and to be able to "force . . . early termination of hostilities on terms favorable to the United States."[10] Only a clear military superiority could achieve this. The administration cited U.S. vulnerability but asked for weapons that would enable it to wage and sustain protracted war and defeat the enemy. This same purpose was evident in its conventional defense strategy as well, to be able to intervene, preempt, force terms on the adversary, and project overwhelming force.

To support its new conventional strategy, the administration proposed a 600-ship navy instead of the 450 vessels proposed by President Carter.[11] The massive strengthening of the naval forces was meant to secure U.S. supremacy on the high seas and to enable the United States to interdict or preempt hostile action and project U.S. military power even in remote corners of the globe. This decision by the administration was based on two important assumptions. First, it believed that the United States could not and should not rely on friends and allies to protect its interests. The failures in Iran, the continuous bickering among the Europeans, the stresses and strains in NATO, the capricious behavior of allies such as Israel and Pakistan, and the vulnerability of most Third World allies to internal upheavals and external aggression made them ultimately unreliable as trustees of U.S. interests. There was no substitute for U.S. presence, military and political, if national interests were at stake. Second, the administration was totally convinced that a "soft-line" policy toward international instability and Soviet gains in the Third World had lost the United States all freedom of action in world politics. It had seriously diminished the U.S. ability to shape events abroad. The administration argued that the United States must abandon this paralyzing posture of "strategic passivity" willfully accepted in the aftermath of Vietnam, and replace it with one of forceful initiative. This freedom of maneuver was critical if the United States was to match Soviet expansionism.

The administration proposed a concerted effort to roll back Soviet influence wherever possible, but particularly in areas that were considered vital to the United States—i.e., Southwest Asia and Central America. This was to be achieved by matching the Soviet presence region-for-region and point-by-point on the map, using U.S. naval forces where appropriate; strategic collaboration with regional powers where possible; the acquisition of base facilities, when these could be secured; arms sales, economic assistance, and diplomatic support when conditions permitted; and, above all, by frequent and public declarations of the U.S. intent to resist every Soviet move.

The administration undertook to expand the conventional forces of the United States to counter a wide range of potential threats and contingencies throughout the globe, but particularly in Europe and Southwest Asia. In the administration's thinking, the two were closely interlinked. Any disruption in the flow of oil, or any further gains for the Soviet Union in that region, would have a devastating impact on Europe and Japan. The Pentagon, therefore, proposed that the conventional defense strategy should be "based on the concept that the most effective deterrent to Soviet aggression will entail combat with the United States forces and those of other friendly powers." In other words, in the event of a Soviet military move, the entire alliance would be mobilized in addition to the "prospect that the war may extend to other areas."

This strategy had two dimensions. First, it called for a U.S. capability to rapidly deploy enough force to hold important positions and to interdict and blunt a Soviet attack. This capability was meant to convince enemy planners, Fred Ikle wrote in the *Strategic Review*, "that they could not count on seizing control of a vital area before United States forces were in place, thereby confronting the United States with an accomplished fact that would deter American counterintervention."[12] This meant that it would be the United States that would take preemptive action before the USSR could do so. Second, the United States would exercise the option of fighting on other fronts and of building up allied strength to the point where the consequences of adventurism became unacceptable to the Soviet Union.

The Reagan administration, therefore, proposed a strategy that revolved around creating the capacity to wage counteroffensive operations in arenas not of the opponent's choosing. In other words, U.S. forces, as well as the strategic doctrine under which they would operate, were readied to engage the Soviet Union anywhere, and even simultaneously in several regions of the world if necessary.[13] In contrast to past policies then, the Reagan strategy would not restrict the United States to countering a Soviet advance where it occurred, but reserved to the United States the right to escalate the confrontation horizontally to other regions or vertically to higher levels of conflict. This departure from the earlier posture was both critical and dangerous. It can be best explained by using the metaphor of football and soccer. Not unlike football, war-fighting strategy of the past had concentrated on holding the enemy advance along the front and trading territory to gain advantage, but what the Reagan administration proposed now was totally different. The United States would no longer seek to confine defense to one area, but would go deeply behind the enemy lines and, as in soccer, move the confrontation to any region on the globe, choosing spots where the Soviet Union was overextended and weak. In such a strategy, regional tensions were bound to escalate quickly into a global confrontation, but the choice of whether or not to do so was to remain with the United States. This also meant that the lines between defensive and offensive or even preemptive moves became totally blurred. So far as the Reagan administration was concerned, such distinctions were of little relevance when the adversary was an "evil" power bent on world domination.

Growing Focus on Southwest Asia

From the above, the next logical step was to build a military capability and achieve a state of readiness whereby U.S. conventional forces could respond swiftly to a wide range of possible threats and contingencies. There were three aspects to this objective. The administration needed, first, to define the nature of threats in a specific region; second, to establish the military and political infrastructure in order to mount a counteroffensive; and third, to create a force formidable enough to deter and, if necessary, cope with the anticipated danger.

As explained earlier, in Reagan's thinking three elements made Southwest Asia the central focus of concern: its energy resources, its strategic location and proximity to the Soviet Union, and its vulnerability to hostile influences. In Reagan's view, all three were intimately connected. Secretary of State Haig stressed this point when he told the editors of *Time* (March 16, 1981) that growing Third World lawlessness threatened U.S. access to critical raw materials and that the growing incidence of wars of national liberation were jeopardizing the U.S. ability to influence world events.

The administration put no store in the argument that Soviet motives could be defensive, or that Third World turmoil was a desperate response of societies long under the oppressive rule of leaders aided and abetted by the West. In testimony before the House Subcommittee on Mines and Mining, Secretary of State Haig stated, "As one assesses the recent step-up of Soviet proxy activities in the Third World, . . . one can only conclude that the era of the resource war has arrived,"[14] i.e., the Soviet Union not only fomented trouble in the Third World to acquire greater influence, it was intent on acquiring control over and limiting Western access to Third World oil, minerals, and raw materials.

As Michael Klare comments, both these arguments, about turmoil and about raw materials, were "predicated on a relentless need for imported materials—and both [relied] ultimately on military force to assure United States access to such materials when threatened by conflict or disorder abroad."[15] The administration stressed that "for at least the foreseeable future, what happens in Southwest Asia will seriously affect the economic well-being of the industralized world."

Here, the administration drew a distinction between threats potentially most dangerous and those most likely to occur. The most dangerous threat would be a Soviet attack, perhaps at the invitation of some faction in a regional state or on a pretext designed to exploit regional instability. Although this was less likely than other scenarios, it could not be ruled out altogether, particularly since the Soviets' strategic superiority gave them the necessary protection and made them bolder in pursuing their regional advantage. Afghanistan was an obvious case in point. In the Reagan assessment, Soviet capabilities in Southwest Asia were formidable. First of all, the USSR was nearer to the entire region than was the United States and bordered on major countries of the region. The Soviet response time to crises was therefore much shorter. The administration subscribed to Shahram Chubin's view that the Soviet Union's being "in the region and unable to get out means that regional nations must shape their policies and actions with an eye always over their shoulder toward their northern neighbor."[16] The Soviet Union could, therefore, merely put its forces on an alert and signal displeasure with events in the region or warn nations of Soviet disapproval. In the event of a crisis, it could bring its most formidable asset to bear in the conflict—land-based power. The Soviet clients— PDRY, Libya, Syria, Ethiopia, and Afghanistan—only added to Moscow's political and military muscle in the region. None of the Southwest Asian nations could deter or stand up to this. In particular, Iran and Pakistan were gravely threatened. Neither was strong internally, and each faced a hostile front with their other neighbors, Iraq and India, respectively. From a purely military standpoint, the occupation of Afghanistan extended the unrefueled reach of Soviet tactical air power to areas critical to the United States, the Persian Gulf, the Indian Ocean, and the Straits of Hormuz. This, coupled with the Soviet presence and military facilities in the Red Sea and Gulf of Aden, gave the Kremlin the power to sever the West's economic jugular in the Gulf.[17] The administration argued that the United States was the only counter to Moscow in this region.

The other and perhaps more likely possibility was an indirect version of this threat, involving predatory activities by a state closely supported by the Soviets, such as Libya or South Yemen. There were other threats to stability stemming from intraregional conflicts such as the ongoing Iran-Iraq war with its potential for destabilizing the entire Persian Gulf (Saudi Arabia versus the PDRY, PDRY versus the YAR, Oman versus the PDRY, Pakistan versus India). The 1980 Iraqi invasion of Iran's oil-rich province of Khuzistan had disrupted oil production in both countries, and although world recession during the early 1980s had moderated its impact, the consequences of war in itself were likely to be dangerous. If Iran were to be defeated and Iraq to emerge the preeminent military and economic power in the Persian Gulf, it could alter the entire balance in the Middle East. Similarly, if fundamentalist Iran were to triumph, the United States had to fear for the internal stability of Saudi Arabia, Oman, Iraq, and even Jordan. Revolutionary activity, whether from Islamic fundamentalists as in Iran, or from hostile leftists such as the Palestinian Liberation Organization, posed a third serious danger to U.S. interests in the region. The conservative, monarchial, or authoritarian nations of Southwest Asia were particularly vulnerable to such internal disorders. There were also situations combining these last two threats, as in the case with the internal war in the YAR, which was supported by the Soviet-backed regime in South Yemen, or as in the civil strife in Lebanon. And last, but not least, there was the ever-present danger of yet another Arab-Israeli conflict.[18]

The Rapid Deployment Force

On all counts, a strong military presence in the region was indicated. The administration decided to strengthen the Rapid Deployment Force (RDJTF) far beyond the tripwire force envisaged by Carter. Instead, it was to be upgraded to force levels that would enable it to meet the most demanding of all threats—a direct Soviet attack. Other threats were to be met by tailoring the RDJTF forces to specific contingency requirements. According to the *Defense Guidance Plan* of May 1982, the RDF was to consist of five army divisions, two marine divisions and air wings, ten air force tactical fighter wings and two B-52 wings, and three navy aircraft carriers and escorts. It could command a total of 250,000 troops on an immediate basis, and more when it began to operate as an independent command directly under the office of the Joint Chiefs of Staff, beginning 1 January 1983.

The creation of the RDJTF, its size, composition, and nature of deployment, all indicated that the administration had changed the operational doctrine of U.S. armed forces, particularly for the region of Southwest Asia and the Middle East. The new doctrine, called Air Land Battle, first of all emphasized "war-fighting posture" and second, envisaged battle on totally different rules of conduct from those subscribed to previously.[19] In such a battle, the "fight" did not proceed along "orderly, distinct lines." Instead, U.S. counterattacks were expected to "carry the battle 75 to 150 miles behind the line of enemy advance." This, the security planners pointed out, was the "only way" to throw the attacker off guard and "seize the initiative." According to the new doctrine, "once political authorities commit military forces in pursuit of political aims, military forces must win something—else there will be no basis from which political authorities can bargain to win politically. Therefore, the purpose of military operation cannot be simply to avert defeat, . . . but rather it must be to win." On this point, the Reagan strategy was certainly consistent. Globally, the aim was to "prevail" and force terms favorable to the United States; regionally, it was to win territory and press advantages even to the point of carrying the battle to the Soviet heartland. The major criterion in both focused on seizing the initiative, preempting advantages, and threatening escalation to arenas different from where the conflict may have originally begun. What did the United States plan to do with its forces 75 to 150 miles behind the enemy line? Was the purpose merely to disrupt enemy divisions, or to seize terrain? The army briefing is quoted as saying, "Enemy leaders must be made to understand clearly that if they choose to move militarily, no longer will there be a status quo ante-bellum— something to be restored—rather the situation they themselves have created is one which will be resolved on new terms."

In the year before Reagan assumed the presidency in 1981, the army ran an exercise called Gallant Knight, designed to "test how Iran could be defended against a Soviet invasion. The game assumed a worst-case scenario: that twenty-six Soviet divisions would try to march across the Iranian border and push south toward the oil-rich province of Khuzistan."[20] It revealed three serious flaws: that such a conflict would need 325,000 military personnel, far beyond what Carter had proposed; that it would take six months to deploy the whole force in the region, a disadvantage that would defeat the central purpose of the RDJTF, which is to deter the enemy; and third, that it would require staging facilities in the region, particularly around and within the Persian Gulf, protected by friendly powers—Egypt, Saudi Arabia, Oman, and perhaps Pakistan. On all three counts during its first term in office, the Reagan administration made substantial progress, although many questions still remained unresolved. Not only was the RDJTF immensely strengthened; the administration was also aggressively using political and economic instruments to secure basing facilities in the region. But that was not all. The *Guidance Plan* directed the RDJTF to force its way in if necessary and not wait for an invitation from a friendly government. This was a major departure from earlier policy that had carefully avoided repeating the mistakes of Vietnam. The new policy underlined the administration's resolve to undertake unilateral intervention, even if it was contrary to every conventional precept of international law.

However, the administration hoped that it would not be called upon to do so. The political difficulties in such a course of action both at home and abroad were too obvious to ignore. This meant that the choice of instruments and timing in meeting the threat was to be critical.

Reagan's Priorities

One thing was clear from the adoption of the strategic doctrine: its vigorous anti-Soviet purpose. But beyond this, many questions remained unanswered. For instance, what nations in Southwest Asia were the Rapid Deployment Joint Task Force meant to guard, and what kind of military infrastructure, weapons stockpile, and basing mode were required to make the RDF an efficient arm of U.S. conventional forces? Under what circumstances would the RDF be mobilized? And finally, what nations would the United States co-opt into its Southwest Asia strategy? It was, of course, possible to design an ideal situation for the new doctrine, but reality seldom bore any resemblance to the ideal. President Reagan had inherited the conflicts and problems of the region. He could not remake them.

However, this is where the administration differed from its predecessors. If a regional conflict could not be avoided, then the administration would use it to augment U.S. influence; if an imbalance in the armed strength between two Southwest Asian nations did not suit U.S. aims, the United States would redress the imbalance; and, if a conflict and its continuation served U.S. purposes, the administration would do nothing to settle it. Egypt, Israel, Saudi Arabia, and Pakistan became the important countries in these calculations.

Basically, the administration had the following concerns.

Access to the Region's Oil

One of the major objectives of the RDJTF is to guard the oil routes along the choke-points and the sea lanes in the Persian Gulf and the

Red Sea, i.e., notably the Straits of Hormuz and Bab-el-Mandeb. According to one estimation, in 1983, the United States accounted for 32.9 percent of world demand for petroleum. Its own domestic productions had already tapered off by the early 1980s. Even then, its percentage share of world demand was considerably lower than the peak demand of 1979–1980. The United States was still the largest consumer of petroleum in the world. Interruption of oil supplies due to war or revolutions in the Middle East was certain to be enormously damaging to it, and to the economies of the industrialized world.

In a 1984 study, Karim Pakravan analyzed the costs of four scenarios of oil disruption in the Persian Gulf: disruption in the amounts of three, six, nine, and eighteen million barrels per day. "They correspond to . . . limited regional conflicts or internal destabilization, generalised regional conflict involving more than two states, total cutoff of Saudi Arabian production as a result of internal or external conflict, and closure of the Strait of Hormuz for one year by the USSR."[21] Only in the case of the three million barrel-per-day scenario does the United States incur a less than 1 percent loss in its GNP; with a six million barrel-per-day loss for a year, the United States GNP is estimated to decline by 2.5 to 2.8 percent. In the situation of a nine million barrel-per-day loss, decline is on the order of 4.8 percent in 1985, and 5.2 percent in 1980. In dollar terms, this interruption would mean a loss of $155 billion in 1987. In the worst-case scenario brought on by the closure of the Straits of Hormuz, the GNP losses add up to an enormous 12.8 percent in 1985 and 14.9 percent in 1990.[22] Another critical finding of this study is the enormous importance of Saudi Arabia. Any conflict involving interruption of Saudi oil adds up to a hefty loss in availability of world petroleum supplies. For instance, a limited regional war involving Iran and Iraq results in a maximum net loss of 2.7 million barrels per day, but one involving Iran and Saudi Arabia is estimated to reduce the world oil supplies by 10.7 million barrels per day.[23]

These disruption analyses and resulting estimates of costs suggest that the RDF will be most probably used in three possible instances: to prevent the closure of the Straits of Hormuz; to contain the Iran-Iraq war within those two nations; and to ensure the security of Saudi Arabia. Whether it will intervene in the event other states in the region also are threatened remains unclear.

A second means of enhancing oil security was to gain preeminent influence in the capitals of major oil-producing countries—Saudi Arabia, Kuwait, the UAE, and possibly Iraq. Improvement of relations with Iran was automatically ruled out because of the fierce anti-

Americanism of the Khomeini regime. However, the United States continued to monitor closely the course of events in Iran and sought to keep its disruptive impact from spreading to surrounding countries.

A gradual weakening in the bargaining position of OPEC was a third means of ensuring long-term access to Persian Gulf oil. A sudden breakup of OPEC could cause great chaos in the world financial markets; it could also endanger the survival of the regimes that the United States was trying to protect. It was entirely possible that, in the event OPEC collapsed, Egypt, North Yemen, Pakistan, Jordan, and Somalia, who all depended on it for large amounts of economic assistance, would also be thrown into a state of turmoil. It was therefore necessary to prevent the collapse of OPEC in the short run. What the administration strove to obtain was stability in production and prices, and a continued, steady supply of oil from the region. In the long run, however, it hoped that OPEC would wither away.

Regional Balances among Nations

In the aftermath of the Iranian revolution and the Soviet occupation of Afghanistan in 1979, Pakistan, Saudi Arabia, and Jordan had moved decisively toward the United States. Camp David had already ensured a pro-U.S. Egypt. Subsequently, Morocco and Sudan also joined the ranks of pro-U.S. moderate powers in the Arab world. The growing tension and outbreak of hostilities with Iran in 1980 pushed Iraq toward the United States. Saddam Hussein needed massive economic and military assistance that, at least in the beginning, Moscow was reluctant to provide. Saudi Arabia and other Gulf nations, on the other hand, extended substantial amounts of assistance to Iraq, mainly because, in their assessment, Iraq was the lesser of the two evils. The repercussions of an Iranian victory were too dangerous to contemplate. Iraq could, on the other hand, weaken and destroy the fundamentalist threat from Teheran. Following the Saudi lead, the Reagan administration concentrated on "containing" the war and neutralizing its impact beyond the two warring nations. It pursued a classic balance-of-power approach. In fact, the United States had much to gain from an impasse in the Iraq-Iran conflict, for its conclusive resolution could alter the regional balance in ways not advantageous to the United States or its allies. Whether the United States would play a more active role in this conflict in the future would depend on a decisive and permanent Iraqi shift away from Moscow and on Iraq's future attitude toward Israel.

Apart from the Iran-Iraq war, the Soviet presence in South Yemen represented yet another source of danger to the Persian Gulf, particularly Saudi Arabia. The approval of massive arms sales to all the Gulf nations—including the transfer of F-15 components, 1,175 Sidewinder missiles and AWACs to Riyadh—indicated that the Reagan administration saw this as a primary means of securing regional stability.[24] The total Saudi arms package added up to an impressive sum of over $20 billion. Between 1980 and 1984, arms transfers and economic aid to Egypt were also stepped up, particularly after Sadat's assassination in 1981. The administration underwrote the security of Morocco, Sudan, and Somalia, each considered critical to Egyptian and Saudi stability.[25] Morocco was to receive 108 M-60 tanks in order to counter the Soviet- and Algerian-backed Polisario guerrillas in the western Sahara, while Sudan was to receive substantial economic aid to help it withstand subversion from Libya. Soviet-backed Ethiopia and its guerrilla arms were perceived to be highly dangerous to the survival of the pro-U.S. Somali regime of Siad Barre. He had agreed to allow the United States the use of base and port facilities at Berbera. The significance of the Berbera base as a springboard for RDJTF action in the Persian Gulf and the Red Sea cannot be overstressed. Acquisition of base facilities there was an important achievement of the administration.

In Reagan's view, yet another pro-U.S. regime threatened directly by Soviet expansionism was Pakistan. President Zia-Ul-Haq faced grave threats from Soviet-occupied Afghanistan, as well as from pro-Soviet India. The administration, therefore, proceeded to shore up Pakistan with promises of forty F-16 fighters and sophisticated radar equipment as part of a $3.2 billion package of military credits and economic aid to be delivered between 1981 and 1987. This was a long commitment indeed.

Base Rights, Overseas Facilities, and Transit Rights

The Reagan administration vigorously pushed regional powers for participation in its Southwest Asian strategy. It secured or reaffirmed agreements to use bases and military facilities in Spain, Egypt, Morocco, Somalia, Kenya, and Oman.[26] Egypt was to be a critical launching pad for possible actions in northern Africa and the Persian Gulf. Strategic cooperation with Egypt took several forms. First, Egypt offered the United States "temporary limited access" to airfields near Cairo and in Ras Banas on the Red Sea. In return, the United States devoted $106.4 million to improving the infrastructure at Ras Banas, including runways for jet fighters and staging areas for ground troops.[27] Although Ras Banas is not in the Gulf, it is a strategic point in the protection of the Suez Canal and the Mediterranean, and may acquire added importance in the future since the Saudis are planning to pump more of their oil through a pipeline to the Red Sea in order to relieve congestion in the Persian Gulf.

Second, Egypt agreed to joint military training and manuevers. On 1 January 1980, the United States dispatched two AWACs carrying 250 air force personnel to the Egyptian air base in Qena to "practice contingencies" such as directing fighter-bombers to targets.[28] The planes flew over Saudi Arabia and joined U.S. warships in the Indian Ocean. It was officially acknowledged that the manuevers were meant to counter potential Soviet action in Afghanistan and threats from Iran. In July 1980, considerable equipment was airlifted and a squadron of bombers landed at Cairo West to test the Egyptian facilities for projection of U.S. air power.[29] In November 1980, the RDJTF, including around 1,400 troops and eight A-7 tactical ground-support planes, participated in a two-week exercise in Egypt. The exercise gave the RDJTF and the participating nations their first experience of joint manuevers and brought to their attention serious problems in operationalizing the concept. Third, Egypt agreed to prepositioning of weapons and equipment to be in readiness for use in a crisis.

It is generally felt that these measures make Egypt an important link in the protection of the Persian Gulf. Its role may not be to provide a station for U.S. troops, but to be a credible deterrent to threats from the fundamentalist regime in Iran. In fact, Egypt has extended considerable assistance to Iraq in it conflict with Iran. The Reagan administration added a similar strategic dimension to its long-held special ties with Israel as well. In the administration's view Israel represented a logical "strategic asset" for the United States in Southwest Asia. In this regard, previous administrations had not been different; they had also stressed Israel's special importance to the regional interest of the United States.

In September 1975, the United States and Israel had signed a Memorandum of Agreement (MOA) that obliged the United States to be "responsive" to Israel's economic and energy needs and to guarantee it adequate supplies of oil. Another MOA in March 1979 allowed Israeli firms to compete with U.S. companies for Pentagon contracts. During this period, Israel extended its military cooperation with the United States to cover situations in Africa, allowing Washington access to regimes in that continent that would otherwise raise congressional objections. In April 1981, a secret agreement was put into effect obliging the United States to buy $200 million worth of Israeli military goods each year. This was incorporated in the Memoranda of Understanding signed in November 1981, and reaffirmed in November 1983. The last envisaged joint strategic planning for implementation of the RDJTF.[30]

Although the RDJTF was designed as the spearhead of Reagan's security strategy for the region, in 1981 it was hamstrung with serious problems. First, the RDF as conceived initially was not strong enough to deter the Soviets, which was its main purpose. Second, it could not be mobilized or landed rapidly enough to fulfill its function. Lack of adequate base facilities in the region and a shortage of transport planes were the main problems.[31] Until these problems could be solved, the United States had little choice but to accept what on-the-scene capabilities it could obtain. By virtue of its geographic location, domestic stability, proven reliability, highly skilled manpower, and potent air, naval, and ground forces, Israel had much to offer the United States, and in 1981, the psychological moment for a strategic alliance with Israel was also right. In fact, Israel eagerly offered its cooperation.

Israel pointed out that although the RDJTF was unlikely to function before 1985, the threats were immediate and the dangers clear. Thus, what the United States needed was an interim "Rapid Reaction Force," more modest in size but capable of instant action in the Persian Gulf, and Israel could collaborate in creating one.[32] That U.S. strategists were thinking about this suggestion was apparent from reports about a special study by the Pentagon in 1981. This demonstrated that arms and armor sufficient for one mechanized division could be flown from Israel to Saudi Arabia within eleven days. It would take twenty-two days from Kenya, twenty-seven days from Diego Garcia, and seventy-seven days from the United States. Since the stated goal of the RDJTF was to land forces in full strength within two weeks, the logistic advantage offered by Israel became critical.[33]

Although the exact nature of the commitment by the United States remained shrouded in mystery, certain things were clear. From Israel's viewpoint, the strategic collaboration brought it a "guarantee," a layer of security to the "line of communication via Eilat to Africa." It also gave continuity and consistency to U.S.-Israeli ties that had been under severe strain since the 1973 oil embargo. This was one way Israel could ensure firm U.S. support even if it gave only a partial autonomy to the Palestinians. As for the United States, strategic collaboration with Israel served several purposes. First, it made available stockpiles of weapons, prepositioned equipment, military bases, and air cover in the event of a crisis in the region. Second, it made available critical intelligence information for countermeasures and diplomacy. Israeli intelligence has a first-rate reputation in this regard. Third, it allowed the United States to demonstrate forcefully its resolve to defend the region against any unfriendly encroachment. And last, it gave Washington bargaining power over Israel since Israel was more anxious for such an accord with the United States than the United States was.

U.S. naval and air base facilities in Oman dominate the entrance to the Persian Gulf, in addition to being a counterpoise to Soviet presence in Afghanistan or to Soviet designs on Iran or the Baluchi province of Pakistan. The United States has improved the facilities at the very tip of the Saudi Arabian peninsula, the Omani territory jutting into the Persian Gulf.[34] This will enable the United States to protect the choke-point at the Straits of Hormuz if threatened by a hostile regime in Teheran or by the Soviet military presence only 250 miles away in Afghanistan. Berbera in Somalia similarly commands the entrance to the Red Sea and, therefore, helps offset Soviet bases in South Yemen and Ethiopia. The port of Mombasa in Kenya offers a point closer to the Gulf and a base for prepositioning U.S. naval forces in the event of an emergency.[35] Morocco has also subscribed to the Reagan RDJTF strategy in the region and offered bases for U.S. forces. This will enable the United States to offset Soviet- and Cuban-backed activities of Libya, Algeria, and Ethiopia in North Africa and Bab-el Mandeb on the Red Sea. Last, but not least, the Reagan administration has enhanced the U.S. naval presence in the Indian Ocean and turned Diego Garcia into a major focal point for an immensely strengthened advance and relatively secure U.S. military fortress serving the Indian Ocean, the Persian Gulf, and the Red Sea.[36]

The Reagan administration must, however, live with the Saudi, Kuwaiti, and Pakistani governments' refusal to allow U.S. bases. Still, it hopes that their deepening dependence on the United States will ensure cooperation at least in times of crisis.[37] Having invested so heavily in the current Saudi and Moroccan monarchy, and in Egypt, Sudan, and Pakistan's military dictatorships, the United States has every interest in maintaining the status quo there.

Internal Security and Stability of Pro-U.S. Governments and Elites

In the Reagan view, the entire arc of Islamic nations stretching from Egypt to Pakistan, including Morocco and Somalia, was vulnerable to pressures from various secular and religious ideologies. The monarchies of Saudi Arabia, Morocco, Jordan, and other smaller kingdoms of the Arabian peninsula were threatened internally by leftist nationalists. In Jordan, this threat was combined with the growing presence of Palestinians committed to an endless struggle to gain self-determination. Their rapidly growing migration to Jordan, Lebanon, and to a smaller extent, Egypt, represented a potential threat to the stability of these states. King Hussein had great difficulty in putting down the 1970s Palestinian attempt to topple his regime. Lebanon was balkanized and plunged into a state of unending civil war. Sadat saw a real threat to his survival as long as the Palestinian question remained unsettled, and Hosni Mubarak sees a threat to his own survival.[38] Saudi rulers, too, cannot abandon the Palestinian cause without endangering their stability. Palestinians represented an internal threat to the extent that the broad political consensus behind the Saudi throne would shatter if the royal family were perceived to have betrayed their causes. On the other hand, the establishment of a leftist and secular Palestinian state in Lebanon or Palestine-Jordan would also pose a threat to the conservative monarchy in Riyadh.

Islamic fundamentalism and its recent resurgence with a state base in Iran was perceived by the United States as the second immediate threat to the fragile policies of the Persian Gulf and West Asia.[39] The 1979 attack on Mecca brought this vividly to world attention. We will discuss the destabilizing potential of fundamentalism at greater length in Chapter 9, but it is important to note that this is perhaps the most difficult challenge future administrations are likely to face.

Ethnic irredentism and separatist movements constituted the third source of threat in the region.[40] For instance, the Kurds have long agitated for a separate state, endangering the internal stability of Iraq. Baluchi nationalism is also a serious threat to both Iran and Pakistan, and since the Soviet occupation of Afghanistan its danger has mounted a hundredfold. In Reagan's view, Pathan and now Sindhi separatism represent a similar problem for Pakistan, while Ethiopia, Somalia, and Kenya can easily fall prey to tribal strife and separatist demands within their nations.

The Reagan administration gave military assistance to enable individual nations to put down ethnic separatist revolts. For instance, Morocco and Sudan managed to crush the internal challenge, while Pakistan was able to devote substantial economic resources to the development of the Baluch and Pathan provinces. It laid down a network of roads, built commerce, and co-opted a large part of the separatist leadership into the support structure for President Zia.

The Palestinians and the Islamic fundamentalists, however, posed the administration's most difficult problems, the first because of the U.S. commitment to Israel, and the second because of fundamentalist resentment toward Western influence. To counter these problems, the Reagan administration developed a series of bilateral security ties with a majority of the nations and provided them with ready assistance when threatened by radical guerrilla activities. The 1982 airlift of equipment to Somalia was a case in point.[41] Similarly, the administration dispatched the aircraft carrier *Nimitz* in early 1983 to the coast of Libya, while AWACS and squadrons of F-16s were dispatched whenever Egypt or Saudi Arabia felt threatened. The entire purpose was to put a damper on the Soviets or Soviet allies and force them to desist from interfering in U.S.-backed nations.

Resolving Regional Disputes on Favorable Terms

Four major intraregional disputes threaten U.S. interests in the Persian Gulf: Arab-Israeli, Ethiopia-Somalia, India-Pakistan, and Iran-Iraq. Only the last one is at the center of the region, while the first three are on the periphery of Southwest Asia. Their impact, however, reaches the heart of the region. In fact, for strategic purposes, the Reagan administration also perceives them as central. The reasons for this are not difficult to see. Every Arab-Israeli conflict immediately upsets the course of bilateral relationships between the United States and the Arab world. Its outcome creates internal threats to the pro-U.S. regimes, and its escalation produces opportunities for the USSR to enter the region on behalf of its beleaguered Arab allies. The India-Pakistan and Somalia-Ethiopia conflicts each involve a close U.S. ally and a pro-Soviet power, or, as in the case of India, an anti-U.S. neutral power. Pakistan and Somalia both play an important part in Reagan's RDJTF strategy. Their defeat would seriously jeopardize U.S. ability to defend the region, the U.S. objective of making the region "hospitable for American ideals," and U.S. access to its resources and minerals. Neutralizing the Indian threat to Pakistan and securing Somalia against Ethiopia was, therefore, important to U.S. interests.

Since regional disputes are extremely divisive, and since the administration was anxious to secure a consensus of anti-Soviet strategic interests there, it tried to avoid issues that would force it to make a clear choice between its regional allies, i.e., Israel and Arab states over the issue of Palestine. In fact, Reagan advisers argued that past administrations had given excessive importance to solving regional disputes. In the process, they had reliable U.S. allies make concessions to not-so-reliable "nonallies"—for instance, Israel and Pakistan. This had directed U.S. energies away from its own strategic interest, which was to secure the region against the Soviets. Growing Soviet military strength threatened India as well as Pakistan, Arabs as well as Israel. Reagan's criticism of Carter's human rights policy, toward Iran under the Shah and toward Pakistan, as well as of Carter's Camp David initiative, stemmed directly from this perception. Resolution of regional disputes was low among Reagan's priorities. The fear that the region would remain relatively exposed until the RDJTF was properly readied (this could not happen until the second half of 1980) gave the administration a sense of urgency to move rapidly toward a consensus of strategic interests in the region.

The participation by regional powers depended largely on their threat perceptions, and although most agreed that the Soviet buildup was ominous, each perceived its own adversary as infinitely more dangerous than the "Soviet threat."[42] These differences of perception led to different priorities for U.S. allies and different degrees of commitment to the U.S. anti-Soviet stance. This will be discussed at greater length in the following chapters. What is important to note here is that the administration sought to integrate the anti-Soviet focus of both its global and its regional thrusts, and reordered U.S. priorities on that basis.

Implications of the Reagan Strategy

What were the implications of this strengthened strategic posture?

The most significant implication of this new military posture was the dramatic change in the balance between diplomacy and coercion in U.S. relations with Southwest Asia. During its first term in office, the Reagan administration sought to faithfully translate its major themes—globalism, unilateralism, and interventionism—into strategic capability. The formation of the Central Command for Southwest Asia, the stockpiles of weapons, access to base facilities, enhanced readiness, and strategic agreements had all given the United States a formidable on-the-scene capability to project military power and to deter its adversaries. But these raised a number of serious questions: first, whether the United States could afford defense budgets of this magnitude; second, whether Reagan's perceptions of military threats were exaggerated; third, whether the new military posture could guarantee enhanced U.S. security and the protection of its interests; and fourth, whether there were not other, less costly alternatives to the course proposed by the administration.

What the administration had proposed added up to a budget that was historically unprecedented in peacetime. It reflected the Reagan analysis of international threats and U.S. military weakness. Not everyone, however, agreed with this analysis. There were serious questions about the requested allocation of resources (i.e., whether the United States needed first-strike weapons such as the MX, the Trident II, and the B-1 bombers) and the political effects of such allocations (whether these new weapons would not destabilize the already frail East-West balance). Given the mounting public debt and projected fiscal deficits estimated to rise to more than 300 billion by 1989, the U.S. Congress was bound to undertake a substantial review of the proposed budgets.[43]

The administration had justified the original commitment to enhance the military posture by citing a "relentless buildup" of Soviet forces and a dangerous "mismatch" between U.S. strategy and the sources devoted to it. However, the evidence presented to the Congress during 1983 did not bear this out. The estimated growth of Soviet defense expenditures was in fact reduced from 4 percent a year to 2 percent between 1976 and 1981, while Soviet procurement of new weapons had remained unchanged. The administration had reasoned that the Soviet Union had major technical advantages in certain categories of weapons, but this too seemed inconsistent with the Pentagon's loud complaints that Moscow was stealing technology from the United States. Nor had the Soviet army scored a decisive success in Afghanistan. The imminent threat of Soviet encroachment on Persian Gulf oil routes had not materialized, nor had Soviet arms in Syrian hands performed well against Israel in 1982. All in all, over the four years the "Soviet threat" in Southwest Asia appeared to have been highly exaggerated.

One obvious conclusion from this was that the administration had accumulated a force structure far beyond what was necessary to protect U.S. global and regional objectives. A number of studies substantiate this contention. For instance, a Brookings Institute study concludes that the administration, when it came to office, "seriously misjudged what needed to be done to strengthen U.S. defenses." It overestimated the magnitude of the defense effort made by the Soviet Union during the previous six years, and it underestimated the extent to which existing U.S. defense capabilities had been modernized and, in conjunction with allied forces, were able to defend essential interests.[44] In other words, had the administration been more objective in estimating Soviet military strength, and had it taken into full account the military abilities of its allies, the magnitude of buildup it proposed would not have been necessary.

What then was the purpose of this "surplus security" and this excessive military buildup? Could it guarantee stability in the region and deter all elements hostile to U.S. interests? There are two major considerations in this. First, it is difficult to assess the future Soviet response to the Reagan military buildup. Although the Soviet Union may not match the United States ship-for-ship and weapon-for-weapon in the

Persian Gulf, greater military effort to counter enhanced U.S. presence would be a logical Soviet step. There is bound to be an attempt on the part of Moscow to hold onto its allies and widen its political options in the region. Second, it is equally difficult to foresee consequences of enhanced U.S. presence on the region as a whole. It is entirely possible that, instead of stabilizing the region, the heightened U.S. pressure may incite popular nationalist reaction against it, and against what is likely to be perceived as U.S. domination.

In any case, strengthened military posture may not be enough in itself. If the RDJTF is to be a stabilizing presence, it should not be seen as a force inimical to the nationalist aspirations of the people in the region. Nor should it encroach upon the freedom and sovereignty of the states in Southwest Asia. Ultimately, the Reagan strategic purpose—enhanced stability and security for Southwest Asia—will depend on a correct mix of coercion and diplomacy in U.S. policy. With President Reagan at the helm, the means of coercion were well in hand; whether the administration had also pursued a political strategy that was effective is a question to which we turn in the next chapter.

Notes

1. U.S. Department of Defense, *Soviet Military Power,* October 1981. Published in its entirety in *Strategic Digest,* Institute for Defense Studies and Analysis, New Delhi (April–May 1982), 231.

2. Ibid., 270.

3. These views were enthusiastically aired by Alexander Haig during the September 1981 testimony before the House Subcommittee on Mining. He insisted the United States was vulnerable to the growing crisis in strategic and critical materials. Not only was the United States "inordinately . . . dependent on foreign . . . supply, but had to increasingly compete with the Soviet Union for influence and control."

4. *Soviet Military Power,* 275.

5. Central Intelligence Agency, *The International Energy Situation: Outlook to 1985,* ER 77-102 UOV (C5A, 1977), 13. See also *The Soviet Oil Situation: An Evaluation of CIA Analysis of Soviet Oil Production,* staff report of the Senate Select Committee on Intelligence, 15th Congress, 2nd session, 1978.

6. Disputing the Defense Intelligence Agency's findings, the CIA, in a 401-page study released at the end of 1982, concluded that the Soviet economy was not on the verge of collapse and had in fact experienced a reasonable growth (3 percent per year) over the decade. See *New York Times,* 5 March 1982.

7. For the main argument in this debate, see Robert Komer, "Maritime Strategy vs. Coalition Defense," *Foreign Affairs* 60:5 (Summer 1982), 1124–1145.

8. William Kaufman, *The 1985 Defense Budget* (Washington, DC: Brookings Institute, 1985), 1.

9. Quoted in *New York Times,* 5 March 1982.

10. An excerpt of this secret document was published in *New York Times,* 30 May 1982.

11. The Reagan administration has attached the highest priority to this. According to John Lehman, secretary of the navy, the goal was nothing short of "maritime superiority over any power or powers." Its purpose was to be visibly offensive in orientation, develop global reach and to be designed to meet any challenge however small or big. To this end, "every psychological leverage will be sought, opportunities seized to maximize U.S. strength and Soviet weakness." See *Strategic Review* 9:3 (Summer 1981), 13–14; "Arming for the 80's," *Time,* 27 July 1981, 15–16.

12. Fred Ikle, "The Reagan Defense Program: A Focus on Strategic Imperatives," *Strategic Review* (Spring 1982), 15.

13. When directly confronted with the question of whether the new strategic doctrine meant preparing for two and a half wars instead of one and a half wars, Defense Secretary Weinberger shied away from the answer but stated that the United States must prepare for wars of "any size or shape and in any region." "Arming for the 80's," 9.

14. U.S. Congress, House Committee on Interior and Insular Affairs, Subcommittee on Mines and Mining, Non-Fuel Mineral Policy Review Hearing, 96th Congress, 2d session, 1980, pt. III, p. 5.

15. Michael Klare, *Beyond the Vietnam Syndrome: U.S. Interventionism in the 1980's* (Washington, DC: Institute of Policy Studies, 1981), 51.

16. Shahram Chubin, "U.S. Security Interests in the Persian Gulf in the 1980's," *Daedalus,* 109:4 (Fall 1980), 47–48.

17. For future discussion, see Robert J. Hanks, *The Unnoticed Challenge: Soviet Maritime Strategy and Global Choke Points* (Cambridge, MA: Institute for Foreign Policy Analysis, 1980).

18. For an excellent articulation of dominant views about potential threats in Southwest Asia, see Chubin, "U.S. Security Interests in the Persian Gulf," 31–67; Richard Cronin, *U.S. Interests, Objectives and Policy Options in Southwest Asia,* Strategic Studies Institute, U.S. Army War College, Carlisle Barracks, 15 January 1982.

19. Deborah Shapley, "The Army's New Fighting Doctrine," *New York Times Magazine,* 18 November 1982.

20. Ibid., 36.

21. Karim Pakravan, *Oil Supply Disruptions in the 1980's* (Stanford, CA: Hoover Institution Press, 1984).

22. Ibid., 139.

23. Ibid., 21.

24. *The Middle East,* 5th ed. (Washington, DC: Congressional Quarterly, 1981), 60–61.

25. U.S. Congress, House Committee on Appropriations hearings before a

subcommittee on Foreign Operations and Related Agencies. *Supplementary Appropriations for 1982,* 97th Congress, 2d session, May 13, 1982. pp. 1–77.

26. Ibid. For a good discussion of Reagan's problems and prospects in acquiring base facilities, see Robert Harkavy, "Military Bases in the Third World," in *The Third World: Premises of U.S. Policy,* ed. Scott Thompson (San Francisco: Institute for Contemporary Studies, 1983), 175–203.

27. *New York Times,* 12 March 1981.

28. Joe Stark, "The Carter Doctrine and U.S. Bases in the Middle East," *MERIP Reports* 80 (September 1980), 8.

29. Ibid., 3.

30. See *Middle East International* (London), August 1984, 18.

31. See Rear Admiral Robert Hanks USN (Ret), "Rapid Deployment in Perspective," *Strategic Digest,* Institute for Defense Studies and Analysis, New Delhi, November 1981, 917; see also Stuart Koehl and Stephen Glick, "The Rapid Deployment Force," *The American Spectator,* January 1981, 18–21; Jeffrey Record, *The Rapid Deployment Force and U.S. Military Intervention in the Persian Gulf* (Cambridge, MA: Institute for Foreign Policy Analysis, 1981); U.S. Congress, House Committee on Appropriations, Subcommittee on the Department of Defense, Department of Defense Appropriations for 1982, Hearings, 97th Congress, 1st session; *Part IV: Rapid Deployment Force* (Washington, DC: U.S. Government Printing Office, 1981); E. Asa Bates, "The Rapid Deployment Force: Fact or Fiction," *RUSI: Journal of the Royal United Services Institute for Defense Studies* 124 (June 1981), 23–32.

32. Shai Feldman, quoting Aharon Yariv, head of the Israeli Center for Strategic Studies, in "Peacekeeping in the Middle East: The Next Step Up," *Foreign Affairs* 59: 4 (Spring 1981), 765–766.

33. Reported in *New York Times,* 2 October 1981.

34. *Washington Post,* 11 October 1980; *New York Times,* 6 June 1980, 28 January 1980.

35. See "Kenya Agrees To Expand U.S. Use of Military Bases," *New York Times,* 28 June 1980; "U.S. Warily Seeking New Outposts Abroad," *Washington Post,* 25 February 1980.

36. The Diego Garcia base and port is to be used to deploy on a continuing basis forward supply ships for the RDF. The regular B-52 sorties were to begin as soon as an adequate runway was completed. "U.S. Studying $1 Billion Expansion of Indian Ocean Base," *New York Times,* 6 April 1980.

37. It is significant that, although U.S. access to Jidda remains unclear, it began to operate AWACS out of Saudi Arabia, reinforcing this arrangement further through additional sales of AWACS and F-15 equipment. This could only result in tightening the U.S.-Saudi security ties. See Gervasi, "Island of Instability," *Harper's,* September 1981, 13–18.

38. For the destabilizing impact of Sadat's policies, the rise of Islamic fundamentalism, and impact of abandoning the Palestinian cause by Egypt, see Mohamed Haikel, *Autumn of Fury* (London: Andre Deutsch, 1983), 103–216.

39. See, for instance, Martin Kramer, *Political Islam, The Washington Papers,* no. 73. (Washington, DC: Center for Strategic and International Studies,

1980); Michael Curtis, ed., *Religion and Politics in the Middle East* (Boulder, CO: Westview Press, 1981); *Islam and Power in the Contemporary Muslim World*, ed. Alex Cudi and Ali Hillal Dessouki (Baltimore: Johns Hopkins University Press, 1981); Ali Hillal Dessouki, *Islamic Resurgence in Arab Countries* (New York: Praeger, 1982).

40. Edmund Ghareeb, *The Kurdish Question in Iraq*, (Syracuse, NY: Syracuse University Press, 1981); Selig Harrison, *In Afghanistan's Shadow: Baluch Nationalism and Soviet Temptation* (Washington, DC: Carnegie Endowment for International Peace, 1981).

41. "U.S. Flying Arms to Somalia To Counter Ethiopian Raids," *New York Times*, 25 July 1982, 1 August 1982.

42. Robert Litwak reviews the regional threat perceptions and interstate conflicts in Southwest Asia. See Robert Litwak, *Security in the Persian Gulf* (NJ: Allanheld and Osman, 1981).

43. By the middle of 1982, the critics of the Reagan defense program had become far more vocal and the Congress was reluctant to support budget requests. Senator Tower, chairman of the Armed Services Committee, noted, "The consensus is . . . still there . . . but the willingness . . . had eroded." See *New York Times*, 15 June 1982, 29 December 1982.

44. William Kaufmann, *The 1985 Defense Budget* (Washington, DC: Brookings Institute, 1984), 5.

6.

Reagan's Approach to the Arab-Israeli Dispute

Reagan's conduct in Southwest Asia was a logical extension of the administration's three foreign policy themes: globalism, unilateralism, and interventionism. As noted in the last chapter, the administration had decided to abandon "strategic passivity" and instead obtain for itself greater freedom of action. A variety of steps were taken to ensure this: the RDF and the strategic agreements, the stockpiled weapons, and visible U.S. military support for its major allies in the region. These programs had fundamentally altered the equation of coercion and diplomacy in Reagan's policy.

In what way did this free the administration from previous restraint, and to what purpose did it use its enhanced ability to project U.S. power? These are the questions to which we now turn. The conduct of Reagan's policy will be analyzed in the context of events and opportunities in Southwest Asia. The realities of politics in the region—the specific distribution of power, the advantages conferred by the strength of allies of the United States, and the position of its foes—will be considered as we examine U.S. policy in Southwest Asia.

Among the important events that shaped the U.S. response, the following will be discussed: in the Middle East, the U.S. involvement in the Lebanon War, the 1 September 1982 peace initiative and its aftermath; in South Asia, the strengthening of U.S.-Pakistani ties, and the changing alignment of power among India, Pakistan, and the United States; in the Persian Gulf, the Iraq-Iran war and the U.S.-Saudi strategic relationship. This and the following two chapters are each concerned with a pair of states important to the balance of power in

Southwest Asia but in conflict with each other: the Arab states and Israel are considered in this chapter, both friends and allies of the U.S.; India and Pakistan under the shadow of the Afghan crisis in Chapter 7, with Pakistan a close ally and India an uncertain friend; and Iran and Iraq in Chapter 8—Iran an enemy state and a major destabilizing factor in the Persian Gulf and Iraq a potential friend of the United States.

The main purpose here is to answer two questions that seem critical to an assessment of Reagan's policy. The first is whether the administration made visible progress in moving toward its objectives, i.e., continued access to Persian Gulf oil, exclusion of the Soviet Union and advancement of U.S. influence, and finally peace. The second is whether its achievements are likely to endure, or whether its success reflects only a temporary edge in the political balance and not a condition of sustained preeminence. The last can be ensured generally in two ways, by increasing U.S. military domination and establishing political hegemony, or by building a structure of peace on the foundation of U.S. power. The two are not necessarily mutually exclusive. It is possible to coerce others into peace but not possible to sustain such a peace for long without committing more and more arms to that objective. History tells us that in the ultimate analysis there is no real lasting substitute for a peace that is built on a general consensus, and one that is sustained by the self-interest of those involved. In this and the next two chapters, we will examine whether or not the Reagan policies reflected this lesson of history.

Even a casual glance at the Reagan policy in Southwest Asia shows that its boldest moves were not in Afghanistan, where presumably the United States had the greatest provocation, but in Lebanon, where its interests were only peripheral. Unlike President Carter, the Reagan administration did not consider the resolution of the Arab-Israeli dispute its first priority. Yet, in 1982, only a year after Reagan had assumed office, the administration had committed U.S. troops to the defense of objectives in the region. This was the first time since 1958 that the United States had sent its Marines to Lebanon. In committing U.S. troops, the Reagan administration had jettisoned the guidelines that had been laid down by Kissinger and Carter, who had believed that the United States should remain an external weight and never a physical military presence committed to a particular outcome in the Arab-Israeli dispute.

What had caused the administration to initially neglect the conflict in the Middle East, and then, only a year later, to commit its armed forces to Lebanon? What did the administration hope to achieve, and how did this action enhance the prospects for peace and stability in the Middle East, if in fact it did?

Perceptions and Priorities

As the year 1980 opened, a new set of regional perceptions and objectives had become visible among the major actors in the Arab-Israeli dispute.

1. The hostage crisis in Iran and the Soviet invasion of Afghanistan had reinforced the perception that the United States was in a geopolitical decline. The Reagan administration was therefore anxious to reverse what it believed were the failures and the weaknesses associated with these two events. The security and stability of the Persian Gulf thus assumed paramount importance, whereas the resolution of the Arab-Israeli conflict became important only insofar as it affected the situation in the Gulf. Explaining these priorities, Haig said, "it is important to handle the Arab-Israeli question and other regional disputes in a strategic framework that recognizes and is responsive to the larger threat of Soviet expansionism."[1]

2. In this perspective, Israel was regarded as a valuable strategic asset. In fact, President Reagan's pro-Israeli position had been visible throughout the 1980 election campaign. He said, "we must prevent the Soviet Union from penetrating the Mideast.... If Israel were not there, the United States would have to be there."[2] In other words, the administration viewed Israel as a bulwark of anti-Soviet and antiradical influence in the Middle East. As subsequent events show, this course of policy was dangerous. In cultivating strategic ties with Israel, the administration was wittingly or otherwise committing itself to the Likud solution for the resolution of the Arab-Israeli conflict. It is true that U.S. and Israeli interests converged on several points, but these had never been identical in the past, and were not so now. The moderate Arab regimes were also meant to serve a similar function, except, in the Reagan assessment, the Arab regimes were internally vulnerable and externally too weak to deter Soviet ambitions or those of its surrogates.

3. The Reagan administration's views on the PLO at least initially coincided wholly with the Begin government's views. Shortly after the elections, President Reagan stated, "I think the PLO has proven that it is a terrorist organization.... I separate the PLO from the Palestinian refugees. No one elected the PLO."[3] In other words, the Reagan administration had retreated from the previous administration's position that the PLO had a legitimate political (as opposed to humanitarian) claim to a homeland.

4. The Reagan administration was generally committed to the preservation of the Arab-Israeli relationship as it was institutionalized in the Camp David agreements. It was also committed to the protection and stability of moderate Arab states, but it was not anxious to exert itself on behalf of the Palestinians, or to further negotiations that would include pro-Moscow radical states such as Syria and Iraq.

5. The Reagan administration did not see U.S. interests served by any attempts at the comprehensive peace so zealously advanced by Carter, nor did it feel any urgency to pursue the step-by-step diplomacy of Henry Kissinger. In fact, the administration did not even replace Sol Linowitz, who had acted as a special envoy under the Carter administration. The Arab-Israeli negotiations were left to the disputing parties themselves or to the professionals in the State Department. There were occasional flurries of activities in response to specific crises, but the administration had no comprehensive approach, no timetable, and no framework that would impart even minimal momentum to the resolution of the outstanding problems in the Middle East.

Israeli Perceptions

In several ways, Washington's priorities suited the objectives of Menachem Begin. Israel had already agreed to return the Sinai and vigorous U.S. pursuit of peace might have forced him to make further concessions that he did not want to make.

The Begin government policy toward the West Bank could not accommodate any interests other than its own. Begin categorically stated that Judea and Samaria (the West Bank) were an integral part of

Israel's sovereignty: "it is our land, you don't annex your own country," he said.[4] Begin had conceded the Sinai to Egypt partly because that was the geopolitical price he had to pay to obtain U.S. support and partly because the Sinai claim did not involve fundamental ideological issues. This was not the case with the West Bank. For Begin, the West Bank was a part of Israel's sacred patrimony, *Eretz Yisrael.*

In Begin's view, "full autonomy" for the West Bank, as mentioned in the Camp David agreements, in no way implied territorial or political separation from Israel. "The five year period granted by Camp David was merely to allow Arab inhabitants of the territories to choose between Israeli and Jordanian citizenship."[5] In other words, the Begin government was committed to the eventual incorporation of the West Bank into Israel.

Anticipating Arab and U.S. objections to this, Begin proceeded on two simultaneous courses of action. First, he ordered the construction of additional West Bank settlements, hoping that this would create a *fait accompli* to which both the Arabs and the United States would eventually succumb. And second, he proceeded to apply the doctrine of "preemption" to the region—a strategy to change, through force, the political situation outside the borders of Israel (i.e., Lebanon and the West Bank). This policy of preemption received its full expression in August 1981, when Begin appointed Ariel Sharon to the defense ministry in Israel. According to Ze'ev Schiff and Ehud Ya'ari, Sharon brought a bold plan to establish a "new political order" in Lebanon in which the PLO was to be driven out of Lebanon and Bashir Gemayel, the longtime friend of Israel, was to be installed as the country's new president.[6]

To prevent Syrian intervention, the Syrian army was to be evicted from Lebanon. Once the PLO had lost its "independent" base in Lebanon, Sharon reasoned, it would be in no position to make demands on the West Bank. The Sharon plan assumed that the political destruction of the PLO would allow a more accommodating, moderate Palestinian leadership on the West Bank to step forward and make a deal with Israel. In this event, Sharon thought, the Palestinians would have no option but to seek accommodation with King Hussein, who, as everyone knew, feared Palestinian machinations and would in all likelihood take the necessary steps to prevent their independent resurgence. If this scenario were to come about, and Sharon had every confidence that the Israeli Defense Forces could accomplish it, Israel would become the unchallenged preeminent power in the Middle East.

An informal alliance with the Christian Maronite Phalange was central to this design. The other need was to secure U.S. acquiescence in the actions outlined. As Don Peretz comments, Likud's leaders are strongly influenced by a revisionist theory that antedates the establishment of Israel, namely, the idea of "an alliance of minorities in the Middle East."[7]

It is important to note that although previous Labor governments in Israel had helped the Kurds (yet another minority) against the Ba'athist regime in Iraq, on the whole, these governments did not subscribe to the concept of a permanent Middle East alliance of minorities. The Labor party feared that such an alliance would foreclose the settlement of the conflict with the Arab states, and seriously damage the chance of a *modus vivendi* with the larger Muslim world.

Arab Perceptions

In contrast to the Begin government's singular obsession with regional supremacy, the Arab states had become hopelessly divided and weakened due to several developments in the early 1980s. The Iranian revolution had strongly underscored the fragility of their domestic political order; the Iran-Iraq war had highlighted the staying power and the ideological strength of their most feared ideological enemy, Ayatollah Khomeini; and the oil glut had deprived them of their most potent bargaining asset. The biggest handicap for the Arab world, however, was the loss of Egypt and the conclusion of the Egyptian-Israeli peace treaty.

Under Likud, Israel's cohesiveness and power had substantially increased. In contrast, Arab unity was in shambles. The eleventh Arab summit, held in Amman, Jordan, in November 1980, exposed to full view the growing divisions in the Arab world. The Amman summit was boycotted by the "radical front"—Syria, Libya, South Yemen, Algeria, and the PLO. The Arab-Israeli issue was hardly raised, while the remaining members concentrated on developmental and financial issues. There was a growing indication that the Arab regimes were becoming increasingly concerned with their individual problems and less concerned with Arab unity or the collective Arab cause. The next summit, at Fez in Morocco in November 1981, however, focused on the Palestinian issue. Saudi Arabia had presented an eight-point plan (the Fahd Plan) for the settlement of the Arab-Israeli conflict. But this too revealed sharp differences among the Arab states. Syria vehemently objected to the plan and charged that it was a "camouflaged American scheme to pass a Camp David–like settlement in Arab garb. They felt that such a plan would exclude the Soviet Union . . . robbing Syria of a strong ally during future negotiations. Further, the Syrians believed that the Fahd Plan would pave the way for an Egyptian return to the Arab arena, thus undermining Syrian stature and bargaining power in inter-Arab dealings."[8]

These events were duly noted in Washington and Tel-Aviv. It was apparent to the Reagan administration that Saudi Arabia had shifted closer to the Egyptian position, although only a year ago, Saudis had categorically rejected the Camp David agreements and broken ties with Egypt. For Begin and Reagan, the critical political fact in the situation was that the Arab world was unlikely to militarily unite or impose a collective oil embargo on the West. It was also apparent to both, particularly to the United States, that at least some Arab states might be willing to trade off their commitment to the united Arab cause in exchange for arms and technology from the United States.

Prelude to War (January 1981–July 1982)

The first phase of the Reagan administration was shaped on the one hand by the asymmetry of power between the Arab states and Israel, and on the other by Washington's obsessive concern with eliminating Soviet influence from the region. A series of crises compelled the Reagan administration to turn its attention to the Arab-Israeli conflict.

In February 1981, Reagan's second month in office, tensions had begun to build up between the Maronites and the Syrians around the city of Zahle in Lebanon, which is the capital of Bekaa Valley and an area regarded by Syria as vital to the defense of Damascus. The Begin government knew that the confrontation was a Phalange ploy to draw Israel into a clash with Syria. However, by early 1981, Begin and Sharon were not averse to the idea, and in fact believed that such a confrontation might be a step toward the fulfillment of their larger ambitions.[9] Israel stepped up its bombings and raids in Lebanon. Syria responded by laying siege to the city of Zahle and deploying SAM-3 and SAM-6 antiaircraft missiles in the Bekka valley. Israel insisted that Syria remove the missiles or Israel would take action to remove them.

Similarly, by May 1981, Israel was frequently raiding and bombing the PLO bases in Southern Lebanon. At first, the PLO retaliated "gingerly for fear that a vigorous reaction would . . . provoke a crushing Israeli ground operation,"[10] but as air attacks continued the PLO abandoned restraint and shelled Israeli towns on the Mediterranean coast. These events let loose a spiral of violence in which Israel bombed the PLO headquarters in the densely populated area of Beirut, killing 100 people and wounding over 600. In June 1981, Israel bombed and destroyed the Iraqi nuclear reactor and in December 1981 it annexed the Golan Heights.

Throughout the missile crisis, confrontations with Syria, and raids on the PLO camps, the Reagan administration remained supportive of Israel. The president blamed Syria for the escalation of violence and for aiming "aggressive" missiles against Israel.[11] As for the PLO, his views were well known. The Reagan administration concurred with the Israeli view that the PLO was a terrorist organization and as such deserved no consideration. Nevertheless, some attempt at peace had to be made. Reagan therefore sent Philip Habib to defuse the missile crisis, but the Habib mission was soon overshadowed by the Israeli raid of the Iraqi nuclear reactor. The raid was carried out by F-16s escorted by F-15s supplied by the United States but without prior consultation with Washington. Israel had undeniably violated the U.S. military sales act. The administration was therefore obliged to protest the violation and admonish Israel for such a precipitate action, but these reprimands remained strictly perfunctory. UN Ambassador Kirkpatrick explained the U.S. position carefully, saying that the United States would support the Security Council resolution "condemning" Israeli action but "nothing in the resolution will affect my government's commitment to Israel's security."[12]

However, Israel's July bombing of the PLO headquarters had resulted in considerable loss of life and aroused a strong international reaction. The Arab states were in fact furious and stepped up their pressure on the administration to restrain Israel. The Reagan administration therefore doubled its efforts to obtain a cease-fire between the disputants, which was finally arranged on 25 July 1981. Promptly on 17 August, Alexander Haig announced that the shipments of ten F-16s and two F-15s to Israel, suspended due to earlier Israeli actions, would be resumed. Begin had roundly denounced the suspension and said that it had been both "absolutely unjust and unjustifiable." The administration was growing somewhat wary of Israeli ambitions and continuous demands on Washington's goodwill and loyalty. The Israeli actions had compromised the U.S. position in the Arab world and placed repeated obstacles in the way of Washington's attempts to draw the moderate Arab states into a network of strategic relationships.

This network of pro-U.S. Arab states was in fact central to Reagan's concerns in Southwest Asia. The administration had wanted to establish an anti-Soviet consensus of strategic interests but feared that Israeli actions might jeopardize its goals. On 23 February 1981, the State Department declared that the United States would not press for a resumption of Israeli-Egyptian talks on Palestinian autonomy, but instead would focus its energy on warding off major strategic threats to the Middle East. In other words, the administration meant to uncouple the Egypt-Israeli negotiations over the Sinai from the fate of the West Bank, and use this leverage not for bringing about comprehensive peace but for the construction of a countervailing alliance against the Soviet Union.[13] It was also clear that the administration was divided over the extent to which it should support various Israeli actions in Lebanon. The secretary of defense favored pressing Israel to give greater consideration to U.S. interests. Nevertheless, until after the invasion of Lebanon, Alexander Haig's views seemed to prevail. Commenting on Haig's April visit to the Middle East, Schiff and Ya'ari observe, "By the time the secretary left Israel, there was no doubt in many minds that with a man of Haig's bent running the State Department, Israel could definitely allow itself to adopt a militant posture vis-à-vis Damascus."[14]

With the intent of binding the pro-U.S. moderate Arab states more closely to U.S. interests and of giving concrete shape to this strategic consensus, the administration decided to sell five AWACS to Saudi Arabia. Israel and the pro-Israeli lobby in the Congress mounted a major campaign to prevent the sale.[15] The Saudis saw the AWACS as a test of Washington's commitment and of Israel's ability to veto such a sale. Israel saw it as a direct threat. The administration argued that Saudi Arabia needed these to defend its oil facilities, and that the United States needed to reinforce Saudi perceptions that Washington was a reliable ally. When Begin was convinced that the AWACS sale could not be prevented, he dropped his opposition. The debate, however, had shown that there were important differences in the regional objectives of Israel and the United States.

Hoping to smooth over the differences over the AWACS, Ariel Sharon visited the United States in November 1981. In his presentations at the Pentagon and the State Department, Sharon bemoaned the spread of Soviet influence in Africa and proposed that, in return for Israeli cooperation in Africa, the United States should allow Israel a free hand in the Middle East. It has been suggested that the administration sought to mollify Israel in November 1981 by offering a pact for strategic cooperation. It is also widely believed that the signing of the Memorandum of Strategic Cooperation in November encouraged Begin to annex the Golan Heights a month later, in December 1981.

Defense Secretary Weinberger was cool to the Sharon proposals, but the White House was favorably disposed toward Israel, and Weinberger's views did not prevail. On the other hand, Haig was persuaded of the advantages of destroying the PLO in Lebanon (which he regarded as a principal source of support for international terrorism) and of weakening the pro-Soviet front (Syria and the PLO) in the Middle East.

By early 1982, it was clear that Israel was rapidly moving toward an armed action in Lebanon. There were frequent reports of Israeli military preparations, and major newspapers in the United States and Europe were noting with growing frequency that the Middle East was heading toward war. The administration could not have missed the signals unless it was being willfully blind. William Quandt points out that in February 1981, four months before the invasion, the head of Israeli military intelligence briefed Secretary Haig on the general plan. The U.S. response was to say, in effect, "not before the Sinai withdrawal."[16] The administration was afraid that an Israeli invasion might jeopardize the proposed implementation of Camp David and the return of the Sinai and undermine the Egyptian-Israeli relationship, which, in the administration's view, constituted the cornerstone of its strategic consensus.

On 29 April 1982, amidst intensifying conflict in Lebanon, divisions in the Arab world, and massive strikes and demonstrations on the West Bank, Israel withdrew from the Sinai. Any one of the above developments would have been sufficient reason for Israel to postpone its withdrawal, but the United States was bent on securing that piece of its overall design, and Israel had other plans. In Israeli Defense Minister Sharon's view, with the return of the Sinai to Egypt, the way had become clear for his next move. In the early summer of 1982, he once again visited Washington and met with Haig. The strategic pact remained officially suspended, and Schiff and Ya'ari suggest that Sharon did not fully disclose the scope and extent of "operation Galilee" either to Haig or his own colleagues in the Israeli cabinet. However, Sharon came away from the meeting reassured that the United States endorsed Israel's right to respond to acts of terrorism. Commenting on Sharon's stratagem, Schiff and Ya'ari write, "Sharon was not in the least concerned about verifying whether the position reflected in his talk with Haig should be taken as the official policy of the Reagan administration . . . the Israeli government had grown accustomed to hearing clashing voices from Washington . . . he returned to Israel with the tidings that Washington was not adverse to an advance into Lebanon."[17]

This meeting was also reported to the White House, which had become somewhat concerned that Sharon would involve the United States in a situation not of its own making and from which it could not extricate itself without damage. It was proposed that Haig should write to Prime Minister Begin expressing U.S. concern and reservations about developments in Lebanon. Haig sent such a letter on 28 May 1982. According to several observers, the tone of the letter was too mild and the phrasing ambiguous enough for Israel to misconstrue the letter as an official U.S. warning, but a tacit approval nevertheless, of Israel's proposed actions in Lebanon. Whether Haig endorsed the Sharon grand plan or was ignorant of its true scope and purpose will long remain a matter of controversy among scholars. Several, however, believe that Haig was at least cautiously approving.[18] It was also clear that neither the White House nor Secretary of Defense Weinberger were fully aware of the extent of the U.S. commitments.[19]

Nevertheless, inasmuch as the president is in charge of the formulation and conduct of U.S. policy, he must be held responsible for its failures. The argument that the administration was unaware of Israeli plans in fact grows less and less credible as one surveys repeated U.S. defense of Israeli actions throughout 1981–1982.

Israel invaded Lebanon on 6 June 1982. This was ostensibly to push back the PLO forty kilometers north of the Israeli border, but Israeli troops soon spread all over Lebanon. It was a major invasion, and its scale left no one in any doubt that Israel had been preparing for it for some time. The timing of "operation peace for Galilee" was significant. Iraq was busy waging a war with Iran, and the Soviet Union was occupied with Poland and Afghanistan. It was also significant that the Reagan administration remained totally silent about the invasion until after Israel was well entrenched on the outskirts of Beirut and had started its terrible bombing and shelling of the city. It was only at this juncture that the United States stepped up pressure on Israel. Relations between the United States and Israel began to deteriorate rapidly. In the administration's view, Israel had not confined its operation to the forty-kilometer limit as it had claimed it would; what is more, it had shown total disregard for Washington's opinion and interests in the Middle East. President Reagan threatened a "comprehensive reassessment" of U.S. ties with Israel. Three weeks after the siege of Beirut, with great reluctance and after tremendous pressure, Israel agreed to PLO evacuation plans, to be executed and supervised by U.S. Marines.

The United States Leans toward the Arab States

The 1982 Israeli invasion had completely altered the political map of the region and brought about the need for a new strategy. In the Reagan peace plan of 1 September 1982, the United States proposed the creation of a self-governing entity on the West Bank and Gaza, linked with Jordan. The Reagan plan sought a compromise between the PLO's demand for an independent sovereign Palestinian state and Israel's demands for annexation of the West Bank and Gaza. The administration could hardly disguise its elation. There were repeated statements about an "unprecedented opportunity" and "spectacular prospects for peace." The administration viewed the war as a historical turning point. Indeed, it could not be disputed that, although the administration denied any hand in the Israeli decision to move into Lebanon, the post-1982 Middle East had drastically altered, and the United States had gained from it. Israel had destroyed the PLO base in Lebanon and inflicted a devastating defeat on Syria. The United States had emerged as the sole peacemaker without undue damage to its position. The Soviet Union, on the other hand, had suffered a serious setback. It had been highly embarrassed by the poor showing of its military equipment and weapons in the hands of the Syrians and had been unable to prevent their defeat. The PLO and Syria faced the humiliating choice of following U.S. initiatives or relying more closely on the Soviets. These developments gave an immense leverage to U.S. diplomacy. As U.S. officials happily declared, the United States had "moved into the diplomatic driver's seat in the Middle East." But it was obvious that these advantages would rapidly evaporate unless the United States made its proposed solutions work quickly. The success of the Reagan peace plan depended on obtaining the cooperation of both Syria and Israel in sustaining a truly independent and neutral Lebanon, a strong central government in Beirut that would maintain law and order, and the simultaneous return of the PLO to the West Bank. The first item on the agenda was then to secure a favorable response to the September initiative and the withdrawal of all foreign forces from Lebanon.

Israel rejected the Reagan plan and demanded a Syrian pullback before it agreed to withdraw; the withdrawal was also linked to a normalization of relations with Lebanon, which meant Gemayel would have to defy Arab opinion and recognize Israel's existence as well as dominance in southern Lebanon. The reasons for Israel's demands were not difficult to fathom. Begin recognized that the military success itself had ironically strengthened the hands of those who advocated territorial compromise on the West Bank. The PLO, weakened and now removed from Lebanon, could no longer be cited as a threat to justify occupying all the Arab land.

In fact, the months following the invasion were marked by growing clashes between the Reagan administration and the Begin government. The Reagan administration had resurrected the Palestinian question by proposing the creation of a Palestinian entity on the West Bank.

Israel had hoped that the destruction of the PLO leadership would free it of such pressures, but in this it was clearly mistaken. The United States appeared to be swinging toward a more Arab-oriented strategy in the post-Lebanon war period, signalled by the departure of Alexander Haig from the State Department and the arrival of Shultz, who was believed to be far more evenhanded between the Arabs and Israel.

The 19 September massacre of Palestinians by Phalangist Christians at the Sabra and Shatilla refugee camps in Lebanon strengthened U.S. resolve to distance itself from Israeli actions. The Arab states charged, and it was later confirmed, that the Phalangists had entered the camps with the full knowledge of the Israeli defense ministry. The administration immediately expressed its "outrage and revulsion" and pressed Israel to withdraw its forces. Reagan accepted Gemayel's request to send peacekeeping forces back into Lebanon. On 21 September, under immense pressure, Israel agreed to pull back from the area.

In a strange paradox not uncommon to the Middle East, Syria wanted some of the same things that Israel desired—a dominant influence in Lebanon, the subservience of the PLO, and veto power over any diplomatic arrangement in the Middle East.[20]

President Assad of Syria has always maintained that Syrian security was closely connected with the situation in Lebanon. The Israeli occupation of South Lebanon was therefore viewed as a serious security threat to Damascus.[21] Syria rejected the September proposal and insisted that Israel withdraw first. It was against any concessions to Israel and proceeded to arm the anti-Gemayel Druse and Shiite militias in Lebanon. Assad systematically replenished his arsenal with Soviet help. Anxious to preserve its only remaining foothold in the East, Moscow complied, although it was wary of Assad's ambitions and feared being drawn into the conflict; still, it did not hold back on providing Syria some $2.5 billion worth of arms and equipment, twice the amount Syria had lost in the 1982 war with Israel. Once again, Syria was ready to fight any military and diplomatic move dangerous to itself.

The PLO also rejected the peace plan, but, unlike Israel and Syria, it equivocated, indicating its willingness to come to some compromise.[22] However, Syria was bent on undermining Arafat, ending his stewardship of the PLO, and bringing the Palestinian organization under a leadership that would be more amenable to Damascus. When Arafat showed a willingness to work toward a compromise and sent feelers to Jordan, Syria moved against him with determination. It openly incited anti-Arafat Palestinians led by Abu Nidal, and helped promote a split within Arafat's Al-Fatah organization. This put an end to the PLO's claims to unity and all but destroyed Arafat. He was trapped between his loyalists and his enemies.

Israel aided and abetted in weakening Arafat. His popularity among the West Bank Palestinians was a direct threat to Israel's plans for the area, so Israel stepped up its campaign of denouncing Arafat as a murderer and a terrorist.

Yet in the time that had elapsed between the June 1982 defeat and mid-1983, the administration could have pushed for some common understanding with Syria. However, Washington offered Syria no incentive to join in the negotiations on Lebanon, and its diplomacy after the invasion revealed little consideration for Syrian security concerns. For instance, the administration had no answer as to how it proposed to meet Syrian security needs in Lebanon or prevent Israel from intervening in Lebanese politics. Nor did Syria feel assured that Reagan would prevent Israel from permanently annexing the West Bank and the Golan Heights. In other words, Syria could have been persuaded to participate in the negotiations, had it seen a clear link between the withdrawal from Lebanon and a U.S. guarantee for the return of the West Bank and the Gaza. It is true that Syria relished its position at the forefront of the Arab cause and hoped to benefit from the growing cracks in the U.S.-Israeli relationship. There was, however, some possibility of bringing Syrians into cooperation in Lebanon had the administration made sufficient effort in this direction. Instead, in a shift of strategy, it abandoned the September plan and focused its energies on securing an Israeli-Lebanese agreement.

Such an agreement was finally signed on 17 May 1983. In support of the May agreement, the administration expanded the role of the U.S. Marines. They were now charged with the task of militarily ensuring the survival of the Gemayel government. It was clear, however, over the summer of 1983, that the May agreement would never survive the conflicting ambitions of Syria and Israel, and their proxy forces in Lebanon. The agreement never got off the ground and was subsequently abandoned.

The Reagan Strategy Unravels

It was obvious by the fall of 1983 that both the Reagan peace plan and the 17 May agreement were dead, Lebanon was caught in a cycle of war and fratricide, Israel had asked for too much, and Syria was prepared to give too little. Even if Israel and Syria had withdrawn their forces, an independent sovereign Lebanon needed a strong central leadership backed by effective military muscle. The Christian Maronite Gemayel and his Lebanese army could provide neither, although both were propped up with massive U.S. support. The U.S. Marines were shielding Gemayel and training the Lebanese, but this involvement was not paying off. It was, in fact, becoming increasingly unpopular in the United States, since the Marines became a target for growing acts of terrorism and violence.

During the closing months of 1983, the Reagan administration was forced to acknowledge this and to concentrate on containing a rapidly deteriorating situation in Lebanon. Its efforts took on an increasingly military character. U.S. warships and planes moved into action, to threaten first the Syrian forces in Lebanon and then the Syrian-backed Druse as well as Shiite Muslims. The battleship *New Jersey* was positioned off the coast of Beirut and began bombardment to prevent the collapse of the Gemayel government. The administration also moved along yet another and now familiar line. To counter Syrian assertiveness, it turned to Israel, and in November 1983, the two countries reaffirmed their intentions to strengthen "strategic cooperation."[23]

The declaration was essentially a warning to Syria and did not at that point envisage a joint U.S.-Israeli military action. Israel was internally divided, and the U.S. public would not have supported action on such a scale. The administration was fully aware that a war with Syria was likely to bring confrontation with the Soviet Union. The reaffirmation of strategic cooperation was mainly a ploy, a diplomatic maneuver that was meant to increase Washington's leverage in Lebanon. But in this it failed.

From October 1983, violence escalated to a new plane in Lebanon. On 23 October 1983, came the suicide bombing of Marine headquarters in Beirut, where 241 U.S. Marine troops were killed. Similar attacks were made on French and Israeli troops as well. These incidents mobilized U.S. public opinion against military involvement in Lebanon. The administration came under increasing fire. There were growing charges of negligence, lack of policy coherence, and irresponsibility. In an attempt to turn the trend of public opinion, on 27 October, the president declared that Lebanon was vital to U.S. interests and warned that the United States would not be bullied out. He argued that the region's oil resources and the West's dependence on them made this vital. He also raised the spectre of a Soviet grand design. But all the same, the administration began to press Gemayel to compromise with the opposition and negotiate with the various factions in Lebanon. The reconciliation talks finally got under way at the end of October in Geneva, but Syria and its Druse and Muslim supporters insisted that no progress could be made until Gemayel abrogated the 17 May agreement with Israel.

As 1984 opened, it was clear that Reagan's peace initiative had gone nowhere. The September proposal was rejected by everyone, and the 17 May agreement was beginning to collapse. At home, Reagan faced fierce criticism for pursuing a "military option" in Lebanon. The marine presence had failed to keep peace in Lebanon, or to stabilize Gemayel. The Lebanese army had proven ineffective; Syria had acquired a veto over the success of all U.S. initiatives; and the strategic ties with Israel had impressed no one.

In the first week of February, fierce fighting broke out between the Shiite militiamen and the Lebanese army. The latter retaliated by shelling densely populated southern Beirut. In protest, the Gemayel cabinet quit and called for Gemayel's resignation. The fighting escalated and engulfed the entire city. The Lebanese army began to simply disintegrate under the pressure of events. It had neither the political power nor the military strength to hold Lebanon together. The administration could no longer justify its presence in Lebanon now that its political base, the Gemayel government, was disintegrating. The Pentagon had in fact laid out a pullback plan in a document that later became a National Security Decision Directive and was accepted by President Reagan on 1 February 1984.

As the Gemayel government crumbled, Reagan ordered a "redeployment" of 1,600 marines off the shores of Beirut and authorized increased naval attacks and air strikes against Syrian-controlled factions. For nine consecutive hours, the 16-inch guns of the U.S. battleship *New Jersey* boomed out, sending hundreds of one-ton shells crashing into the hills behind Beirut, but the United States had pulled out of Lebanon. A few weeks later, Gemayel abandoned the 17 May agreement with Israel. In the third phase of U.S. involvement in Lebanon, every single piece of Reagan strategy had come undone.[24]

Conclusions

Several conclusions can be drawn from the Reagan conduct in the Middle East. The 1982 U.S. debacle in Lebanon was anchored in aggressive ambitions on the part of Israel's Defense Minister Ariel Sharon, grave miscalculations on the part of Prime Minister Begin and his cabinet, and a serious lack of foresight and coherence in Washington. Both Israel and the United States contributed to the awful tragedy in Lebanon, but neither emerged triumphant. Lebanon was also a story of delusion and deceit. Ariel Sharon never discussed his plans in full detail with his colleagues and attached the most specious interpretation to U.S. support. In the process, he unwisely violated the established parameters of Israel's policies. The Lebanon war cost Israel dearly. It tarnished Israel's image throughout the world, produced friction and divisions in many Jewish communities abroad, and hastened Israel's economic decline. The strategic and political benefits of its adventure in Lebanon, however, remained inconvincingly meager.

On its part, the Reagan administration deluded itself into thinking that the Sharon plans would work. It ignored mounting evidence about the real scope and purpose of Sharon's proposed Operation Galilee. Of course, one could argue that the administration was misled by the Begin government and that, in any case, the United States at any given time has only a limited ability to control events abroad. Even if this were true, it does not explain the administration's repeatedly giving in to the Israeli interpretation of events, nor does it explain why the president remained in the dark about Sharon's real intent in Lebanon. Finally, it does not explain why the administration publicly defended the often unprovoked but invariably aggressive Israeli actions. particularly when its own intelligence community had repeatedly warned that Israel was forcing a showdown in Lebanon. The Reagan administration made a serious error in thinking that in one fell swoop the Israeli invasion would remove the obstruction (the PLO and Syria) to an Arab-Israeli accommodation and at the same time deal a decisive blow to the Soviet position in the Middle East.

It is also important to ask why the administration made these errors in judgment. After all, the United States does not have vital interests in Lebanon. The administration, however, insisted that to contain the Soviet threat and politically backstop Soviet allies, U.S. military involvement in Lebanon was necessary. There was never any consensus on this proposition. The administration argued that the outcome in Lebanon would seriously affect the course of the superpower contest. Again, in reality, Syria, Israel, and the PLO were the major contestants for influence in Lebanon. In fact, the Soviet Union was known to be reluctant about supporting Syrian and PLO schemes in Lebanon during 1981–1982. The Reagan administration was on shaky ground in claiming that Lebanon was vital to the United States, or that a show of force was necessary to win the superpower contest. When the U.S. Marines began to take casualties, the Congress reacted sharply, exposing the fact that it too had not fully bought the administration's reasoning.

Similarly, the administration never backed up its September peace proposal with convincing and forceful diplomacy. The peace plan envisaged security and recognition for Israel, an end to Palestinian militancy, stability for the pro-West regimes of Egypt and Jordan, and finally, exclusion of the Soviet Union from every step of the process. But the plan relied on Israel and Syria to restrain their regional ambitions, on Palestinians to unite under a moderate leadership, and on Jordan to abandon its overcautious stance. It also required the United States to be truly evenhanded between its Arab friends and Israel.

Reagan's early initiatives were anything but evenhanded. First, he used Israeli military power to secure political advantages and then pinned his hopes on universal belief in Washington's goodwill and neutrality. Not surprisingly, even Israel felt betrayed. Second, once the PLO was a weakened force, it could not negotiate with any degree of credibility. Having experienced humiliating defeat, Syria could not be persuaded of Washington's honorable intentions; it was bound to rearm and try to reverse the course of events once again. There had been an opportunity when, in the weeks following the invasion of Lebanon, Washington, with Israel's compliance, could have secured an agreement.

But the administration remained averse to any real and sustained dialogue with Syria. Admittedly, Assad was a tough negotiator, but he was not impervious to diplomatic persuasion. Several experts were of the opinion that the administration could have done much more in securing Syrian cooperation for at least some of its initiatives.[25] Syria's arms relationship with Moscow was, however, given too much weight in Washington's assessments. As a result, the administration lost important opportunities for a successful and speedy conclusion of the reconciliation among Lebanon's warring factions. It was obvious that, to gain Syrian cooperation, the United States would have had to extract greater concessions from Israel, and this it was not prepared to do. The peace plan was therefore doomed from the very start.

The administration was also mistaken in its belief that Gemayel could unify Lebanon and remain impervious to Syrian pressure, and it misjudged the depth of local hostility to the U.S. Marines. The marines were never seen as a neutral "peacemaking force." Israel had rejected the Reagan plan, as had Syria, while the Gemayel government was neither popular nor representative of the Lebanese nation. The administration had committed its forces to a task that was never properly defined and in support of a government that could not govern. The deployment of 1,600 marines could not make up for these errors in political judgment. Besides, the military resources needed for such a task were beyond what the United States was willing to commit. According to the Pentagon, bringing order to Lebanon would have required not 1,600 but 100,000 U.S. troops, and even then the depth of sectarian hatred would have made the task impossible. Coercion had not obtained the desired results, neither for Israel nor for the United States. The U.S. naval bombardment had no discernible effect on the swings in the political fortunes of the various factions within Lebanon. If anything, it merely underlined the lack of connection between military power and political advantage: The first had not guaranteed the second.

In its preoccupation with strategic matters, the administration failed to apply sufficient pressure on Israel and wrest appropriate concessions in exchange for Washington's support. This turned out to be a major weakness of its policy. As early as 1975, Kissinger had succinctly summed up the pitfalls in the U.S.-Israeli ties. He said, "I ask Rabin to make concessions, and he says he can't because Israel is weak. So I give him more arms and he says he can't because Israel is weak. So I give him more arms and he says he doesn't need to make concessions because Israel is strong."[26] The administration would have done well had it absorbed this lesson from the past.

President Reagan had deepened and widened U.S. commitment and responsibility in the Middle East beyond the guidelines laid down by the previous three administrations. He had some early successes, but his choice of options resulted in serious setbacks. The Institute of Strategic Studies (London) warned in its 1982–1983 survey, "American influence in the region had increased but so had the burden. If the U.S. does not succeed in bringing about enduring settlement, its gains can turn into longterm losses." By the end of Reagan's first term in office, the United States had lost direction in Lebanon. And there was every danger that Lebanon was lost to internecine warfare and Syrian domination—the very outcome Reagan had done everything to avoid.

Notes

1. "Middle East Regional Security" (Washington, DC: Bureau of Public Affairs, Department of State, 23 March 1981).

2. Quoted in Hendrick Smith, "Reagan: What Kind of World Leader?" *New York Times Magazine*, 16 November 1980, 174–175.

3. Ronald Reagan press conference of 6 November 1980, reported in *New York Times*, 7 November 1980.

4. Comments during an appearance on the U.S. television program *Issues and Answers*, 22 May 1977, cited in Bernard Reich, "Israel's Foreign Policy and the Elections," in *Israel at the Polls: the Knesset Elections of 1977* (Washington, DC: American Enterprise Institute, 1979), 272.

5. Quoted in *Jerusalem Post*, 30 April 1979.

6. Ze'ev Schiff and Ehud Ya'ari, *Israel's Lebanon War*, trans. Ina Friedman (New York: Simon and Schuster, 1984), 35.

7. Don Peretz, "Israeli Approaches to a Solution," in *Alternative Approaches to the Arab-Israeli Conflict,* ed. Michael Hudson (Washington, DC: Center for Contemporary Arab Studies, Georgetown University, 1984), 57.

8. Saad Eddin Ibrahim, "Settling the Conflict: Arab Approaches," in *Alternative Approaches to the Arab-Israeli Conflict,* 99.

9. For an interesting insight into Israeli leadership thinking, see Avraham Tirosh and Avi Bettleheim, "Report on the Unfinished War: From Operation Peace for Galilee to the Lebanon War," *Maariv,* 3 June 1983.

10. Schiff and Ya'ari, *Israel's Lebanon War,* 35.

11. Bernard Reich, *The United States and Israel: Influence in the Special Relationship* (New York: Praeger, 1984), 97.

12. Quoted in *New York Times,* 20 June 1981.

13. See Haig's speech about the "consensus of strategic interests" reported in *New York Times,* 20 March 1981.

14. Schiff and Ya'ari, *Israel's Lebanon War,* 31.

15. For one view of the Israeli lobby's attempts to influence the AWACS debate, see Stephen Rosenfeld, "Dateline Washington: Anti-semitism and the U.S. Foreign Policy," *Foreign Policy* 12 (Summer 1982), 172–183.

16. William Quandt, "Reagan's Lebanon Policy: Trial and Error," *Middle East Journal* 38 (Spring 1984), 238.

17. Schiff and Ya'ari, *Israel's Lebanon War,* 74.

18. Schiff and Ya'ari, *Israel's Lebanon War;* George Ball, *United States Policy in the Middle East* (Washington, DC: Center for Contemporary Arab Studies, Georgetown University, April 1984). "It is not that the PLO is a real military threat to Israel. Their forces in Lebanon are nothing really. But if we wipe them out militarily they will lose their political power. That is what we are really aiming at. You can see the same pattern on the West Bank," a senior official told the London *Sunday Times,* 2 May 1982.

19. This argument is implicit in Bernard Reich's discussion of Reagan's Middle East policy. See his *The United States and Israel,* 87–139.

20. For a discussion of Syrian objectives, see Adeed Dawisha, "The Motives of Syria's Involvement in Lebanon," *Middle East Journal* 38 (Spring 1984), 228–237.

21. British Broadcasting Corporation, *Summary of World Broadcasts,* The Middle East, 4941/A/7, 28 June 1975.

22. For a Palestinian perspective on the Lebanon war and U.S.-Israeli ties, see Rashid Khalidi, "The Palestinians in Lebanon: Social Repercussions of Israel's Invasion," *Middle East Journal* 38 (Spring 1984), 255–267.

23. For Arab and Israeli reactions, see David Shipler, "Shamir Asserts Accord Contains No Secret Commitments," *New York Times,* 6 and 12 December 1984.

24. Bernard Gwertzman, "U.S. Said To Halt Hunt for Formula To Save Lebanon," *New York Times,* 28 February 1984.

25. Quandt, "Reagan's Lebanon Policy," 253.

26. Quoted in Edward R. F. Sheehan, *The Arabs, Israelis and Kissinger* (New York: Reader's Digest Press, 1976), 199.

7.

Reagan's Initiatives: Pakistan, Afghanistan, and India

The Strategic Environment in South Asia

In South Asia, as in the Middle East, the Reagan administration faced critical choices in anchoring its containment policy. It could continue with Carter's India-centered strategy, although, with the invasion of Afghanistan, Carter had promptly extended U.S. security and backed Pakistan with economic and military assistance. However, the amounts involved and the kind of assistance given were not meant to alarm India. The Carter administration had in fact dispatched a special envoy to New Delhi so that India could be reassured of U.S. intent. To continue this evenhanded policy was certainly one option the Reagan administration could follow. The other was to focus exclusively on Pakistan and incorporate it in the U.S.-sponsored consensus of strategic interests. For Reagan, the choice in the strategically dangerous environment of the 1980s was clearly the latter, and all other arguments—about dovetailing U.S. policy to regional interests, supporting a stable democracy in India instead of a military dictatorship in Pakistan, pursuing a collective security arrangement instead of depending on U.S. military presence to deter the Soviet Union—were unrealistic. President Reagan insisted that there was a clear and continuing danger emanating from the Soviet occupation of Afghanistan.

The dilemma that has confronted various presidents since Truman, whether to back India or Pakistan, did not detain the Reagan administration for long. In fact, it was worried that Carter's procrastinations had already cast Pakistan adrift in search of a viable solution for its security problem. There was some evidence to suggest this at the end of the 1970s. Pakistan had sought a firm commitment from the United States. Zia had wanted a formal treaty ratified by the Congress so as to avoid a year-by-year review and unfavorable congressional reappraisals based purely on changes in the political climate at home and abroad, but the Carter administration was united in its opposition to such a commitment. Zia threatened that lack of active participation would leave Pakistan no choice but to recast its policy in light of this new reality. Zia now turned for support to the Islamic nonaligned nations and China. At the extraordinary session of the Islamic foreign ministers' conference hosted by Pakistan in January 1980, it joined others in condemning Soviet military aggression in Afghanistan, demanded the immediate withdrawal of Soviet forces, and refused recognition to the Karmal regime, but Pakistan also supported others in warning "Western powers which were attempting to exploit the new situation of the dire consequences of their policies." Agha Shahi explained the rejection of Carter's offer with a statement that "it would not be prudent to be dependent on any single power." By the time the second Islamic conference took place in May 1980, Pakistan had cautiously begun to respond to Soviet diplomatic overtures by underlining a "comprehensive solution of the Afghan crisis." This could be both a tactic to put greater pressure on the United States and a genuine attempt to keep all options alive.[1] In the meantime, arms negotiations between Pakistan and the United States had become deadlocked. Carter did not think the United States could even come close to all that Pakistan was demanding. The Pakistani arms requests were adding up to $11 billion, and Pakistan did not think it could accept an arms deal that did not measure up to its own threat perceptions.[2] In September 1980, Pakistan's Foreign Minister Agha Shahi met with Gromyko at the UN and signalled that Moscow was flexible about the issue of convening talks over Afghanistan, if this could be done under UN auspices. Pakistan was definitely drifting toward a nonaligned, regional solution to the Afghan problem, and this carried the inherent danger of legitimizing the Soviet-backed Karmal government and making permanent the Soviet presence in Afghanistan.

The Reagan administration took immediate measures to halt this development. The central thrust of this was the $3.2 billion package of military and economic aid extending over a six-year span. Under-Secretary of State James Buckley clearly articulated the administration's intention. This was "to recognize that arms transfers, properly considered and employed, represent an indispensable instrument of American policy that complements and supplements the role of our own forces."[3] The offer included 40 F-16s, the most advanced aircraft in the U.S. arsenal, 100 M48A5 tanks, recovery vehicles equipped with 1,005 I-TOW missiles, howitzers, and attack helicopters. The military equipment was purchased through FMS (Foreign Military Sales) credits.

Pakistan insisted on purchasing this equipment rather than accepting grant aid, since Saudi Arabia had agreed to assist Pakistan substantially in this transaction. The aid package was designed to meet Pakistan's air defense needs along its western front. For Pakistan in many ways the agreement on F-16s became a touchstone for the earnestness of the U.S. commitment. Zia justified the arms request by pointing to the "window" that might exist between the onset of the new relationship with the United States and actual receipt of the promised weapons, and insisted that the first six F-16s be delivered by 1982. For Pakistan, this was a "period of peril." Such allusions fitted well into the administration's global concerns. It responded to this by agreeing to divert the first six F-16s from European production lines by December 1982, with the remaining to be delivered beginning in April 1984.

The important element of the new relationship was the upgrading of the quality of the commitment the United States would make to Pakistan. This was apparent in the easing up on the nonproliferation issue, as well as by frequent supportive statements about the danger to Pakistan as a "frontline" state and, as a result, to vital U.S. interests if Pakistan were to collapse under pressure from the Soviets.

The administration requested and received a waiver of the Symington Amendment to the Foreign Assistance Act. This amendment debarred aid to any country suspected of acquiring a nuclear weapon capability. The administration justified the waiver on the grounds that "establishing a relationship of confidence" and "addressing the security concerns that motivated the nuclear program" were the best way to prevent Pakistan from acquiring nuclear technology.[4] The Reagan administration had repeatedly stated that the new relationship with Pakistan had no anti-India content, but the overall weight of evidence in light of the history of military alliance between the two could not fail to alarm India. Pakistan's "security concerns" were mostly India-oriented, particularly those that motivated it to embark on acquiring a matching nuclear capability.[5] Thus, implicit within the U.S.-Pakistani arms deal was the notion that this deal would not only underline the U.S. commitment to Pakistan, but would also restore the arms balance in the subcontinent where India was believed to have a substantial lead. The administration argued that the May 1980 arms deal between India and the Soviet Union had only further widened the gap between the two adversaries. However, there were obvious holes in this. For one thing, Pakistan could not be planning to take on the superpower to its north, and the critics were quick to point this out. Indeed, many commentators criticized the administration and under-lined the harm this new tilt was likely to do to U.S. goodwill in India. They pointed to the dangerous consequences of deliberately altering the arms balance between the two and shoring up Pakistan with what many in India and outside it believed to be an offensive capacity.[6] But the Reagan administration, in its anti-Soviet mood, was deaf to all such arguments and felt particularly resentful of the Indian refusal to condemn outright the Soviet aggression in Afghanistan. In Reagan's view, India, always pro-Soviet by virtue of its avowedly socialist sym-pathies, had made a clear choice between East and West and had, therefore, to bear the consequences of its decision. In any case, in Reagan's judgment, the commitment to Pakistan was likely to be far more advantageous since it would serve several U.S. purposes.[7]

Pakistan's Role in Reagan's Strategy

First, if Soviet influence was to be contained, whatever Pakistan's posi-tive value, it had considerable negative value as a client or an ally of the Soviet Union. In Reagan's view, Soviet control over Pakistan would push the entire South Asian coastline from Kuwait to Thailand into the hands of regimes unsympathetic to the United States (note the inclu-sion of India). This had to be avoided, particularly since the revolution in Iran and the Soviet presence in Afghanistan made Pakistan, by virtue of its geographical location and historical ties to both those countries, simultaneously a target and an obstacle to Soviet ambitions in the area. The second advantage in the new relationship to Pakistan was that it would facilitate direct U.S. aid to the Mujahadeens in Afghanistan. This would enable the United States to increase the cost to the Soviets of continued occupation of Afghanistan. In other words, the Soviets would not be able to "resolve" the Afghan crisis unilaterally even if they so wished, while the United States by its support of the Mujahadeens could keep the issue alive. First of all, this tied Soviet forces down in a civil war, and second, it gave the United States an important bargaining card when and if it chose to work out a com-prehensive understanding with Moscow on the balance of political power in that part of the world.

Pakistan could also serve as an extremely important entrepot for the RDJTF moving into the Persian Gulf from the east, i.e., Diego Garcia or the Philippines. Although Pakistan denied making arrangements for providing naval base facilities for the U.S. Sixth Fleet, the official and academic literature in the United States is full of proposals for the development of the ports of Karachi and Gwadar, as well as base facilities in Peshawar. A more complete scenario for the use of these facilities was given by Admiral Thomas Moorer (former head of the U.S. navy) and Alvin Cotrell. Talking of "alternatives to the Island of Masirah in Oman, in view of the Kingdom's reluctance to allow American soldiers on its soil," they wrote, ' . . .one such territory is the former Omani territory across the Arabian Sea from Oman: the Pakistani port at the fishing village of Gwadar in Baluchistan."[8] Bhutto had offered this to the United States in 1973–1974 in lieu of lifting the arms embargo, but the offer was not taken up by the United States. "Gwadar," they say, "is an ideal spot just where the Gulf of Oman becomes the Arabian Sea." And what did Moorer propose for Masirah in Oman, to which Gwadar was an alternative? According to him, Masirah could be "a staging post for 25,000 American troops, a first springboard for the RDF." Moreover, Pakistan could offer the proposed RDF an air defense and other backup support in case of a crisis. A June 1980 article in the *Wall Street Journal* reviewing U.S.-Pakistani military collaboration noted the topnotch skills and combat readiness of the Pakistani pilots and their ability to fly sophisticated planes.[9]

In addition to its strategic location, Pakistan had developed important military and economic links with the Muslim world, particularly since the loss of the east wing in 1971. Pakistan's Persian Gulf connections could provide a critical link in the security infrastructure for the entire region, especially Saudi Arabia. Pakistan is reported to have twenty-two military missions in the Third World, with the largest contingents in Saudi Arabia, Jordan, Libya, and Abu Dhabi.[10]

Of these, Saudi-Pakistani connections are particularly important for the United States. Although the nature of military collaboration between Saudi Arabia and Pakistan remains shrouded in mystery, this was the main topic of discussion during Prince Fahd's visit to Pakistan in December 1980.[11] It was reported that among specific arrangements discussed were, first, the number of Pakistani soldiers to be assigned to Saudi defense and whether they would be stationed in Pakistan or Saudi Arabia, and second, the extent of Saudi financial aid to Pakistan. The educated guess in the media and elsewhere has suggested the number to be 10,000 Pakistani troops. The experts at the Institute of Defense Studies and Analysis in New Delhi believed the figure to be closer to 20,000 or more. Even if one were to accept a conservative estimate, it would still constitute a substantial part of the Saudi defense, since the Saudi national guard number some 20,000 and its armed forces about 31,000.[12] The Pakistani military units could help maintain internal order as well as man the air defense batteries that protect Saudi cities. They could protect Saudi Arabia from possible incursion from Iraq in the north and from South Yemen, both Soviet-backed adversaries of Saudi Arabia. They could also play an important role in training Saudi pilots to fly F-15 and F-16 planes and to gain important experiences in managing the forty F-16s that Pakistan itself was about to acquire in the next few years.

This was all undoubtedly in the U.S. interest, particularly since protection of Western access to Gulf oil is the key to this region. If Pakistan's well-trained and well-tried armed forces could do this without the active and visible involvement of U.S. soldiers, which in any case the Saudis would not allow to be stationed on their soil although they depended on the United States for its defense, then Pakistan could perform the forward defense function for the United States. As noted earlier, the administration was divided on the question of whether or not to acquire a visible military presence. The strategic advantages of a forward-deployed force in a crisis were too obvious to dispute. In peacetime, however, visibility of U.S. soldiers evoked images of colonial and imperial domination and created internal strains for pro-West moderate powers in the region. The example of Iran was too vividly recent to be overlooked. This pointed to the advantages of relying on more subtle and less visible forms of influence such as military and economic aid, public declaration of support, and strategic agreements. It also made a convincing case for greater dependence on indigenous or local forces to act as instruments for protection of U.S. interests. The Pakistani-Saudi military collaboration was, therefore, highly beneficial for the United States.

It was suitable also for yet another reason. If the United States were to adopt a maritime strategy (and again, as noted earlier, the administration has so far tried to ride both horses, building an extensive navy to operationalize maritime strategy and developing coalition defense to meet the Soviet threat on the ground), Pakistani commitments to Saudi defense on the ground became critical. Since the Reagan administration had yet to make a clear choice between the two alternative strategies, the Pakistani option had to be kept available even if the United States were not to depend on it entirely. If the United States had to make do without an adequate base structure in the region, it had no choice but to lean toward a maritime strategy in periods of crisis. However, it is widely believed that both Pakistan and Saudi Arabia were more than likely to allow U.S. facilities in an emergency, even though they had no formal obligation to do so.[13]

There are, however, serious apprehensions in some quarters within Pakistan about this emerging alliance with the United States. At a seminar held on 30 June 1981 in Lahore under the auspices of the Council of Pakistan's Newspaper Editors, many expressed doubts about the reliability of the United States as a partner in Pakistani defense. Mr. Mian Arshad Hussain articulated the question that was topmost in everyone's mind. "No bases would be given and no foreign troops would be stationed.... In other words, the new agreement would entail no challenge whatsoever in the present policies of Pakistan," But "in life generally you seldom get something for nothing; in international affairs never. Reciprocity . . . governs negotiations. For all the advantages we are hoping to get, there is a quid pro quo, if so, we would like it to be spelled out."[14] Pakistani Foreign Minister Agha Shahi was categorically negative on the question of bases, but Zia-Ul-Haq himself has been vague and more equivocal on the subject. In June 1981, in an interview with *Newsweek International,* responding to a question as to whether Pakistan would offer the United States bases or port facilities in return for U.S. arms, or agree to any similar bilateral security arrangement, he said, "There has been no request by America nor any offer by us, yet we feel free to extend the hand of friendship to the U.S.—even though we are non-aligned."[15]

From the U.S. point of view, the principal consideration in an instance of crisis would have to be the Soviet Union. If Soviet forces were to invade Iran, and the Pentagon's RDJTF exercises suggest that this is the scenario the U.S. is preparing for, the presence of Pakistani soldiers in Saudi Arabia could prove advantageous in several ways. According to a special report prepared by Tahir-Kheli and Staudenmeir for the Institute of Strategic Studies U.S. Army War College, "First, Pakistanis could play a role in defending vital military installations in Saudi Arabia; installations that the U.S. might need if Saudi Arabia asked for our [U.S.] aid."[16] Second, assuming the Pakistanis had combat units of divisional size in Saudi Arabia, they could deter countries in the region that had a history of hostile relations with Saudi Arabia (Iran, the PDRY) from using this opportunity to settle old scores. On the other hand, the Soviet Union could pressure Pakistan to remove their forces by increasing military activity in the northwest border area. Third, if a regional war got out of control and the superpowers were engaged in direct combat, it was conceivable that the Pakistanis could fight against the Soviets. A more plausible scenario, however, was one in which the Pakistanis were used as Saudi proxies (U.S. proxies once removed) to fight against Soviet proxies (Cuba, East Germany) in a renewal of fighting against the PDRY. The authors of the report conclude that "using the maritime perspective, the interests of Saudi Arabia, Pakistan and the U.S. converge and the strategic trilogy of Saudi wealth, U.S. military technology, and Pakistani soldiers, makes eminent sense in terms of the Persian Gulf security."[17]

There are two more elements in the emerging "new and durable" ties between the Reagan administration and Pakistan. First of all, Pakistani efforts to acquire nuclear capability had introduced a major new uncertainty in the region. The administration's position was that it could better influence policies in Islamabad on this question as a benefactor than if Pakistan were left to fend for itself. To this end, it agreed to some restrictive conditions on the exemption granted to Pakistan. These were: (a) the waiver was to be restricted to a period of six years, coinciding with the period of aid to Pakistan; (b) Congress had to be provided with an annual classified report on Pakistan's nuclear program; and (c) the aid was to be cut off to any country, including both India and Pakistan, provided they detonated a nuclear device. The president could, however, get a waiver on all of the above for thirty days of continuous congressional session if he believed that the continuation of aid was in the national interest of the United States. This waiver could be either approved or vetoed by the Congress during that time by a resolution passed by a simple majority in the two houses. Thus, the restrictions on Pakistan were eased up, but the administration retained the final judgment on how far it would allow the Pakistani nuclear program to proceed and at what point it would perceive it as an obstacle to U.S. interests in the region.

The second element in this relationship concerned the reaffirmation of the 1959 bilateral agreement between the United States and Pakistan.[18] The new version of this agreement is vague about the nature of U.S. counteractions in case Pakistan is threatened by aggression from a Communist or Communist-dominated state. The earlier version committed the United States to assistance in the event of crisis. The new version merely reaffirmed the understanding under the 1959 treaty, but did not stress assistance. In view of Pakistan's anxieties about U.S. commitments and its understandable reluctance to identify with the United States without the latter's formal obligation to assist, the acceptance of the present revised version is curious and leads one to believe that, in spite of its strategic ties with the United States, Pakistan means to preserve a degree of freedom in its relationship with the U.S. It has taken at face value the reassurance from Moscow that the Soviet Union has no designs whatever on Pakistan or on the oil in the Persian Gulf. On its part, Pakistan has made an extra effort to emphasize that the major part of the arms package is purchased at nonconcessionary rates, and that it would welcome and work for a political solution to the

Afghan problem. The Pakistani insistence on delivery of the first six F-16s before December 1982 also signaled its fear that the Reagan tide might turn or the opposition might get organized in Congress and obstruct commitments made earlier. The U.S. side of this relationship also reveals a certain degree of doubt about the extent and ways in which the ties with Pakistan could become a working part of the U.S. strategic consensus. The Reagan administration was fully alive to the dangers of an excessive dependence on a regime that was unpopular at home and buffeted by pressures from secular and liberal as well as Muslim fundamentalist forces. Too close an embrace by the United States could very well lead to a repetition of the Iran scenario.[19]

Whatever the nature of doubts on both sides through 1981, the general impression was that Pakistan had moved into the U.S. orbit and had become an integral part of the defense of Southwest Asia against Soviet expansionism. Over the first half of the 1980s this cooperation made substantial progress. The July 1984 issue of *Middle East* (London) reported that the Pakistani navy was marking waters alongside the American flotilla in the Gulf. The Pakistani ships were providing rations, while Karachi harbor, the best-equipped port in the region, was being used by the U.S. navy's Fleet Air Arm to monitor Gulf traffic. It further reported that, in the joint U.S.-Pakistan strategic planning, Pakistani naval helicopters, armed with Exocet missiles, could be used in the Gulf if the United States felt it was necessary. Zia repeatedly stressed that Pakistan was a frontline state, and the administration reaffirmed its support of Pakistan. Despite differences over formal commitment, Pakistani Foreign Minister Agha Shahi was able to declare confidently that, "as far as the administration of the United States is concerned, the Reagan administration, we can take its word as its bond. . . . What the Reagan administration has told us is that it will be in power till 1984 and it will abide by the understanding we have reached."

Regional Realignment and U.S. Diplomatic "Corrections"

Nonetheless, in early 1982, the regional situation had begun to shift perceptibly, and the Reagan administration felt it would miss an important opportunity to strengthen the U.S. position there if it failed to respond to the shifting balance of alignments among India, Pakistan, and China.[20]

There was a slight but discernible thaw in Sino-Indian relations. Pakistan had also made friendly overtures to India, perhaps on its own account, but no doubt with prodding from Washington. And India had signaled its displeasure with Soviet policies, distanced itself from Moscow, and indicated interest in improving relations with the United States.[21] But above all, there were new tensions between the United States and Pakistan, mainly because many of the reservations and ambiguities that had lain dormant during the Afghan crisis had now begun to surface. Pakistan had followed a two-track policy. It had solicited arms and political backing from the United States and articulated its fears in ways that spoke directly to strategic concerns in Washington; at the same time, it had held back on arms and supplies to the Afghan fighters, blown hot and cold on the proposed rapprochement with India,[22] and kept a door open for limited contact with the Soviet Union.[23] None of these actions were particularly to the administration's liking.

Pakistan's reliability as a strategic ally had also begun to be questioned within the Reagan administration. There was growing criticism in Congress of Reagan's one-sided approach in regional disputes. Many expressed doubts about the durability and longevity of Zia's regime, and others criticized the administration for overlooking the importance of keeping India genuinely neutral and the dangers of tying U.S. fortunes to a weak power in South Asia.[24]

The first real sign of a shift in attitude came during August 1982 when Mrs. Gandhi visited the United States and was given enormous publicity, expressions of goodwill, and red-carpet treatment. The U.S. press talked about a new era, a turning point in Indo-U.S. relations. In concrete terms, the United States agreed to allow the French to supply fuel to the Tarapore nuclear power plant, an issue that had long clouded the relationship between India and the United States, and promised a more sympathetic response to India's requests for loans and credits from the IMF and the World Bank.[25] On Afghanistan, there was no real change in India's position, which favored quiet pressure over public condemnation, but it was possible to discern a general shift in India's assessment of the Soviet presence in Afghanistan and in its own stance on the subject.

Although India remained inflexibly opposed to Pakistan's militarization, the worst fears of a hostile China-U.S.-Pakistani alliance against itself had not materialized. U.S.-China relations appeared bogged down in controversy over arms sales to Taiwan, while Reagan's irritation with Pakistan's two-track policy was becoming increasingly clear. The Indian government was slowly reconciling itself to the fact that the new Cold War had come to stay in the region and that the Soviet Union did not seem inclined to withdraw from Afghanistan. On the other hand, the United States had immensely enhanced its presence in the Persian Gulf and the Indian Ocean, a reality with which India must come to terms. India had the power neither to prevent this nor to oppose it, although against Pakistan it felt fairly confident, particularly if the conflict was a protracted one.[26] There also was no significant threat from China, which meant that India could afford to equivocate in its relationship with the Soviet Union. India's pro-Moscow image on Afghanistan was proving particularly harmful in its ties with the Muslim nations of the Persian Gulf and the Middle East. All of the above added up to a need for India to pull back from its excessive identification with the Soviet Union.

It is also important to bear in mind that, in India's view, Pakistan's two-track diplomacy was a spectacular success. For all practical purposes, Pakistan had received massive U.S. commitment without compromising its standing in the nonaligned world. And then it had scored additional diplomatic points by offering India a "No-War Pact." This had caught India off-balance and had undercut her charges that Pakistan's militarization had a specifically anti-India purpose.[27] These were the reasons behind India's willingness to improve the tone of Indo-U.S. ties—and, indeed, the Reagan administration was equally ready to correct the earlier stance.

The enthusiasm with which Mrs. Gandhi was received by the White House left no one in any doubt that the administration had given the event of her visit top priority. Many began to wonder if the United States had not now decided to tilt toward India, and whether it was not swinging to a more evenhanded approach to the region. In any case, it seemed probable that the United States could have had second thoughts on its commitments to Pakistan. For the moment, the Pakistan arms package had passed the Congress, and there was much to gain from encouraging both India's attempts to distance itself from the Soviet Union and Pakistan's attempt to reduce the tension with India by offering her the No-War Pact.[28] The possibility of an armed conflict between the two had to be avoided at any cost since that was likely to draw the United States into a regional conflict on the side of its ally, Pakistan, and perhaps even lead to a confrontation with the Soviet Union, since the latter had become extremely sensitive about U.S. moves in the region. Supporting Pakistan in a regional confrontation was bound to look as if the Reagan administration was choosing to support a military dictatorship over a democracy. A regional settlement between India and Pakistan independent of Soviet mediation was therefore the best arrangement from the U.S. point of view. The Soviet

Union had played the peacemaker role before, first during the 1965 war between the two and then again after the Bangladesh War. In both instances, the Soviet role was an implicit acknowledgment of its preeminence as an external power in the region. Given the threats in the Persian Gulf and the Indian Ocean, the Reagan administration was in no mood to concede any such preeminence to Moscow. If India could be convinced that Zia's offer was genuine and that the United States sincerely backed it, it could be brought to consider it seriously.

Pakistan had, however, undermined its credibility by once again raising the question of Kashmir in international forums and by making provoking statements on the conditions of Muslims in India. These statements had irked India, since it believed that internationalizing the Kashmir dispute all over again was in violation of the Simla Agreement of 1972, where both had agreed to resolve their problems bilaterally without the interference of a third party, be it another country or an international agency.[29] The Reagan administration, therefore, felt that it needed to serve notice on Pakistan that the U.S. relationship with India need not be frozen into hostility and that amicable settlement was what the United States desired most. Again, so far as the United States was concerned, Pakistan could not do what Israel did and force a compromise on the adversary from a position of territorial conquest and military superiority.

It made every sense to rescue Indo-U.S. ties from the atmosphere of suspicion and resentment into which they had sunk. Reagan officials were quoted as saying, "We need to allay Indian fears that our interest in Southwest Asia is inimical to hers and that Pakistan is the spear carrier for some Sino-U.S. conspiracy to undermine Indian influence in South Asia."[30]

These developments no doubt introduced an element of greater balance in U.S. relations with both India and Pakistan; they also allowed the United States greater flexibility in its foreign policy objectives. However, such shifts were hardly meant to change the fundamental long-term strategic decisions that had been made in early 1981. The planning, preparation, and funding for these proceeded full speed ahead, without pause. This was borne out by the fact that two months before Mrs. Gandhi's August visit, the Pentagon issued its new comprehensive *Defense Guidance Plan* to the United States armed forces.

How did the administration propose to reconcile its August 1982 initiatives with its long-term plan for strategic and military goals? Obviously, the first was not to interfere with the second. In the wake of the threat perception of 1980, the United States had to secure the defense of its interests first, but that did not rule out exploring other diplomatic options appropriate during periods of relative calm. And it was obvious that the Soviet Union, caught in the midst of a succession crisis, was temporarily immobilized. It faced a dangerous situation in Poland, a war in Afghanistan, and unmitigated hostility from Washington. From the U.S. point of view, a diplomatic option therefore made sense.

Following Mrs. Gandhi, Pakistani President Zia also visited the United States, during which time the snag in the transfer of the F-16's was solved, and the United States reaffirmed its commitment to Pakistan. The improvement in U.S.-India ties was not meant to substitute for U.S.-Pakistani strategic planning for Southwest Asia and the Persian Gulf. It merely gave the United States freedom of action in the region.

Consistency in Reagan's Approach to West and South Asia

There are important similarities and differences in the **Reagan** approach to the Middle East and his calculations in South Asia. Faced with the dilemma of bitter regional rivalry between India and **Pakistan**, and having to choose between them, the administration followed the course of policy it had pursued in the Middle East. It proceeded to underplay and deemphasize regional disputes and to concentrate on strategic imperatives. In the Middle East, this had greater success than in South Asia, in that the Arab powers did not unite as a bloc to oppose U.S.-Israeli strategic consensus, there were no embargoes, and no one broke off relations with the United States. In South Asia, on the other hand, this policy gave a terrible jolt to India, although the Soviet occupation of Afghanistan prevented India from making any overt gestures to reaffirm its ties with that country. In the Middle East there was a possibility that the administration encouraged Israel to change the very conditions that defined the Palestinian problem; in South Asia, the United States could not pursue a parallel option. In fact, it had to do everything to prevent a forcible resolution of disputes between India and Pakistan. Initially it cautioned India from making any attempts against Pakistan, and later, in the changed political environment of 1982, tried to defuse Indian hostility by underwriting the No-War Pact.

In all this, the administration was careful to seek domestic political support for its policies. Initially it was assured of such support and was, therefore, confident its proposals for arms aid and unequivocal diplomatic backing for Israel and Pakistan would be approved. It was, however, equally aware that, following the usual rhythm of politics, the opposition would surface and begin to erode its conservative political

base. Its peace initiatives of August 1982 for South Asia and of 1
September 1982 for settlement of the Arab-Israeli dispute went a long
way in defusing these criticisms. For once the administration appeared
to have something other than the military option on its mind. The
regional powers, both Israel and Pakistan, the administration's principal allies, responded to the United States with full knowledge of the
domestic swings in U.S. politics.

However, South Asia was not as important in Reagan's scheme of
things as were the Middle East and the Persian Gulf. Although never so
stated, it would be quite safe to assume that the heart of Southwest Asia,
Saudi Arabia and the other oil-producing Arab states in the Gulf and
Iran, is far more critical to the outcome of superpower rivalry than the
fate of Afghanistan, although it is here that the Soviet Union's alleged
expansionism was in full view. Afghanistan does not possess oil, nor
does Pakistan. Nor is either directly on the route for oil tankers passing
through the Gulf onwards to Europe and the United States. Afghanistan was nevertheless important, and so was Pakistan. The first gave
Soviet forces the necessary purchase to extend their activities within a
criticial distance of the Gulf oil, while in the unlikely event of Pakistan's
collapse, the Soviet Union would secure what it desired most, a preponderance in South Asia and adjacent regions. Again, the value of the
Afghan struggle was not lost on the United States. During the hearings
of the Senate Committee on Foreign Relations on 8 March 1982, many
in and out of the administration concurred with the opinion voiced by
Professor Goutierre. He pointed out that to ignore the Afghan struggle
was a

> foolish repudiation of American self interest because the Afghans
> are defending the Persian Gulf, which is vital to our security. At the
> moment, they are better than an American RDF because they are
> an instant deployment force, already fighting and successfully
> barring Soviet expansionism. They are pinning down nearly
> 100,000 crack Soviet troops, thus restraining the USSR in Poland
> and relieving intolerable pressures on Pakistan and Iran.[31]

In fact, in late 1982 the administration appeared to be developing
some differences with Pakistan on the Afghan question. The overall
reduction in tension among India, Pakistan, and China had generated
a search under the UN auspices for a peaceful solution to the Afghan
problem during the second half of 1982, and Pakistan had responded
to this favorably. The Soviet Union had also voiced support for the UN
plan, which revolved around a timetable for the departure of Soviet
troops; guarantees by each side that neither would intervene against
the other; an endorsement of this guarantee by the United States, the

Soviet Union, and China; and return of Afghan refugees from Pakistan and Iran with assured amnesty and promise of complete civil rights by the government in Kabul. Under-Secretary General Diego Cordovez had visited Kabul and Islamabad in January 1983 to seek agreement on these four points.

The initiative was, however, bogged down over questions of troop withdrawal. Pakistan and the United States insisted that this should occur first, although Pakistan was willing to make concessions on this point while the United States was not. The United States also insisted on a return to the *status quo ante,* that is, a creation of a genuinely nonaligned independent government. On this, too, Pakistan along with India displayed greater flexibility.

Early 1983 brought a return to Cold War rhetoric and stepped-up criticism of the Soviet Union from the administration, largely due to the exigencies of budget politics at home. The Reagan administration had to evoke the image of the Soviet Union as the focus of all evil in the modern world in order to push its defense budget through the Senate and Congress. Nonetheless, the Reagan policies displayed a certain rhythm and a degree of flexibility that succeeded in securing for the administration a fair amount of room to maneuver. But its choices were fundamentally flawed.

The other points of difference between its Middle East and South Asia policies must be noted. Access to oil and containment of the Soviet influence had made both sides in the Arab-Israeli conflict important. The administration had, therefore, pursued a vigorous two-track policy, each angle meant to limit the damage caused to the other and both together meant to steer the course in the Middle East to Washington's advantage. The situation in South Asia did not require such a balancing act. Thus, the initial alignment with Pakistan quite ruthlessly ignored security concerns for India; it also discarded Carter's India-centered policies. In Reagan's judgment, a genuine neutrality was the best it could hope for from India. Nor did India serve any specific security interest the United States considered important to its position in the region. If anything, India had been vociferous in its opposition to Reagan's strategy and unwilling to concede to the United States a legitimate right to counter the Soviet military buildup in the region. The choice between India and Pakistan was less difficult and onerous than that between the Arabs and Israel. But once the choices were made, the administration did worry about the escalation of tension and armed conflict between India and Pakistan. This stood in stark contrast to its justification of Israeli raids and attacks and its tacit support of the invasion of Lebanon, at least until the siege of Beirut, which indicated that, in Reagan's view, if the ally was powerful and could guarantee results, it ought not to be restrained. No such guarantee could exist in the case of Pakistan. True to its strategic doctrine, then, the Reagan team believed in a controlled use of force to alter the political environment and did not particularly object to its allies' reading between the lines and doing the needful. Where such advantages were not possible, it was not unmindful of developing a more evenhanded approach, but such attempts were more symbolic than real. In Reagan's view, a stable and pro-West Pakistan was a critical link in the attempt to build a string of strategic collaborations and security understandings; but it was essentially a weak link, and for that reason alone, a flexible policy was more advantageous.

Notes

1. Shirin Tahir-Kheli points out that Zia's advisers argued that "since the United States could no longer be aroused to take note of Soviet inroads in Southwest Asia, Pakistan's interest would be best served in making peace with the Soviets." *The United States and Pakistan* (New York: Praeger, 1982), 75.

2. Francis Fukuyama, "The Security of Pakistan: A Trip Report," Rand, N-1584-RC (September 1980), 28.

3. Testimony before the Senate Foreign Relations Committee, 28 July 1981, *Current Policy* 301, 28 July 1981.

4. State Department spokesman David Passage was reported to have offered the justification that a show of greater support for Pakistan's security concerns was the best way to influence its decision on a nuclear program. *New York Times*, 15 June 1981.

5. See President Zia ul-Haq's interview, *Times of India*, 1 March 1981.

6. See George Kennan's testimony before the Senate Foreign Relations Committee, Hearings on *U.S. Security Interests and Policies in Southwest Asia*, 96th Congress, 2d session (Washington, DC: U.S. Government Printing Office, 4, 18 March 1980), 49.

7. For the basic arguments and justification on the administration's policies, see Fukuyama, "The Security of Pakistan."

8. Admiral Thomas Moorer and Alvin Cotrell, "The Search for U.S. Bases in the Indian Ocean," *Strategic Digest* (New Delhi) 11 (January 1981), 30. For more details see also Maya Chadda, "Reagan's Strategy in Southwest Asia," *India Quarterly* 38:344 (July–December 1982).

9. *Wall Street Journal*, 29 June 1980.

10. Reported in the *New York Times*, 9 December 1980.

11. CBS, "Face the Nation," 18 March 1979. For a succinct discussion of Pakistan's westward connection see John Cooley, "Iran, the Palestinians and the Gulf," *Foreign Affairs* 57 (Summer 1979).

12. The State Department was of the view that Pakistan could play an important role in the security of the Gulf nations. For details, see "Pak Purchase Co-ordinated with Gulf Countries," *POT* Pakistan series 9, part 126 (24 June 1981), 1469; "Press Comments on U.S. Aid Programme," *POT* 9, part 128 (26 June 1981), 1490.

13. *Pakistan Times,* 12 July 1981.

14. *Strategic Analysis* 5:7 (October 1981), 281.

15. Shirin Tahir-Kheli and Staudenmeir, *Saudi-Pakistani Military Relationship and Its Implications for U.S. Strategy in Southwest Asia,* ACN 8 1026 (1 October 1981), 20.

16. Ibid., 16.

17. See "U.S. Assistance and Arms Transfer to Pakistan: A U.S. Congressional Staff Assessment," prepared for the Committee on Foreign Affairs of the U.S. House of Representatives, 20 November 1981. Republished in *Strategic Digest* 12:2 (February 1982), 92–94.

18. Ibid., 75–78.

19. For a detailed analysis, see Chadda, "Reagan's Strategy in South Asia"; Jyotirmoy Banerjee, "Hot and Cold Diplomacy in Indo-Pakistani Relations," *Asian Survey* 23:3 (March 1983), 280–301.

20. Zalmay Khalilzhad, "The Strategic Significance of South Asia," *Current History* 8:475 (May 1982), 194.

21. Pakistan began talks in January 1982, broke them off in February, and resumed them again in June 1982. See *Dawn* (Karachi), 11 and 17 June 1982.

22. Soviet Deputy Foreign Minister N. P. Firayubin was welcomed in Pakistan in August 1981.

23. Selig Harrison, George Kennan, and the former Ambassador to India, Robert Goheen urged the Reagan administration to correct its tilt toward Pakistan. For congressional views, see N. Shankar, "Pakistan and U.S. Congress," *Strategic Analysis* 10:10 (January 1982), 503–513.

24. *New York Times,* 30 July 1982; *Hindustan Times* (New Delhi), 4 August 1982.

25. This was the majority opinion among experts on strategic balance between India and Pakistan at the New Delhi Institute of Defense Studies and at the Jawaharlal Nehru University.

26. *The Statesman,* 17 September 1981; see also Banerjee, "Hot and Cold Diplomacy in Indo-Pakistani Relations," 287.

27. On the eve of Mrs. Gandhi's visit to the United States in August 1982, Deputy Secretary of State Walter Stoessel announced that the United States was prepared to sell military hardware to India, including F-16's. *The Statesman,* 4 April 1982.

28. *The Statesman,* 4 November 1982, 1 April 1983.

29. *Far Eastern Economic Review,* 6 August 1982, 13.

30. Hearing before the Senate Committee on Foreign Relations, *Situation in Afghanistan,* 97th Congress, 2d session (Washington, DC: U.S. Government Printing Office, 8 March 1982), 71.

8.

Military Containment in the Persian Gulf

Although Afghanistan presented the Reagan administration with its greatest provocation and Lebanon with an opportunity to display military muscle, it was in the Persian Gulf that the administration encountered its greatest challenge. There is a growing view among scholars that the "decision to commit its own armed forces for the defense of the Gulf oil supplies under the Carter doctrine was not . . . caused primarily by the Soviet invasion of Afghanistan." It was "primarily influenced by the Iranian revolution and its aftermath, including the hostage crisis, the seizure of the Great Mosque at Mecca and the burning of the U.S. embassy at Islamabad."[1]

In other words, both the Carter and then the Reagan administrations feared the revolutionary potential of Islam and tried to contain it with enhanced U.S. military force. Implicit in this view of Islam was the conviction that, unless protected, the Persian Gulf states would fall like so many dominoes threatening vital U.S. interests in the region. The advent of the Islamic regime in Iran was not merely another routine change in government; it was an event of historic significance, a fundamental challenge to the status quo in the region, and a powerful appeal to the nations of the Islamic world to take charge of their collective destinies. By 1980, this ideology had acquired a state base in Iran and had become a force fiercely independent of and virulently opposed to the United States. However, the United States was not its only target. Conservative, pro-West monarchies and military regimes in the Persian Gulf and the Middle East also came under fierce fundamentalist attack. Moral fervor was not, however, matched by a corresponding strength in arms. Moreover, in 1980, Iran was in a state of chaos, its economy in turmoil, and its armed forces in a state of disarray. A majority of scholars agree that it was this weakness that had tempted Iraq to attack Iran.

It is also important to note that the main lines of U.S. strategy in the Gulf were shaped by the belief that Iran would not be able to project power with any great effect across the Persian Gulf.[2] The administration did not therefore think it necessary to "understand" the Islamic revolution, but merely to militarily contain it. Only history will tell if this was an appropriate response, since much depends on the course of the revolution itself and the outcome of the Iran-Iraq war. The main thrusts of President Reagan's strategy had, however, become fully visible by the end of his first term in office.

In the following we will discuss the implications of the Iranian revolution to the security of the Persian Gulf, the ramifications of its war with Iraq, and the Reagan administration's response to it. It is hoped that this will expose its overall strategy in the Persian Gulf and the calculations behind its various actions. The main question is: Did the administration formulate a comprehensive policy, not only to ward off the immediate threats but also to secure a more durable peace in the Persian Gulf?

Implications for Gulf Security

Three aspects of the Iranian revolution became critical to the preservation of the security of the Gulf states and to the formulation of U.S. policy: the revolution's political objectives, its continued survivability, and its exportability.

Khomeini's credo is that "the duty of the ulema and all Muslims is to put an end to injustice and to seek to bring happiness to millions of people through destroying and eliminating the unjust governments."[3] These governments are those of "tyrannical self-seeking rulers" who have betrayed their people by serving imperialist interests. In Khomeini's view, they have separated various elements of the Islamic *Umma* (community) from each other and created nations out of these elements that have no popular legitimacy. The Khomeini goal is to spread the revolution and establish an Islamic order that is universal. According to Joseph Malone, the IRP (Islamic Revolutionary Party) program is "even more explicit on the export of the Islamic revolution to the entire Muslim world. It calls for the employment of propaganda, material assistance, and armed force in the fulfillment of the objective."[4]

The war with Iraq was considered the logical first step in the achievement of these goals. In November 1982, at a special ceremony in Teheran, the IRP created the Council of the Islamic Revolution of Iraq under the leadership of Bakr Hakim. After the fall of the Bazargan government in November 1979 in Iran, the relations between Iraq and Iran deteriorated rapidly. Khomeini called for the establishment of an "all Islamic" state and addressed his appeal to all "oppressed" Iraqis and Sunni, and to Shiite, Kurdish, and Arab as well as Iranian residents in Iraq. Khomeini supporters attacked the Ba'ath ideology and never failed to point to its lack of a mass base when compared to the popularity of the Iranian revolution. Khomeini insisted that Ba'athism was an imported ideology and alien to the precepts of Islam. This was a direct challenge to Saadam, who at the time was anxious to assume the leadership of the Arab world and thought it well within his grasp since Egypt, his major rival, had abrogated its role and opted for Camp David instead, and Iraq's other rival, Iran, was in a state of chaos; its ethnic minorities were up in arms and the Shah's armed forces had become weakened from defections and frequent purges. It can be argued that Iraq attacked Iran, first to contain the Islamic revolution from spreading elsewhere, particularly to Iraq, and second, to stake out Iraq's claims to the leadership of the Arab states. Territorial claims against Iran and legal disputes over access to the Persian Gulf were not perhaps its only or even its main reasons.

Saudi Arabia was the second but no less important target of the Islamic revolutionaries in Teheran. The hostility toward Riyadh sprang from Saudi Arabia's previous, as well as continuing collaboration with the Shah and with the United States. During the Nixon and later the Carter presidency, Saudi Arabia, along with the Shah, had acted as one of three main pillars of U.S. strategic policy in Southwest Asia. The Saudis had supported the Shah in his attempts to stem the tide of the revolution. Memories of these past Saudi actions, together with the ideological differences over the "correct" interpretation of Islam, spawned bitterness and intense rivalry between the two Gulf powers. Khomeini's millenarian populist Islam when combined with Persian patriotism was bound to collide with the essentially conservative, Royalist Islam of Saudi kings. Khomeini's Islam rejected the legitimacy of the Saudi royal family, and the Saudi guardianship of the holy sites of Mecca and Medina.

In the summer of 1982, Iranian pilgrims to the holy sites staged several political rallies, and the hard core among them campaigned to discredit the Saudi government. Ayatollah Montezeri called the Saudi rulers a "bunch of pleasure seekers and mercenaries" and posed a rhetorical question, "How long must Satan rule the House of God?"[5] Khomeini regarded the Saudi territorial state as the "lands of Najd and Hijaz," the original provinces before the formation of the Saudi state, and Wahhabism as "blasphemous." The fundamental differences between the two were clearly apparent in the letter King Khalid wrote to the Ayatollah in October 1982, protesting the behavior of the pilgrims from Iran. This the king said was "contrary to the aims of the pilgrimage and the honor of holy places." The Ayatollah not only rejected the king's version of events but insisted that in Islam, pilgrimage was completely linked to politics: this was how it had been, he argued, under the prophet of Islam.[6] The separation of religion from politics in the Ayatollah's view was an idea borrowed from the West. Other Gulf states also bore the brunt of the Ayatollah's anger. In December 1981, Bahrain, which has a sizable Shiite minority, had to put down an attempted coup instigated by Teheran.

Viewed as the bastion of imperialism and the foremost source of oppression everywhere, the United States was the third target of the Islamic revolutionaries in Teheran. In Khomeini's demonology the United States occupied the place of a "great satan," an evil influence that penetrated the region through its "lackey governments" made up of corrupt kings and emirs. The dependence on U.S. arms and technology shared by all the Gulf states, and their political ties with Washington, came under fierce attack from Khomeini. Ramzani, reporting a Saudi leader's observation, writes, "the insurrection of the ultrafundamentalists led by Juhayman ibn Muhammad al-'Utaybi at Mecca in 1979 . . . was directed as much against the close Saudi ties with the 'infidels' (especially the United States) as it was aimed at creating a genuine Islamic State." In reply to the October letter by King Khalid, the Ayatollah wrote that if the king had made use of the religio-political ceremony of the Haji, Saudi Arabia "would have no need of America, AWACS planes . . . we know that America has put these planes at the disposal of Saudi Arabia so that America can make use of them in its own interests and in the interest of Israel."[7]

The Islamic fundamentalists were obsessed with Palestine and Israel. While he was in exile in Najaf, the Ayatollah noted that the Shah's government had purchased weapons from the West so that Israelis could train on them. This was obviously a reference to Israel's assistance in setting up and training the SAVAK (the intelligence organization under the Shah) and some units of the Iranian military forces. In Khomeini's view, "Israel is in a state of war with the Muslims—whoever helps and supports Israel is in turn in a state of war with the Muslims." Since gaining power, the fundamentalists in Teheran have rejected all peace plans that may recognize the state of Israel. During the 1982 Lebanon war, Iranian volunteers were sent as "liberation forces" to aid the PLO. Khomeini supporters were said to be behind the six car bombings in Kuwait during December 1983, and some 2,000 Islamic guards were reported to be positioned just inside the Syrian border, and from there they made frequent trips into Lebanon to train Shiite terrorists. A group calling itself the Islamic Jihad was responsible for the truck bombs that killed 241 American and 58 French troops in Beirut during October 1983.[8] The government in Teheran did not acknowledge connections with these incidents, but the fact that the October bombings in Beirut were celebrated in Iran as "the action of patriotic heroes" provided a glimpse of the depth of its hatred for Israel and the United States.

While the United States seeks to stabilize the present Gulf regimes, enhance its influence through arms diplomacy, and protect the state of Israel, the fundamentalists seek to dethrone the present rulers, eliminate U.S. influence, and liberate Jerusalem by destroying the state of Israel. It is apparent that the fundamentalists are armed with a powerful ideology and capacity for sacrifice; whether the Iranian revolution will continue to survive and whether its ideology is exportable, however, depends on Iran's political stability and military strength.

The evidence on this score is somewhat unclear and, in fact, highly contradictory. On the one hand, the initial popularity of the revolution appears to have waned under the pressure of war and political factionalism; however, on the other, the IRP seems to have consolidated its position and ruthlessly stamped out opposition. Contrary to all expectations, the war helped consolidate the power of the clergy and institutionalized the organizations and political network of the fundamentalists. According to Elaine Sciolino, the revolutionary regime "used every new crisis as a means to implement a successful two-pronged strategy: systematic extermination of enemies, and ongoing state building that relied more and more on direct clerical leadership."[9] This meant that even if Khomeini were to die, the revolution would continue to survive. Two things helped in this regard: the improvement in the economy and the war. In mid-1980, the economy had virtually ceased functioning, but by 1982, the situation had improved markedly. There were also indications that revolutionary terror was easing up. The Mosque network and the Islamic Revolutionary Party had, on the other hand, acquired extraordinary control at the grass roots level. It was believed that through this network over 100,000 mullahs were engaged in supervising regulations, collecting taxes, recruiting war volunteers and funneling rationed goods to the masses. They were also running schools and courts. The state revenue from oil and taxes was not spent on consumer items as in the days of the Shah, but went to large-scale subsidies of the revolutionary apparatus, which was meant, in one view, to ensure a substantial level of acceptance from the masses.[10] The war also provided the Islamic revolutionaries with an excuse to rid themselves of all opposition, whether from the left or the center. According to one observer, "in successive stages, the clergy under Khomeini in alliance with the urban proletariat, shed its erstwhile partners—the liberal intellectuals, the secular nationalists, the minorities and the left—moving inexorably toward a populist dictatorship."[11]

The consolidation of the IRP and the stalemate in the war meant that all who hoped to discredit the Khomeini regime failed in their efforts. However, these oppressed groups are likely to be the source of future challenge for the religious dictatorship in Teheran. Some of these fissures were already apparent. According to Joseph Malone, the majority, or Maktabi faction within the IRP's Central Council, supports a program of centralized planning, control of commercial activity, deemphasis on consumer industries, and redistribution of land to the peasantry that is anathema to the bazarris and many of the educated classes whose support was initially a critical element in the success of the revolution.[12] During the revolution, Khomeini had managed to meld together a coalition of modernizers who were frustrated by the "trickle down" policies of the Shah, and traditionalists who were squeezed out by the pace of forced modernization. But these were unnatural allies, and the tension between their opposite views—no longer submerged by the hatred of the Shah—had begun to surface. Nor was the leadership at the top united on the issues regarding the spread of the fundamentalist Islam. A conservative faction among them favored normalization of ties with the Arab world, disengagement from the war, and greater pragmatism in Iran's dealings with the superpowers. The other faction favored continuation of radical and revolutionary activities.[13] These fissures erode Iran's ability to export revolution abroad and also raise serious questions about the future course, if not the survival, of Islamic fundamentalism in Teheran.

Iran's military ability to project power across the Persian Gulf or to intervene there in any major way seems greatly limited. For one thing, it simply does not have the weaponry to match the arsenal in possession of the Gulf powers; also, its war with Iraq fully engaged its resources and already strained its ability. Any additional burden is likely to endanger its very survival. Nor did Iran have the economic base to mount such an operation. The future course of the revolution, its survivability, and its export will therefore depend on the evolution of factional conflict within Iran. Some observers of gulf politics have suggested that the emergence of a military dictator is entirely likely.[14] In any event, at least in the foreseeable future, fundamentalism is likely to hold sway in Iran—if not ruling it unopposed, at least shaping its politics and society.

Implications of the Gulf War for the United States

The war between Iran and Iraq has dragged on for the entire first half of the 1980s, claiming over 200,000 dead, twice that number wounded or taken prisoner, millions of barrels of oil lost to the world market, and millions lost to the warring parties in oil revenue. The fighting has gone through several phases.[15] Beginning with the massive air strikes on 22 September 1980, Iraq rapidly advanced to Khuzestan, capturing the city of Khorramshahr, besieged Abadan, threatened Iranian oil facilities at Dezful and Susangerd. Despite these advances, the Iraqi assault was a strategic failure. Iran did not sue for peace; its military formation was not destroyed; nor was Khomeini discredited. The last was a key political objective of Saddam Hussein. Subsequently, Iran launched a counteroffensive, attacked Iraqi oil installations, and closed off its oil export routes through the Persian Gulf. What is more, Iran recovered most of its territory lost to Iraq during the latter's initial thrust. Between 1981 and 1984, Iran launched several ground offensives, but its ability to wage air warfare remained strictly limited. In April 1982, Iran negotiated the closure of the Syrian-Iraqi pipeline by agreeing to sell Syria oil at concessionary prices. This meant that Iraq could export its oil only by the pipeline through Turkey.[16] In 1979, Iraq exported 3.5 million barrels a day; by 1983, its oil exports had dwindled to a trickle. Iran had been successful in damaging nearly 80 percent of Iraqi oil export capacity. As a result, Iraq has been forced to draw down its foreign exchange reserves by about $30 billion and would have been hard put to continue its war effort without assistance from the pro-West Arab countries. External aid from the Arab countries added up to about $30 billion by the end of 1983.

Since 1982 the war has escalated; Iraq was reported to have used chemical weapons, while Iran employed young teenagers, its Basij Corps, in frontline suicide operations across the border. In October 1983, Iraq received five highly sophisticated Super Etendard fighter-bombers equipped with lethel Exocet missiles. Since early 1984, Iraq increased pressure on Iran with repeated air strikes against "enemy vessels and naval targets." In response, Iran threatened to close the

Gulf of Hormuz and stepped up its air surveillance. It declared that if Iraq attacked its oil facilities, it would close the Straits of Hormuz to all shipping. If Iran could not export, Teheran declared, it would not allow anyone else to export oil either. This phase, popularly known as the "tanker war," was clearly an attempt by Iraq to widen the conflict in the hope that this would tilt the military balance in its favor. It did, in fact, inject a new sense of urgency among the Arab states and the United States to find a solution to the conflict. But these efforts were in vain. The conflict remained stalemated.

In 1984, the Gulf situation was as follows. First, Iraq has failed in both its political and military objectives and faces a possible defeat and the danger of a coup against Saddam's regime. Second, despite purges and weakening through defections, the Islamic government in Iran has shown remarkable determination and grit; what is more, it has used the conflict to consolidate its position within Iran. Third, the Iraqi efforts to internationalize its conflict and to draw in other Arab states on its side failed, although Saudi Arabia, Jordan, and Egypt have extended substantial economic and military assistance to Iraq. Fourth, the general expectation of collapse and ruin of the IRP in Teheran has not materialized, although the war effort has limited its ability to export revolution to other Gulf countries. And last, despite repeated threats on its part, Iran has failed to close the Straits of Hormuz or choke off international shipping through the Persian Gulf. It has lacked the military capacity to do so, but apart from that, one can see that Iran has little to gain from stopping the Gulf traffic since that would cut off its own exports of petroleum as well. Fear of U.S. retaliation may also have persuaded Teheran of the wisdom in being cautious and refraining from demonstrating its revolutionary fervor as some factions of the IRP had been advocating. All in all, the war has been "contained" to Iraq and Iran.

There is no guarantee, however, that the stalemate will continue indefinitely. By September 1984, the consensus among experts was that the military balance had tilted in favor of Iraq.[17] On the other hand, observers also agreed that, for the past forty months, the military initiative had remained with Iran while the Iraqi domestic situation had been shaky at best. In other words, the outcome of this war cannot be predicted with any confidence. This has serious implications for the United States.

It is possible that a continuation of the war could yet topple the current Ba'athist regime in Iraq. The danger that Iraq could fall under a Khomeini-dominated Islamic revolutionary regime makes this the most feared contingency in the Gulf. If this were to happen, most people, including U.S. State Department officials, believe that Khomeini forces will not remain content with Iraq, although it is not possible to predict which direction they will turn from Baghdad—south toward the Gulf or west toward the arena of the Arab-Israeli conflict. As the foregoing discussion on fundamentalist objectives suggests, Khomeini is obsessed with Israel and Palestine. On the other hand, Iran's natural sphere of interests lies in the direction of the Persian Gulf. If the fundamentalists turn their energies toward the Gulf, with the Iraqi "shield" gone, Kuwait would be subjected to serious military pressure and terrorism. With a large Shiite majority, Bahrain would be next in line. Once Iranian forces are entrenched in Iraq, Kuwait, and Bahrain, it would be only a matter of time before the UAE also succumbed. Finally, an Iranian victory in the Gulf War would drastically reduce the local and regional political influence of Saudi Arabia, the most important U.S. ally in the Gulf. This would undoubtedly alter the structure of OPEC and its present policies toward the rest of the world. An Iraqi defeat may radicalize the Shiites in Lebanon and produce tremendous external and domestic pressure on Jordan and even Syria. With Baghdad as a basis of further expansion and Jordan as well as Syria under pressure, the Palestinian community may see greater advantage in forging an alliance with the Islamic forces. In any event, Israel, the closest U.S. ally in the Middle East, would face an extremely dangerous war coalition on its eastern front.[18]

Is this scenario plausible? An important segment of the U.S. foreign policy community argues that it is. However, there is no reason to believe that events would follow such a course of disasters. There is substantial indigenous opposition to fundamentalism in the region. The Sunni-Shiite division in Islam, and the fact that a majority of the Arab countries are predominantly Sunni, suggest that the dominoes will not fall quite as easily as assumed above. The revolutionary potential of Islam would become truly frightening, however, if Shiite fundamentalism were to seek an accommodation with other strains of Islam and successfully integrate these without losing its own revolutionary fervor. Fundamentalist expansion could become a reality if it did not seek to impose its dogma on the rest of the Islamic world. In this regard, it is possible that visible U.S. ties with corrupt rulers could become both a symbol and a justification for a common Islamic response. It should be noted that the domino theory sketched above has been promoted mostly by the pro-Israeli lobby in the United States. They argue that Iran is really the important country in the region. Although this argument is obviously self-serving and reflects the lobby's anti-Arab bias, there is no gainsaying the fact that Iran is of pivotal importance to the balance of power in the Persian Gulf. During the reign of the Shah, Iran had acted as a proxy for and a surrogate to U.S. interests. Now that it opposed the United States, it acquired an added importance, even if only as a negative force that needed to be contained. Therefore, even if events do not quite follow the scenario sketched above and the domino principle does not operate in that manner, Iran's triumph over Iraq will certainly have a profound impact on the power balance in the Gulf.

Iraqi victory over Iran may have less drastic but no less significant effects on the region. Indeed, it is precisely this eventuality that encourages Israel to extend Iran arms and ammunition. Nor are the Gulf states particularly anxious to see Iraq decisively triumph over Iran. They suspected Iraqis of regional expansionist ambitions. These apprehensions persisted, although for the moment the Arab states gave generously from their treasuries and extended considerable logistical assistance to Iraq.

U.S. Response to the Gulf War

The Reagan administration carefully designed its policies to avoid being caught on the horns of a dilemma: a decisive conclusion of the war in favor of either Iraq or Iran, particularly the latter, or expansion of the war across the Gulf to the pro-West Arab states. These two considerations have produced four distinct thrusts in the administration's policies.

Enhancing U.S. Military Presence

First, the administration has clearly stated that it will keep the Straits of Hormuz open to oil traffic. Accordingly, it strengthened U.S. naval presence in the Gulf area with nine warships, including the aircraft carrier *Midway* with its formidable air power that neither Iran nor Iraq was likely to match. In February 1984, when the air war in the Gulf heated up, U.S. destroyers warned off an Iranian patrol plane and frigate that had violated the five-mile safety zone declared by the U.S. government. President Reagan established a special cabinet-level group to coordinate government contingency planning for the Gulf. On 23 February, administration officials stated that President Reagan was prepared, if necessary, to send ground troops to the Gulf region in order to protect the flow of oil through the strategic entrance to the Gulf waters.[19]

These moves did not, however, cover the full range of possibilities. There were in fact other threats that were potentially more likely than a closure of Hormuz, i.e., direct Iranian attacks against Arab oil loading facilities, and terrorist attacks on or assassinations in small Arab states that had helped support Iraq's economy, for instance, Kuwait. To counter these lower-level local threats, the Reagan administration stepped up arms assistance to pro-American Gulf states, particularly Saudi Arabia. At the end of May 1984, the administration sold and dispatched to Saudi Arabia 400 anti-aircraft missiles plus 200 shoulder-held launchers to fire them. The Stingers, which have a range of three miles, are meant to protect Saudi ports and oil fields. It also decided to deploy a fourth and larger U.S. air force tanker aircraft in Saudi Arabia. This was to be used to refuel the patrolling AWACS and the Saudi F-15s purchased from the United States during 1982.[20] Aided with AWAC surveillance, the combined combat forces of Kuwait and Saudi Arabia—totaling about 200 combat fighters equipped and purchased mostly from the United States—was expected to establish a credible air cover above Saudi Arabia and Kuwaiti ships and oil facilities. In this regard it should be noted that, beginning in 1984, the administration showed increasing interest in closer cooperation with the Gulf Cooperation Council (GCC), which consists of six peninsular oil states (Saudi Arabia, Kuwait, Bahrain, Qatar, the United Arab Emirates, and Oman). The main purpose of the GCC is to ensure the stability and security of the Gulf states, but immediately its objectives are to (1) find a nonmilitary, diplomatic solution to the Gulf War; (2) maintain freedom of navigation in the Gulf; and (3) strengthen and coordinate regional efforts to ensure GCC members' security. These objectives obviously coincide with U.S. interests. The Reagan administration has therefore supported the GCC and encouraged its role in ensuring internal security. However, in the administration's assessment, in the event of a serious threat the GCC has a very limited capacity to defend its security. Besides, the council's desire for an independent status has discouraged the Reagan administration from seeking closer connection with the GCC.

Ensuring Oil Supplies

In another move to ensure a continued supply of oil, the Reagan administration steadily added to its petroleum reserves at home. According to the *New York Times* report of 11 March 1984, U.S. oil reserves totaled 387 million barrels. These were expected to last 90 days if all U.S. imports were cut off, up from 17 days in 1980. If only the Persian Gulf oil was lost, the reserves were expected to last 900 days. By 1983,

Gulf oil accounted for only about 5 percent of the total U.S. petroleum imports. However, among its allies, Western Europe relied on the Middle East for 20 to 40 percent of its oil and Japan for about 55 percent. If the Middle East oil flow were to be disrupted for any length of time, the United States would have to share its reserves. This altered the picture somewhat, but still the United States had acquired a comfortable cushion of oil reserves for emergencies by the beginning of 1983.

Containing the Gulf War

Officially, the administration had adopted a position of neutrality and had in fact made no effort to end the war. For one thing, it had little leverage in the situation; the United States had diplomatic ties with neither Iran nor Iraq. Since the advent of the fundamentalist government in Iran, that country had declared itself the enemy of the United States, while Iraq had been long considered a Soviet ally. As long as the war did not spill over across the Gulf, the United States was content to have these two countries exhaust each other in a protracted conflict. There were in fact some benefits to be reaped from this. To begin with, the war helped contain fundamentalism within Iran and possibly weaken its hold even there. The United States hoped that the terrible costs of the war and the possibility of defeat would discredit the extremists in Teheran and open up opportunities for a more pragmatic leadership there. Second, as long as the war did not embroil the United States or its allies, the sense of danger it provoked only helped to consolidate U.S. strategic ties with Saudi Arabia, Egypt, and Oman. The war made its Arab allies far more amenable to U.S. diplomatic solutions elsewhere in the region, i.e., in Lebanon and on the West Bank. And third, the Islamic revolution in Iran and Arab fears strengthened the U.S. role in the region far more than that of the Soviet Union. It is the last two of the above considerations that shape U.S. policy in the Persian Gulf. The war made the Persian Gulf in particular, and Southwest Asia as a whole, far more accessible to U.S. influence and much more receptive to enhanced U.S. military presence. During 1981, when the fundamentalists were installed in Iran, the administration in its exaggerated fear of communism had thought that Moscow might take advantage of the chaos in Teheran and advance Soviet influence into the very heart of the Persian Gulf. This did not happen. Soviet diplomats were expelled from Teheran in 1983, and Khomeini had cracked down hard on the Tudeh and the left-oriented groups in Iran.[21] The Islamic fundamentalists hated the atheist Soviet

Union only a little less than the imperialist United States. Still, fundamentalism continued to endanger the Persian Gulf.

The United States continued to monitor the situation in Teheran and secretly began assisting covert operations in the event the Khomeini regime collapsed.[22] Drawing on the conclusions of an in-government study on the future prospects of fundamentalism in Iran, the administration began to secretly aid two Iranian paramilitary and political exile groups.[23] The larger of the two consisted of about 600 to 800 men, stationed in eastern Turkey under the command of former Rear Admiral Madani. Admiral Madani had been the commander-in-chief of the Iranian navy under the Shah and briefly the defense minister under the Khomeini government. The second unit of about 2,000 men was led by Bahram Aryana, the chief of the Iranian army under the Shah. He was reported to have close ties with Shahpur Bakhtiar, the last prime minister under the Shah and the man whom the Carter administration so desperately tried to promote, but failed. This program of financial support was said to run into tens of thousands of dollars and was reported to include arms and ammunition as well. It was generally believed that these operations were supported for three reasons: as a potentially useful instrument to harass the flanks of Soviet armed forces should they invade Iran, to counter the feared Soviet penetration of the Ayatollah's government, and to have available some force that could move into Iran in a civil war or domestic upheaval and protect pro-U.S. centrist forces there. The purpose was not to immediately overthrow the Khomeini government, but to stake out the U.S. position and prevail in case the Ayatollah's regime fell and the situation became fluid.

The administration's policy toward Iraq also evolved in response to developments in the region and the balance of military forces between the conflicting countries. From a position of strict neutrality in 1980, the United States slowly edged toward Iraq. This was partly in deference to the wishes of its Arab allies, but also because the administration thought it necessary to offset the military balance that seemed to tilt in favor of Iran during 1982 and 1983. This shift in attitude became apparent in the summer of 1984. U.S. officials made strong statements on Iran's culpability for the continuation of the war. The most explicit of these came from the president himself, who, in an interview just prior to the London economic summit of 1984, credited Iraq with "playing by the rules of war" and said, "Iran is now the one that seems to resist any effort" to end the war. Similarly, the administration appeared to have effectively diminished the flow of arms to Iran from Israel and Korea. And finally, after long months of hesitation, the U.S. Export-

Import Bank approved about $570 million to finance construction of the Iraq-Jordan oil pipeline that Iraq has been so anxious to build.[24] In the view of most observers, since the economic justification for the pipeline was weak, the extension of the credit was mainly a political decision.

Nevertheless, the administration was reluctant to get directly, militarily involved in the Persian Gulf conflict. Even though in the summer of 1984 Iraqi attacks on ships around Kharg Island damaged several tankers and raised the insurance premiums sky-high, U.S. officials downplayed the political and economic seriousness of the conflict. This reluctance to enter the fray led some to ask, "What has happened to the gung-ho enthusiasm for the Rapid Deployment Force (or Central Command) which was created to cope with just such a crisis?"[25] Among the key reasons given for this "backing away" were the following. (1) Providing cover for fifty to sixty tankers strung over 500 miles of sea would require that the U.S. mount a major operation, but aircraft carriers were vulnerable in shallow and restricted waters. (2) "Death-loving" Iranian Shiites could launch kamikaze attacks, forcing the United States to retaliate in ways not warranted by its present stakes in the war. (3) Ample oil was available, and any temporary cutbacks in Iranian, Kuwaiti or Saudi production could be easily made up by oil from alternate sources. The Saudi east-west pipeline had an idle capacity of at least one million barrels a day. This could be brought into use, and tankers could lift the Saudi oil at Yanbu on the Red Sea if traffic through the Gulf became too risky. Besides, Saudi Arabia had sent an emergency floating reserve of about fifty million barrels of oil to sea aboard tankers positioned near Japan and the Caribbean. The world oil markets could therefore cope with any shortfalls on a short-term basis. (4) The Iranian air force was too small and too weak to sustain a blockade for any length of time. (5) Ultimately, Iran was the prize in the Gulf. It was strategically located, richly endowed in natural resources, and had a large enough population to develop and evolve into a major influential industrial power in the region. Therefore, the United States should in its long-term interest, some argued, refrain from openly taking sides and alienating the Iranian people, even though it received nothing but hostility from the present Islamic regime in Teheran. The Khomeini regime was, however, unstable, the argument went, and could collapse under the pressure of events. It seems plausible that the administration subscribed to the above views. This, however, suggests that it had not necessarily changed the military focus of its policies, but that the events had not as yet palpably jeopardized its interests. Fundamentalist Iran and the continuation of the Gulf War were both potentially dangerous to the United States, but thus far the threat had not materialized and the conflict had remained within manageable limits for the United States.

Protecting Saudi Arabia

The Reagan administration was, however, particularly concerned about Saudi security and the impact of the war on the Saudi role in the Persian Gulf. It had encouraged Saudi Arabia to take a more active role in the protection of the Gulf and the preservation of the status quo in the region as a whole. The significance of Saudi cooperation in the Reagan strategy for Southwest Asia can hardly be overemphasized. Through its financial diplomacy, the Saudis had kept Egypt afloat, Somalia cooperative, Iraq edging toward the West, Pakistan firmly aligned to the United States, and the PLO moderate. The Saudi royal family's anti-Communist, pro-West orientations may have been the reason for this, but there is little doubt that the United States depended on Riyadh to "persuade" reluctant Arab states to keep their distance from Moscow. Apart from the fact that Saudi Arabia possesses the largest known deposits of oil in the world, Saudi investments and purchases of U.S. financial securities added up to an impressive figure. The exact figures are not known, but according to one estimate, Saudi investments in the United States added up to anywhere from $110 billion to $180 billion in 1983.[26]

Indeed, the U.S. perception of Saudi Arabia's importance to its own strategy has led to a curious ambiguity in U.S. policy. The president declared in 1981 that Saudi Arabia would not be allowed to go the way of Iran, implying U.S. military intervention, should such a situation arise, but all the same, it was not entirely sure how best to ensure Saudi security. Saudi refusal to allow U.S. military bases confounded the administration's RDF strategy. Moreover, it was aware that a visible U.S. military presence would embarrass and even endanger the Saudi royal family. It is this lack of clear options that led to sporadic U.S. attempts to pressure Saudi Arabia into giving the United States base facilities.

For instance, during the "tanker war" phase of the Gulf conflict in early 1984, according to press leaks, the administration approached the Saudi government to provide U.S. forces access to the air base at Dhahran in return for U.S. air cover for Saudi and Kuwaiti shipping.

> According to U.S. officials, the administration's contingency plans called for 100 to 150 combat aircrafts, along with supporting tankers, command controls and electronic counter measure aircrafts. This means that the smallest land based U.S. force that is

> conceivable for Dhahran would number 50,000 men. Since the
> contingency plans also called for preemptive strikes to destroy the
> Iranian airfields from Bushehr to Bandar Abbas . . . what the ad-
> ministration's reported offer . . . really means is an enormous, visi-
> ble U.S. military presence on Saudi territory.[27]

The administration denied making this proposal, but it seemed probable that those Pentagon officials who had long coveted the Dhahran
facilities might have been tempted to take advantage of Saudi fears. If
such a request was made, the Saudis did not accept, and obviously the
administration quickly withdrew it. The entire episode did, however,
expose the administration's predilection for military solutions.

Conclusions

It is possible to make several observations about President Reagan's
policies in the Persian Gulf during his first term in office. First, the
Reagan administration's response to problems in the Persian Gulf has
been mainly military, whether it was extending the strategic cooperation with the Gulf states, reinforcing U.S. naval presence, or supplying
arms. Its principal objective was to contain the Iran-Iraq war to those
two countries, and prevent Islamic fundamentalism from spreading.
To this end, it adopted strict neutrality in the beginning but gradually
tilted in favor of Iraq. However, its support for Saddam Hussein was
qualified by a deference to the pro-Israeli lobby in the United States,
wariness about Soviet-Iraqi ties, and reluctance to take sides in a war
that it could not control or stop.

Second, stalemated as it was over the first half of the 1980s, the Gulf
conflict kept both Iran and Iraq out of the power equation in Southwest
Asia and produced significant payoffs for the United States, i.e., in the
Lebanon War, in consolidating its strategic ties with the Arab states, and
in weakening the Soviet position throughout the Gulf. The administration carefully avoided direct military involvement and sought to manage the conflict rather than see it concluded. Not until early 1984 did
the administration make any noticeable effort to underline its support
for peace. Its influence in this regard was undoubtedly weak, but it was
content to leave the situation alone.

Third, although it is difficult to predict the map of the Persian Gulf
once the war comes to an end, it is safe to assume that both Iraq and
Iran will reenter the picture and look for ways to rebuild their war-
ruined economies. It is not clear, however, if the United States has a
policy to adequately deal with fundamentalism, whatever shape it may
take, in the aftermath of the Gulf War. Nor is it clear whether the

United States understands the nature of the fundamentalist challenge, apart from viewing it as a base for terrorism. Such a view of fundamentalism may justify its present military approach to the region, but it is a poor guide for the future. What if fundamentalist Iran survives the present conflict intact and seeks to expand its realm through selective accommodation with local Islamic sects? Present U.S. policy has depended excessively on military containment, on providing a military umbrella for its pro-West allies, and on the Islamic revolution eventually becoming a discredited force. Each of these assumptions is, however, questionable, and may not come to pass.

It is entirely possible that the U.S. umbrella may fail to shield its allies from the compelling pull of Teheran. It is likely that even if they do not embrace fundamentalism, the Gulf states may seek to distance themselves from the United States in sheer self-protection. And finally, it is also entirely possible that fundamentalist ideology may not lose all its appeal for Muslims in the region even if Iran were to lose the war. The continued preeminence of U.S. influence is balanced on the knife-edge of stability and instability in the region. Its reinforced military presence does not, however, provide any guarantee against popular resort to nationalism or revolt against economic injustice and political oppression. Nor can it stem the tide of Islamic resurgence, whatever form or shape this may take. Yet the success of Reagan's policies will depend on their ability to contain and prevent precisely such a course of events. What, then, is the balance between probable stability and turmoil in the region? How strong and reliable are major U.S. allies in holding onto the status quo if confronted by external and internal challenges? These questions are important to the course of U.S. policy in the future, and it is to them that we turn in the next chapter.

Notes

1. R. K. Ramzani, "The Arab-Iranian Conflict: The Ideological Dimensions," in *International Security in Southwest Asia*, ed. Hafeez Malik (New York: Praeger, 1984), 70.

2. For the Iraqi views of the causes of the conflict, see *Text of the Foreign Minister's Statement, Ministry of Foreign Affairs, the Republic of Iraq, Iraqi-Iranian Dispute: Facts vs. Allegations* (New York: October 1980), 57–62.

3. From Ayatollah Khomeini's address to theology students of Najaf, 1969, "Governance of the Jurisprudence," otherwise known as "Islamic Government," cited in Ramzani, in *International Security in Southwest Asia*, 48.

4. Ibid.

5. *FBIS*, 10 October 1982.

6. Ramzani, "The Arab-Iranian Conflict," 65.

7. Ibid.

8. *Time*, 12 March 1984, 39.

9. Elaine Sciolino, "Iran's Durable Revolution," *Foreign Affairs* 61:4 (Spring 1983), 925.

10. Theda Skocpol, "Rentier State and Shiia Islam in Iranian Revolution," *Theory and Society* 11 (1982), 265–283.

11. Shahram Chubin, "The Soviet Union and Iran," *Foreign Affairs* 61:4 (Spring 1983), 925.

12. Joseph Malone, in *International Security in Southwest Asia*, 46.

13. *Time*, 12 March 1984, 38–39.

14. See Ramzani, "The Arab-Iranian Conflict," 70.

15. For reports on various phases of the war, see "The Gulf War at a Glance," *New York Times*, 17 May 1981; *The Economist*, 25 February 1984, 33; *The Economist*, 2 June 1984, 25; *Time*, 12 March 1984, 37–39.

16. Sterett Pope, "The Gulf War," *World View* 27:5 (May 1984), 6.

17. See the *New York Times*, 12 September 1984; *Middle East International*, 1 June 1984, 3.

18. For a similar scenario, see *Middle East International*, 9 March 1984, 14; Mark Heller, "Turmoil in the Gulf," *The New Republic*, 23 April 1984, 19.

19. *Middle East International*, 9 March 1984, 14.

20. *The Economist*, 2 June 1984, 26.

21. In February, Iranian authorities arrested Communist Tudeh party head Nureddin Kianuri and others on charges of spying for the USSR. In May, Iran dissolved the Tudeh and ordered Soviet diplomats to leave the country. The Soviets denounced the move.

22. Reported in the *New York Times*, 17 November 1982.

23. *New York Times*, 7 March 1982.

24. *Middle East International*, 29 June 1984, 6.

25. *Middle East International*, 1 June 1984, 4.

26. *New York Times*, 25 April 1983.

27. Ibid., 5.

9.

Prospects for Stability in Southwest Asia

As previous chapters have shown, the three major buttresses of President Reagan's policy in Southwest Asia were (1) in West Asia, unlimited military support for Israel to maintain and strengthen its absolute dominance, reinforced by the neutralization of Egypt through growing economic and military assistance; (2) in South Asia, the continued military buildup of Pakistan both as a buffer and a "tripwire" to discourage any further southward expansion by the Soviet Union; and (3) the promotion of a strong and stable Saudi Arabia as the pivotal force in the Persian Gulf.

All these are backstopped by a vastly reinforced U.S. military presence, signified by its base facilities in Egypt, Somalia, Oman, and Morocco, and by its large military stockpiles, the launching pad of Diego Garcia, and Rapid Deployment Force. While the avowed objective is to roll back Soviet influence, the basic or minimum goal to which the United States is aspiring is not significantly different from the one espoused by Kissinger in the years after Vietnam. Not surprisingly, the configuration of U.S. allies is remarkably similar. What has changed is the immense reliance on force, and the much higher level of confrontation that this has brought into being. The principal fear resulting from Reagan's policies is that the greater the reliance on military might, and the higher the resulting level of tensions, the greater is the risk of open conflict with direct U.S. involvement, if one or more of these buttresses should collapse.

To assess, therefore, the long-term effectiveness of the Reagan strategy, it is necessary to examine the reliability of its allies, Egypt,

211

Pakistan, and Saudi Arabia, and their capacity to cooperate with the United States in the achievement of U.S. global objectives. It hardly needs to be pointed out that such cooperation has to be voluntary, as indeed it has been for the most part. The United States does not have the means to force any of these countries to cooperate with its global policy aims now, any more than it had in the 1950s and 1960s. Thus the long-term effectiveness and eventual successes of the Reagan strategy depend on a variety of factors not within U.S. control. This chapter is devoted to an examination of the limits of this cooperation, and the ways in which it can be endangered.

These limits are defined by three basic factors. The first is the degree of convergence in objectives between the United States and these three countries; the second is the socioeconomic transformation that is occurring in all of them; and the third is the force of the Islamic fundamentalist challenge in each.

The Limits of Convergence in Objectives

As shown in the foregoing chapters, the events of 1979 (the Islamic revolution in Iran, the Soviet intervention in Afghanistan) led to closer strategic cooperation between the United States and Egypt, Pakistan, and Saudi Arabia during the early 1980s. But this apparent alignment against a "common threat" has glossed over deep and abiding differences in their respective aims and policies. Over the past few years, many of these cracks have become increasingly visible. Chief among these are the differences over access to oil and the disposition of the surplus petrodollar, determining the source of threat for the region, weapons procurement, and diplomacy.

Access to Oil

After a decade of stormy relations, the oil embargo, and upward surges in oil prices, both the United States and Saudi Arabia seem to agree that a steady supply of oil and stable prices would be to their mutual advantage. The Saudis must sell oil in return for technology, arms, and goods; the United States needs to cultivate a close connection with the Saudis, who possess the largest known deposits of oil in the world.[1] But this relationship has never been purely business. Political considerations have always played a critical role in Saudi production and price decisions. On these and other related issues, such as investment and disposal of petrodollar surpluses, the United States and Saudi Arabia have often worked at cross-purposes. The United States has generally demanded that Saudi Arabia should produce oil at a high rate, keep the prices moderate and predictable, act as a "swing producer" in emergencies, and assist in filling the U.S. Strategic Petroleum Reserve.[2] On their part, the Saudis have been willing to moderate OPEC prices and step in to meet a rising demand for petroleum, but they have done this to gain at least some political leverage over U.S. policy in the Middle East, particularly regarding the Palestinian issue, the West Bank, Gaza, and the future of Jerusalem. In this regard, the Saudis have two major advantages. First, they have vast financial reserves to tide them over in a lean period; and second, they have great flexibility to quickly adjust production to demand. These two together give the Saudis considerable leverage and political influence. According to one estimate, the Saudi development and other expenditures can be met by producing about 8.5 million barrels a day, but the Saudi oil facilities can produce at 11 to 12 million barrels a day. It is further estimated that the Saudis have a flexibility to produce 1.5 million barrels per day on either side of that 8.5 million minimum without disrupting their own or the world oil market. This represents the range of Saudi oil power.[3] However, if the demand were to decline drastically below that figure, as during 1983–1984 (when Saudi production had fallen to 6 million barrels per day), Saudi oil power would correspondingly erode.[4]

Saudi latitude in oil production and the resulting influence on OPEC as well as on the United States are a source of serious tension in Saudi domestic politics. The more conservationist-minded Saudi officials favor stretching out the useful lifetime of the nation's main resource, while the more nationalistically inclined argue that Saudi Arabia should demand from the United States a concrete quid pro quo in terms of support for the Arab cause.[5] With the exception of the 1973 oil embargo, the Saudis have generally refrained from explicitly linking oil decisions to the Arab-Israeli conflict. Instead, they have attempted to influence the overall agenda and priorities of U.S. policy while carefully avoiding actions that might be misconstrued as blackmail. According to Quandt, although the conservationist and the nationalist voices have yet to gain influence, the events in the Middle East may propel them into greater preeminence. If this were to happen, and "if Saudi Arabia felt less vulnerable, or, if it sought to maximize its power, it may use its oil resources more aggressively."[6]

In any case, the future is most uncertain. No one is able to predict with any confidence the world demand for oil in the coming decades, or the likely economic growth in the industrialized world. It is these factors that will ultimately determine the international demand for oil.

The balance of opinion, however, favors a steady recovery in the world economy and a rising demand for OPEC oil, although such increases are predicted to be proportionately less than the increases during the decade of the 1970s.[7] If this scenario is correct, then Quandt's reasoning may bear out, and the issue of how much to produce, and at what prices, will continue to occupy an important place on both the U.S. and the Saudi agenda. In that case, differences over the role of "oil power" and the purpose to which it is used will continue to plague the U.S.-Saudi relationship.

Differences over Threat Perception

There are sharp differences between the regional states (Saudi Arabia, Egypt, and Pakistan) and the United States over the entire range of issues concerning their mutual security. Although all agree that the Soviet military buildup of the recent past has given Moscow the required ability to intervene in the region, they do not think this very probable. They are one in perceiving the need for a countervailing U.S. presence but prefer that the presence should remain over the horizon and off the shore. Nor is there a consensus on what would be an appropriate response to regional threats. Both Egypt and Saudi Arabia regard Israel and not the Soviet Union as the main threat, and hence tend to see U.S. military presence as Israel's "strategic reserve" that could be used against them and in the interest of both U.S. and Israeli hegemony. This perception has made them acutely sensitive to the danger of extending military bases to the United States. They believe that U.S. bases would impinge on their independence and sovereignty, restrict their freedom of action, make them ready targets of countries against whom the use of bases might be evoked, aggravate local tensions by making U.S. military personnel too visible in their countries, and make their governments a focal point of domestic political opposition from both the ideological left and the right.[8]

Saudi Arabia, in fact, fears that the ultimate objective of the RDJTF is not to protect the oil producers but to seize the oil fields and even to intervene in Saudi domestic affairs to ensure a steady supply of petroleum for the United States and the West. These suspicions are deep-seated and have surfaced repeatedly during the rancorous debates over the administration's requests for military assistance for the Arab states. All three states view the events of the recent past—the U.S. "amber light" to the Israeli invasion of Lebanon, the evidence that certain officials in the U.S. Defense Department had passed on to the Israelis details of the Saudi air defense system to make the Osirak raid of June 1981 possible, U.S. failure to obtain Israeli support for President Reagan's September peace initiative, the strategic cooperation agreements with Israel— as clear signs that the United States cannot be counted on to support the Arab cause.[9]

The Arabs' distrust is further reinforced by their experiences over the politics of weapons procurement in Washington and the formidable power of the Israeli lobby in the U.S. legislature. The Saudi experience over the sale of sixty F-15s proposed during the Carter administration and the acrimonious debates over the sale of AWACS during the Reagan presidency produced grave suspicions about future U.S. commitment to the Persian Gulf. The abrupt cancellation by Congress of Stinger missiles to Jordan in early 1984 (despite King Hussein's ready cooperation in providing a local rapid strike force for the RDF) and a similar cancellation of arms for Kuwait at the same time that U.S. arms were pouring into Israel were equally harmful and produced a profound bitterness about the pro-Israeli biases of U.S. policy. By early 1984, it was clear that the Arab world had major doubts about its overdependence on the United States.

In April 1984, the Saudi government announced that it was purchasing $4 billion worth of arms from France and West Germany. The Saudi ambassador in Washington angrily declared, "We are determined to defend ourselves and we will get those weapons [the Stinger missiles] anywhere."[10] Two days later he hosted a dinner for the Soviet ambassador in Washington. The next day, the newspaper *Al Rai A-Aam* commented that the dinner "should make the U.S. realize that its all out commitment to Israel will cost it everything." Although many observers dismissed this as "an elaborate game of bluff," there has been growing evidence that the Gulf states are in the process of reevaluating their future stance toward the United States. *Middle East Magazine* quoted a source "close to recent behind the scene discussions" to point out that, although the Saudis were antipathetic to Soviet communism, the pressure from Kuwait (which has diplomatic ties with Moscow) and Jordan to establish diplomatic ties with the USSR was beginning to make an impression.[11] An Arab diplomat was quoted as saying that Saudi Arabia had given a "green light" to other Gulf states to establish links with the USSR. By early August, Egypt had also moved closer to the Arab world, its relations with Israel had cooled, and Hosni Mubarak had begun to explore the possibility of reestablishing ties with the Soviet Union that had been broken off by Sadat in 1981.

In fact, conflict between the Arab states and Israel has often paralyzed U.S. diplomacy; it has blocked peace and limited the extent of cooperation given to U.S. efforts by the Arab states. The situation in

South Asia is no different. The United States faces a similar dilemma in Pakistan. Despite the $3.2 billion six-year assistance package to shore up Pakistan against the Soviet threat, Islamabad has been reluctant to grant formal bases to the United States. The bitter experience during the Bangladesh War, the Nixon embargo on the sale of weapons to the subcontinent, and the Carter attempt to treat India and Pakistan evenhandedly have taught Pakistan caution and made it extremely reluctant to court Soviet displeasure.[12] As long as the Soviet occupation of Afghanistan continues, there is the ever-present danger of Soviet incursions across the Durand Line. Pakistan has therefore refused all U.S. requests for a visible military base and held back on arms to the Mujahadeens fighting in Afghanistan. It has also participated in UN-sponsored talks to negotiate a timetable for the withdrawal of Soviet troops from Afghanistan and, instead of depending totally on the United States, has looked to the Arab world to underwrite Pakistan's weapons procurement program.

There is the ever-present fear in Pakistan that improved relations between India and the United States may adversely affect Washington's willingness to support Pakistani interests. Nor is Pakistan fully convinced that the United States would intervene on its behalf in the event of war with India. It worries that the United States might reappraise its entire policy toward the subcontinent in light of the growing political assertiveness and economic importance of India. In short, not unlike Saudi Arabia, Pakistan is apprehensive about the reliability and steadiness of its superpower ally. In self-protection, it has moved closer to the Islamic nations of the Persian Gulf and the Middle East, but this renouncing of its South Asian identity cannot solve its problems because, ultimately, its main conflict is with India. Any change in Saudi Arabia, as in Iran during 1979, will alter the whole balance of power in the Gulf and in all likelihood jeopardize Pakistan's "westward look."

In Pakistan, as in Saudi Arabia and Egypt, there is a keen awareness, almost a fear that an alternative in the guise of regional cooperation might be more popular and in the long run a wiser course to follow than the policy of bilateral strategic collaboration and U.S. arms that they have pursued. For instance, Ali Dessouki comments that in the 1980s Egypt faces two competing role perceptions: military considerations propel it toward closer coordination with the United States, but its traditional role as a bloc leader in the Arab world and among the nonaligned nations requires it to distance itself from the United States. And, he continues, "under President Hosni Mubarak, Egyptian decision makers are more sensitive to the image of Egypt and have made a point of projecting one of independence and non-alignment."[13] In this regard, Egypt's reluctance to publicize the annual "Bright Star" exercises during 1983, compared to the fanfare and wide press exposure that accompanied them in 1980 and 1981, shows that President Mubarak is worried about popular backlash and thinks it wiser to tread softly over the controversial subject of strategic cooperation with the United States. Each nation fears that this alternative may become the focus of the opposition within their country and beyond it in the region. The example of Iran is too recent to ignore and colors all perception in the capitals of the region. In other words, these regimes are aware that there are real dangers in being seen as pawns in a U.S. hegemonic design; they are also aware that the delicate balance in cooperation with and independence from the United States hinges first and foremost on preserving stability at home and on convincing at least the articulate and influential segments of their societies that the present course of cooperation is truly in their national interest.

The Issue of Domestic Stability

How stable are Pakistan, Egypt, and Saudi Arabia, and what is the nature and source of their internal opposition?

Recent literature on this subject has provided no clear answer. For instance, Seth Tillman believes that the political culture of Saudi Arabia and the ruling style of the Saudi monarchy make it less vulnerable to internal destabilization than is generally acknowledged.[14] The orthodoxy and traditionalism of the Saudi rulers and their alliance with the *ulema* protects them from fundamentalist attacks, while the institutions of *majils* and *shura,* although different in form from the participatory liberal democracy of the West, give the Saudi people an open access to their rulers. In addition, the Saudi royal family itself is large in number (about 5,000 princes) and has the ability to co-opt aspiring rivals, notable families, or tribal chiefs through marriage or kinship. This way they are able to give ambitious individuals and groups a stake in the continuation of the status quo. Above all, the availability of vast oil revenues has allowed the royal family to spread the economic benefits to the masses and undertake an ambitious program for development.

The conditions in Egypt inspire less confidence among scholars. Nonetheless, many have commented on the rapid growth in the GNP (about 9 percent in 1980); the massive infusion of U.S. aid; growing revenues from oil, tourism, and remittances of Egyptian labor in the Gulf; and the tremendous construction boom of recent years.[15] For them these are signs that things are better in Egypt, that the *infitah* (economic liberalization) policies instituted by Sadat are finally paying off and will produce sufficient investment from within and without to lift Egypt out of mass poverty and stagnation.

As evidence, they point out that, after Sadat's assassination in October 1981, state power was peacefully transferred to Mubarak, a clear sign that the population wanted the continuation of peace with Israel and the "open door" policies initiated by Sadat. Similarly, the 27 May 1984 elections are cited as a further proof of popular support for Hosni Mubarak.

As to Pakistan, advocates of the optimistic scenario point out that the Zia regime has lasted longer than any since 1947, including the popularly elected civilian government of Zulfikar-Ali Bhutto. They are convinced that the good harvests, the impressive growth in the GNP (about 7 percent in the early 1980s), the infusion of sizable economic aid from the international aid consortium as well as from Washington, and large remittances from the Gulf will keep the economy free of disruptive strain and unwanted hardship.[16] In the political sphere, they point out that a number of astute moves by Zia have improved his prospects. Chief among these are the co-optation of the religious establishment by rapid Islamization of law and society, selective application of suppressive measures, periodic purges of dissident elements from the army, and clever manipulation of the opposition's failures to unify.

While it is true that the prophets of doom and collapse have so far been proven wrong, and that the expected upheavals have not occurred, future prospects for stability in this region are rapidly growing dim. Even if these regimes may have so far managed to survive, domestic strains within their societies remain barely contained. What success they claim is mainly cosmetic and temporary in nature and reflects more their weakness than their strength. On the other hand, the changes that oppressive measures are meant to contain may gather momentum in the near future. Indeed, there are many signs that this is already happening.

The growth in the GNP and the general evidence of prosperity cited earlier are highly deceptive. These statistics obscure growing imbalances within the economy, the lack of any real improvement in productivity, and increasing disparities of wealth and income.[17] A false facade of calm has spread over the frustrations of the young who are blocked out of opportunities, the urban underclass and the rural poor who are trapped in poverty, and the growing number of adherents to Islam who are drawn from all sections of the society and who believe that the moral decay undermining Islam is a direct result of its slavish imitation of the West. Though the saliency and strength of this growing challenge varies from one country to another, there is no doubt that it gravely undermines the established order in these societies.

Analyzing Sadat's and Mubarak's economic policies, Malcolm Kerr observes that the new "commercialism and the accentuation of social inequality will erode the political passivity of Egypt's great mass of urban immigrants." He points out that the open-door policies have led to "unrestrained Americanization of everything in Egyptian life from foreign policy to consumption habits."[18] Foreign and domestic investors have ignored the industrial and agricultural sectors, which are really the key to a sustained economic development; instead, they have focused on real estate, tourism, luxury imports, and construction, creating an illusion of prosperity. The great expectation of breakthrough via massive investment and private enterprise has failed to materialize in Egypt. In fact, the *infitah* policies have ushered in a mercantile model (reminiscent of Lebanon before the civil war) that is singularly inappropriate for an economy of the size and scale of Egypt's.[19] Kerr further points out that since this mercantile model, based as it is on banking and business, had failed to serve even Lebanon, it was improbable that it would succeed in Egypt. According to most observers, the *infitah* has allowed the government to ignore basic social and economic ills and instead has made it dependent on windfall revenues from abroad. These have been flowing into Egypt since the Camp David accords, but, as pointed out by Kerr, in the wrong channels. In the meantime, the country's productive strength has steadily deteriorated because of accumulated strains and growing tensions in its economy. The most recent outburst of popular resentment took place in October 1984, when the government raised the price of bread. According to one analyst, like the oil-rich states of the Gulf, Egypt has become a "rentier state." Its ruling elite, however, is courting grave danger in pursuing this path, for unlike the Gulf states, Egypt's revenues come from outside and are not generated within the country.

The prospects for stability in Egypt thus depend on the continued profitability of the *infitah* for the growing circle of businessmen, bureaucrats, and military officers on one hand, and on the other, on the continued passivity of Egypt's rural and urban masses who know the *infitah* is not paying off for the nation as a whole but have remained patient. If either fails, the present order will be undermined. According to Kerr, the prognosis for the longevity of the present system is negative "because the beneficiary of such a system may find their position undermined as time passes."[20] There is indeed a limit to how much growth can be expected from oil production, the Suez Canal,

remittances, and construction. As the international demand for oil
fluctuates, so will each of the above. In any case, the real problem is also
the alienation and rapid social dislocation among the masses, who may
resort to the Iranian solution or reach back into their own past and
resurrect the fiercely independent, populist policies of Gamal Abdul
Nasser.

Some of the same pressures operate in Pakistan as well: poverty,
unequal distribution of national wealth, blocked opportunity for the
educated young, growing militarization of society, social disruption
caused by Zia's economic policies, and finally, U.S. aid and remittances
from the Gulf. The last has produced a new paradox in Pakistan, one of
high expectations for continued prosperity and growing anger at the
denial of political liberty.[21]

There have been repeated protests, riots, and demonstrations in
Pakistan throughout 1982 and 1984 and several abortive attempts by
disaffected elements in the military. This has steadily forced Zia on the
defensive. What is more, the deliberate "Islamization" has offered no
guarantee against dissent, since the basic tension between religion and
the state remains unresolved in Pakistan.[22]

In fact, unlike Egypt and Saudi Arabia, Pakistan's problem is even
more fundamentally serious: It is the intractable question of national
identity. Should Pakistan move toward, and in step with, the conservative Islamic states of the Gulf as it has been doing since 1977, or should
it nurture the secular, liberal tendencies in the tradition of South Asia?
Should Islam become the ruling force shaping every law, institution,
and action in Pakistan, or should it remain merely an overarching
principle, a spiritual beacon to guide the nation toward its destiny?
Where does the future of Pakistan lie? In finding an independent place
within the South Asian subcontinent, or as a strategic entrepot, tied to
the ebb and flow of superpower competition in the Gulf?

According to Foreign Minister Yakub Khan, "Pakistan, Janus-like
has two faces: one looking **westward and another eastward.**" But there
is dangerous tension **between the two claims on Pakistan's national**
identity. First, it produces **confusion and ambivalence in foreign policy,**
in its relations with the **United States, Saudi Arabia, Iran, and India:**
second, it leads to intolerance and oppression in domestic policy, toward its Pathan, Baluchi, and Sindhi minorities. In one recent view,
these contradictions explain why Pakistan has always fallen back on
military dictatorships, but, tragically, the military solution has not offered a way out of the dilemma. On the contrary,

> Army rule has brought all the contradictions of the Pakistani state
> to a head. Lack of political democracy, economic inequality and the

> oppression of minority nationalities have become deeply embed-
> ded in the consciousness of masses which increasingly begin to
> question the very basis of the state. It does not, after all, require a
> university degree to realize that something has gone seriously
> wrong with the state of Pakistan.[23]

During the 1970s, oppressive domination of then East Pakistan led to
the loss of that part of the country and gave birth to Bangladesh; it also
caused a near-civil war in Baluchistan, while in 1983, the province of
Sindh burst into open revolt. There were pitched battles between Zia's
security forces and the demonstrators, resulting in considerable loss of
life and property. Although the Sindh agitation led by Zia's main
opposition, the Movement for the Restoration of Democracy (MRD)
failed to spread to the key province of Punjab, political conditions in
Pakistan as it enters the second half of 1980 are far from normal. The
continuation of Zia's rule has so far depended on effective neutralization of the bazaar, the working class, and the mosque. Benefits from the
present economic growth will not, however, meet the rising aspiration
of Pakistan's rural and urban poor. Employment opportunities in the
Gulf countries are retrenching, as was evident from the return in 1984
of over 60,000 Pakistani workers from Libya, and the religious establishment, although sympathetic to Zia, is still in a state of indecision
about its future strategy. In fact, the Islamic groups as well as Islami
Jamiat Tuleba (the Islamic student group) have increasingly edged
closer to the position adopted by the MRD.[24] This tentative alignment
may become a solid front against Zia if the coalition that supports him
disintegrates or if his economic program fails.

The major sources of instability in Saudi Arabia are inherent in the
contradictions of Saudi power. On the one hand, Saudi Arabia sits on
the world's largest deposits of oil, but on the other, it is militarily and
politically a weak state. The first condition catapulted Saudi Arabia into
great prominence as a major financial power capable of underwriting
arms purchases for its allies, dominating OPEC, and bankrolling its
diplomacy with cash and hard currency. While this has bought friends
for the ruling family, it has failed to guarantee influence. The failure to
persuade Syria to negotiate in Lebanon and back Yasir Arafat during
the 1982 war are the most recent of these setbacks. Lack of military
power has, on the other hand, greatly heightened the Saudi sense of
vulnerability. Security guarantees from the United States have become
its single most important bulwark against external aggression. This
new role, regional influence combined with political and military
weakness, has enormously increased the possibility of domestic unrest.
First, as pointed out earlier, the nation has produced far more oil than it

has needed, resulting in a huge surplus of petrodollars and forcing the Saudis to import equally huge quantities of goods and services from abroad. This has aggravated tensions in the ruling family between the older generation and the younger set of princes, many of whom are influenced by liberal and Nasserite ideologies and seek to reshape Saudi political life. The latter group is loath to see their future wealth squandered so carelessly.

The rapid economic transformation of the past decade has also produced a new class of technocrats, middle-level officials, and small businessmen, many of whom have been educated abroad and resent the venality and corruption of some members of the ruling family. In fact, the overambitious development plans, the increase in military spending, the influx of foreigners, and the growth of these new groups seeking political expression have created in Saudi Arabia an unstable environment ripe for a military coup or a civilian dictatorship. For the Saudis, wealth and preeminence have not only enlarged the areas for potential influence, they have paradoxically brought greater vulnerability to setbacks. These could be diplomatic failures in Washington (weapons procurement, U.S. reluctance to restrain Israel, the Palestinian question) or in Arab capitals. Nor has such wealth brought a clear sense of direction. The Saudi ruling family, in fact, remains uncertain about how to absorb the changes inherent in the process of economic transformation. Thus, revolutionary changes in the region, whether of the fundamentalist variety as in Iran or the Marxist variety as in the PDRY (South Yemen), pose a real danger to Saudi rule.

It is understandable, therefore, why the Saudi monarchy depends on U.S. military presence, although it protests U.S. intervention unless such intervention is on its own behalf. Egypt under Mubarak also depends on the U.S. strategic and economic network, which ironically includes a former foe (Israel) and an uncertain friend (Saudi Arabia). Pakistan under Zia, too, bases its security on U.S. economic and military aid in the hope that this will countervail Soviet and Indian ambitions and stem the tide of domestic unrest.

The Threat of Islamic Fundamentalism

Economic frustration and political oppression, dependency and failures, and the loss of solidarity and ideals have produced an explosive reaction in the name of Islam throughout the region.

The trauma of the Iranian revolution and the fall of the Shah in 1979 dramatically focused world attention on the militant potential of Islam. But a number of events before and since indicate that Egypt, Saudi

Arabia, and Pakistan were already in the grip of Islamic ferment. Saad Eddin Ibrahim, in his study of Islamic groups in Egypt, states that the January 1977 food riots and the bloody confrontation in July of the same year between the Sadat government and the members of a militant Islamic group known as the Repentance and the Holy Fight group (RHF) were clear signs that the government had reason to fear an Islamic-fed revolution in Egypt. He comments that the "January riots reflected the mounting frustrations of the lower classes and the lower middle classes in Egypt vis-à-vis the negative pay off of President Sadat's socio-economic policies."[25] The confrontation in July 1981 also reflected the growing "despair of the youth of the lower strata," who sought salvation in Islamic militancy.[26] But this was not the first time that Sadat had faced Islamic militancy. In April 1974, the Islamic Liberation Organization (Al-Fanniyya al-Askariyya group) had attempted a coup d'état. The plot proved abortive, but the "attempt was spectacular in volume, planning and timing." In October 1981, Sadat was assassinated by a group of young Islamic fundamentalists, who formed the hard core of the new Islamic revival in Egypt.

Analyzing the events leading to Sadat's assassination, Mohamed Heikal, a former editor of *Al-Ahram* and a respected observer of the Egyptian scene, writes, "As the year 1981 developed, tensions inside mounted . . . corruption was the word on everybody's lips . . . the rapprochement with Israel was bitterly disliked . . . because it . . . isolated Egypt from the rest of the Arab world . . . there was almost universal resentment at Sadat's willingness to let Egypt be used as the springboard for the abortive American raid in the summer of 1980 to rescue the hostages in Tehran."[27] It is obvious that the contradictions and tensions within Egyptian society had culminated in Sadat's assassination. To the assassin, this was an act of supreme sacrifice for his country and for his God. It was also a warning to "all who come after him and to teach them a lesson." In the words of one conspirator, "my aim at this stage of the struggle is to deter all those rulers who follow."[28]

Although the conspirators were arrested and executed, Islamic fervor has steadily gained ground in Egypt. For example, the Egyptian weekly, *Al Liwa al Islami* (the *Islamic Standard*) had increased its circulation to 750,000 by 1983. Attendance at mosques and religious observances has also steadily increased.

The strength of Islamic protest in Saudi Arabia was fully evident during the seizure of the Grand Mosque of Kaaba in 1979.[29] In one view, the band of 200 led by Juhayman ibn Muhammad al-'Utaybi may have been motivated by tribal rivalry, but religion played an important part in that uprising as well, as in the one that occurred around the same time in the oil-rich eastern province of Saudi Arabia. Here, the Shiite population is in the majority. Throughout 1982, the Saudi regime became extremely sensitive to this danger. In December, King Fahd announced the plan to crack down on corruption within the ruling elite "to counter the widespread image of many Saudi princes and officials as playboys—who squander huge sums on high living."[30] The Saudi regime seemed bent on nipping in the bud any potential fundamentalist opposition. The ruling family dismissed some 180 Saudi officials suspected of ties with the fundamentalists. Since then there has been stricter adherence to the Koran, and a firmer enforcement of the Sharia, the Islamic law in Saudi Arabia.

Pakistan has also experienced a strong Islamic revival. The attack on the U.S. embassy and rioting triggered by the false rumors about U.S. involvement in the uprising at the Grand Mosque, the reintroduction of the Islamic laws, and the conversion of public institutions to correspond with the principles of Islam, all suggest that religion has become a potent force that can no longer be denied its place in Pakistani politics and society.[31]

A close scrutiny of the growing literature on the subject of Islamic revival suggests that there are two major explanations why, unless the rulers mend their ways, it is likely to cause major political upheavals.[32] First, there is the anomie theory. According to this, religion becomes the sheet anchor for individuals who are cast adrift into the anonymity of mass society. Confused by rapid economic growth and frustrated by the erosion of traditional values, they find a ready explanation of, and a familiar solution for, their rootlessness in Islam. In both Iran and Egypt, Islamic militants were drawn from the migrants to urban centers, or they were individuals who were denied political participation, social mobility, and a higher standard of living. In these two countries, repression has strengthened the fundamentalist opposition more than the leftist alternative. The mosque has provided the former a ready sanctuary, while support for the latter has eroded.

The situation in Saudi Arabia is different. Here the second explanation becomes operational. It has to do with the political culture and religious attitude of the people. According to this, the fundamentalist movement may represent an attempt by "traditional groups" who have been pushed aside by modernization and economic growth to revive the past and regain their status in society. These groups include "the artisans and the shopkeepers of the great cities, the merchants and the middling landowners of the provincial town and —the Ulema."[33] There is little reason to believe that blocked mobility or status displacement, poverty, or even desire for political participation is behind the fundamentalist challenge in Saudi Arabia. The Saudi theocracy is by-and-large supported by the clergy and the leading tribes. It has also considerable popular support. Nonetheless, there is a feeling in an indeterminate number among the ulema that their rulers are overly tolerant of modernity and change. In fact, the Saudi regime symbolizes religious orthodoxy. As one scholar observes, "by identifying with Wahhabism, the Saudi monarchy seeks to benefit from the prestige of a traditional religious movement with deep roots in the Arabian peninsula. The association also appears to fulfill the old Islamic ideal of the legitimate state, in which the ruler is a devout Muslim ruling with the advice of the ulema and in accordance with the Sharia."[34] The fundamentalist challenge in Saudi Arabia is likely to grow if Saudi rulers are seen to deviate from the orthodox precepts of Islam. The piety and religious political culture of the Saudi people offer any dissenting elements an exploitable opportunity to agitate against change. The chances of an upsurge of fundamentalism in Saudi Arabia are therefore less likely than in Egypt, where it is ruthlessly suppressed. Pakistan combines features of both these states. On the one hand, it has given official expression to the new religious fervor, but on the other, Zia remains wary of militant Islamic groups. If these were to question his legitimacy and join the opposition, Zia might be forced to root them out as ruthlessly as Sadat did during 1980–1981. In any event, this would mean a major political crisis in Pakistan.

Several scholars have noted the revolutionary potential of Islam.[35] This arises from the tragic clash between the state and religion that has characterized Islamic history since its beginning. On the one hand, only the strengthening of the "Islamic state could save the identity and conversion of the Islamic community," an ideal that is contrary to Islam, but on the other, "as it grew stronger, the Islamic state moves further and further away from the social and ethical ideals of Islam." Resistance to this process of change and a struggle to restore radical dynamism to Islam are therefore inherent in Islamic societies. Each of America's close allies, Egypt, Saudi Arabia, and Pakistan in particular, must defuse this revolutionary potential of Islam and build a stable order in their countries that is more in sympathy with popular sentiments.

The Saad Ibrahim study of the ideological beliefs of the imprisoned militants in Egypt in 1977 found that their objective was to force the elite either to conform to the precepts of Islam or to step down. In other words, a serious challenge to the status quo is a built-in component of any militant Islamic ideology. The militants claim that the present political system is both corrupt and inept, while all the external setbacks and the internal socioeconomic ills of Egypt and other Islamic societies were attributable to these two evils.

This clearly shows why the present rulers in Saudi Arabia worry about external diplomatic failures, why the ruling circles in Egypt and Pakistan have decisively moved toward Islamization of their societies, and why each country wants to keep U.S. military presence at arm's length. This also tells us why it is that the words of Hasan-al-Banna, Sayyid qutb, Abdul Ala-Maudadi, and the Ayatollah Khomeini, who attack modernization and the West, are eagerly followed by the masses in the Middle East and the Persian Gulf.

Islamic fundamentalism has not only dimmed the prospects of domestic stability, it has contributed substantially to tensions and conflicts among the states of the region. The senseless war between Iran and Iraq is the most obvious instance of this new confrontationist environment in Southwest Asia. The Saudi interference in North Yemen, tensions between Jordan and Syria, Somalia and Ethiopia, Egypt and Libya, Morocco and Algeria, Syria and Iraq, and finally between Syria and the PLO attest to the growing incidence of rivalry and contest within the region. The aim of many of these regimes is to bring about the downfall of an opposing government (Libya in Chad, Saudi Arabia in Yemen, Ethiopia in Somalia). To this end they are willing to aid and incite minority revolts in the adversary country. This is a dangerous trend, given the existence of numerous ethnic and religious minorities strewn across national boundaries in Southwest Asia. The tragic disintegration of Lebanon is the most extreme instance of this new danger in the region.

Conclusions

The implications of these old and new instabilities for future U.S. policy in Southwest Asia are not difficult to see. It is obvious that the sources of social disruption are deeply rooted in several recent changes within the region: Future turmoil may be a result of economic imbalances, social and political frustration, excessive oppression, or popular demand for a return to Islamic orthodoxy. In the recent past, these forces have not only weakened the region against itself but made it an easy prey for the superpowers. Present U.S. dominance is the direct result of these developments. However, there is a serious danger that such domination, while a desirable goal for Washington to pursue, might become a red flag for the frustrated militants in the region. The only way for the United States to build enduring influence is by building an enduring structure of peace. In the absence of the latter, influence may quickly erode, producing uncertainty and anxiety all around. President Carter confronted just such a configuration of threats and opportunities during his last year in office. As shown in Chapter 3, he could not have stemmed the tide of revolution in Iran or prevented the Soviet Union from invading Afghanistan, nor could he have done anything about the initial wave of fundamentalist ecstasy sweeping through the region. However, only a short time before those events took place, U.S. influence was at a high point in the region. All its allies were intact, and its mediation had triumphed at Camp David. This situation did not, however, last long. Similarly, at the end of Reagan's first term in office, the United States stands militarily unchallenged in the region, but its easy preeminence provokes the very elements it seeks to neutralize. The main allies of the United States in Southwest Asia—Egypt, Saudi Arabia, and Pakistan—are fully in control of neither their politics nor their economies, although present U.S. policies depend on their remaining both stable and reliable.

Notes

1. Karim Pakravan estimates Saudi proven resources to be 110,000 million barrels. See *Oil Supply Distribution in the 1980's* (Stanford, CA: Hoover Institution Press, 1984), 6; *Oil and Gas Journal,* 27 December 1982.

2. William Quandt, *Saudi Arabia in the 1980's* (Washington, DC: Brookings Institute, 1981), 139–140.

3. Ibid., 125.

4. *Petroleum Economist* (February 1983), 38.

5. For detailed discussion of the ideological, tribal, and other conflicts within the Saudi royal family, see Quandt, *Saudi Arabia in the 1980's,* 127.

6. Ibid., 135.

7. Pakravan, *Oil Supply Disruptions in the 1980's,* 29; "Predicting Long-Term Oil Demand," *Petroleum Economist* (July 1983), 254–255; "Oil Demand in Perspective," *Petroleum Economist* (August 1984), 254.

8. Lenore Martin, *The Unstable Gulf* (Lexington, MA: Lexington Books, 1984), 134. Speaking for all the Gulf nations, Abdulla Bishara, secretary-general of the Gulf Cooperation Council (GCC), stated that the Gulf nations had no desire for foreign troops; security could be preserved by the littoral states themselves. See *American-Arab Affairs* 7 (Winter 1983–1984), 42.

9. Stephen Green, "Strategic Asset, Soviet Opportunity," *American-Arab Affairs* 9 (Summer 1984), 52.

10. *The Middle East* (June 1984), 13.

11. Ibid. The *Washington Post* reported on 25 June 1984 that Kuwait had concluded a $327 million arms deal with the Soviet Union for aircraft and short-range ballistic missiles as well as tanks.

12. For succinct analyses of foreign policy options for Pakistan, see Ghulam Mustafa Khar's article in *Economist* 31 (October 1981), 25–30.

13. Ali E. Hillal Dessouki, "Egypt and Gulf Security: The Dilemma of Two Role Perceptions," in *International Security in South West Asia,* ed. Hafeez Malik (New York: Praeger, 1984), 141.

14. Seth Tillman, *The United States in the Middle East* (Bloomington: Indiana University Press, 1984), 73–123; also see Quandt, *Saudi Arabia in the 1980's,* 105–106.

15. According to John Merriam, Egypt's foreign exchange earning from remittances, Suez, and tourism rose from $370 million in 1970 to $2.9 billion, and about $900 million more in 1981. Workers' remittances amounted to about $3 million in 1981. "Egypt after Sadat," *Current History* 81 (January 1982), 7–8.

16. See House Subcommittee Hearings on Asian and Pacific Affairs and on Human Rights and International Organization, "Reconciling Human Rights and U.S. Security Interests in Asia," 2d session, 10 August 1982, 175.

17. "For the Arab world, a crude calculation separating high income oil exporters from the other states supports the common observation that income disparities have grown markedly over the decade. In 1970, 8.2 percent of the population of the Arab states accounted for 30 percent of the total domestic product of these states, while 72.5 percent of the people shared 50 percent of the GDP. In 1979, 9.7 percent shared 55 percent of the GDP while 71 percent had access to only 25 percent of the product. In 1981, 11.8 percent of the population shared 72.8 percent of the wealth, and 88.2 percent shared 27.2 percent." Joe Stork, "Ten Years After," *MERIP Reports* (January 1984), 6.

18. Malcolm Kerr and El Sayeed Yassin, eds., *Rich and Poor States in the Middle East* (Boulder, CO: Westview Press, 1982), 455.

19. Ibid., 453.

20. Ibid., 456.

21. "The Wobbly Bit of Pakistan," *The Economist,* 8 October 1983; also see *The Economist,* 3 September 1983.

22. G. H. Jansen, *Militant Islam* (New York: Harper & Row, 1979), 175–176.

23. Tarik Ali, *Can Pakistan Survive? The Death of a State* (London: Penguin Books, 1983), 145.

24. *The Middle East* (July 1984), 11.

25. Saad Eddin Ibrahim, "Anatomy of Egypt's Militant Islamic Groups: Methodological Note and Preliminary Findings," *International Journal of Middle East Studies* 12 (1980), 425.

26. Ibid., 424.

27. Mohamed Heikal, *Autumn of Fury* (London: Andre Deutsch, 1983), 227.

28. Ibid., 265.

29. Alexander Bligh, "Opposition Activity and Recent Trends," in *The Arabian Peninsula: Zone of Ferment,* ed. Robert Stooky, (Stanford, CA: Hoover Institution Press, Stanford University Press, 1984), 75.

30. *Washington Post,* 20 December 1982.

31. Jansen, *Militant Islam,* 190–193.

32. Alexander Cudsi and Ali E. Dessouki, eds., *Islam and Power* (Baltimore: Johns Hopkins University Press, 1981); Martin Kramer, *Political Islam,* vol. 8, no. 73 of *The Washington Papers* (Beverly Hills, CA: Sage Publications, 1980); Elie Kedourie, *Islam in the Modern World* (New York: Holt, Rinehart and Winston, 1980); Jansen, *Militant Islam.*

33. Cited in Lucien Vandenbroucke, "Why Allah's Zealots? A Study of the Causes of Islamic Fundamentalism in Egypt and Saudi Arabia," *Middle East Review* 5:16 (Fall 1983), 32.

34. Mohammed Ayoob, "The Revolutionary Thrust of Islamic Political Tradition," *Third World Quarterly,* no. 3 (Spring 1981), 269.

35. Edward Mortimer, *Faith and Power,* the Politics of Islam (New York: Vintage Books, 1982); Bernard Lewis, "The Shi'ites," *The New York Review of Books,* no. 13 (August 15, 1985), 7–10.

Conclusions

Ever since the events of 1978–1979, there has been great concern in the United States about the precipitous decline in U.S. power, growing uncertainty in the world, and the increasing ability of lesser-order powers to challenge U.S. world leadership. This concern has resulted in a highly emotional and passionate debate about the causes and consequences of this decline. Those who subscribed to the "decline thesis" pointed to the Soviet military buildup and aggressive Soviet activities in North Africa and the Persian Gulf and claimed that the Soviet Union was probing into the most vulnerable and defenseless area of Southwest Asia, which was, by virtue of the West's dependency on oil, also the area most vital to U.S. interests. The alarmists among these insisted that the region was engulfed in a wave of crisis that stretched from the Fertile Crescent to the Maghreb, and from the Persian Gulf all the way to Afghanistan; no one was safe from Soviet aggressive designs, and in this deadly zero-sum game, the United States had steadily lost. Those who challenged this view pointed out that both the estimates of Soviet buildup and the assumptions about Soviet need for Persian Gulf oil were highly exaggerated. The Soviet conquest of the world was not inevitable; neither was every U.S. loss a certain Soviet gain.

A logical corollary was the question of what to do, and how to protect U.S. interests against this perceived threat. Those who had subscribed to the "decline theory" insisted that lack of strong leadership, vacillation, and a wrong-headed approach to human rights had been responsible for U.S. weakness; therefore, what the United States had to do was to build up its military strength and project it to match and deter Soviet actions everywhere—but, as a priority, first in Southwest Asia. In contrast, those who challenged the "decline thesis" raised moral objections and argued that the political and financial cost of such a buildup was not only debilitating to the U.S. economy, it was entirely misplaced. They further stressed the hard-learned "lessons of Vietnam," and the dangers of overextending U.S. responsibilities.

Ronald Reagan's victory in the 1980 elections left no one in any doubt which advocacy had finally triumphed. But not everyone supporting the new hard line advocated it for the same reason. For some, the Cold War view was born of deeply held ideological convictions about the nature of Soviet power. These could be called the theologians. There were others, however, who saw a matching U.S. military buildup as a matter of pragmatic necessity, though they did not believe the U.S.-Soviet clash was either inevitable or unavoidable.

Nevertheless, there was a general consensus in the United States about the international significance of the events of 1979 in Southwest Asia. Both sides of this debate, however, constantly seemed to overlook an important point that had far-reaching implications for U.S. policy. It was true that the United States could no longer exert unequivocal power in the world, but U.S. decline was not a result of diminishing military prowess—if anything, in the 1980s the U.S. arsenal had grown more formidable—but a natural outcome of objective conditions in the postwar world economy, and of politics. The emergence of Europe and Japan, the evolution of some Third World economies (i.e., India, Mexico, Brazil, and Saudi Arabia), and the growing force of nationalism, all had diminished the area within which the United States had been relatively unopposed. By the 1980s, the world consisted of several centers of power: The growth in the sheer number of nonaligned states attested to this. This meant that even less powerful nations had obtained greater ability to foil the designs of superpowers. U.S. setbacks in Iran and the Soviet expulsion from Egypt clearly underlined this. Thus, U.S. and for that matter Soviet ability to influence others had become conditional, and increasingly constrained by the plurality of competing states and their zealous regard for their independence.

What the great powers could hope for, then, was a situation of relative preeminence: greater ability than others to shape issues and agenda and to influence the terms of interaction between states and the distribution of resulting payoffs. The intrinsic properties and nature of U.S. power have not declined, but the United States and others are now required to recognize and face up to the situation of relative loss. The United States is still first among all world powers, with the Soviet Union following a close second. The "thesis of decline" has ignored this development and confused objective realities of power with what is essentially a subjective perception. The second important point to note is that political power is situational. The United States can simultaneously be less influential in Africa and remain an undeniable influence in the Persian Gulf. Thus, the setbacks of 1979 were at least to some extent a result of systemic changes in international politics.

In retrospect, the events of 1979 were hardly advantageous to the Soviet Union. The revolution in Iran, the hostage crisis, the fourfold rise in oil prices were not instigated by Moscow. It did not benefit from these. As it turned out, fears that it meant to control the "oil jugular" and strangulate the "lifeline of the West" proved grossly exaggerated. The Soviet presence in Ethiopia, Yemen, and Afghanistan had failed to give it any leverage; if anything, its continued occupation of Afghanistan had seriously handicapped Moscow in winning trust and goodwill in Southwest Asia. Similarly, the Gulf War confounded the Soviet policy. With no purchase in Iran, and with Iraq steadily slipping away, the Soviet Union has been left with Syria as its only major ally in the region; but here, Hafez Assad has routinely ignored Soviet advances. This is not to justify or ignore Soviet opportunism or its jockeying for position, but merely to suggest that the U.S. decline has multiple causes, that its weakening in one region need not bring similar weakening in another, and that the Soviet position in Southwest Asia suffered important setbacks over the decade from 1973 to 1983.

It is in view of this that this book has raised questions about the fundamental problems of President Reagan's policy and taken issue with the "thesis of decline" as it was applied to Southwest Asia in the aftermath of the events of 1979.

The theologians in the Reagan administration claimed that the dangerous decline of U.S. power, so apparent in the late 1970s, could in fact be traced to the last years of the Vietnam War, and to the detente diplomacy of Henry Kissinger. In their view, this policy of "appeasement" had allowed the Soviet Union the time and opportunity to become a formidably armed adversary. Chapter 2 tried to show that, contrary to this belief, arms negotiations and the agreement on principles of reciprocity and equality concluded with the Soviet Union in 1972 had in fact persuaded Moscow to restrain its major allies in the Arab world—Egypt, Sudan, and Libya—and to cooperate in defusing tensions after the war of 1973. The activities of U.S. proxies, Iran and Saudi Arabia, had successfully neutralized radicalism in Oman and North Yemen, while it was Washington that mediated the cease-fire agreements between the Arab states and Israel after 1973.

However, even in achieving this, Kissinger had laid the groundwork for a confrontation between the superpowers that came in the 1980s. After Egypt's estrangement from the USSR, in which the United States had played a significant role, U.S. policy objectives shifted to exclusion of Soviet influence from the region. The weapon was still primarily diplomacy, but the element of coercion had subtly increased—was in fact implicit in the more aggressive nature of the objective itself. It is arguable that Soviet intervention in Angola and the Horn of Africa was a direct response to this, and not part of a grand design. But what is indubitable is that its much greater support of the PLO and the PFLOAG in the mid-1970s was a direct response (arms delivery and advice). This shifted the focus of West Asian conflict to Lebanon. In a broader sense, therefore, although Kissinger achieved his objective of excluding the USSR, he set the stage for a much-heightened level of conflict in the future, with a much-increased potential for military action. This was eventually realized in Lebanon.

What Carter tried to do was essentially defuse this potential by shifting the emphasis back to negotiations. He did this most dramatically by SALT II, efforts to convene the Geneva conference on the Middle East, and the conclusion of the Camp David talks. Indeed, at the end of 1978, the United States had acquired great leverage to influence the course of diplomacy in Southwest Asia and was in a much stronger position than it had been at the end of the Kissinger epoch. The activities of the Red Sea Entente (Egypt, Saudi Arabia, Iran) had undermined the Soviet position in Sudan and Somalia. The loss of Berbera had been a serious blow to Moscow. It had suffered further reverse in North Yemen, and because of its activities in North Africa, its ties with Iraq had perceptibly cooled.

In contrast, the chief U.S. ally, the Shah, appeared to be fully in control within Iran, and the key states of Saudi Arabia and Egypt had come to depend increasingly on U.S. arms and diplomacy. Carter's achievements had been premised on greater sensitivity to more fundamentally destabilizing issues in the region (although he did not altogether ignore the advantages of pursuing arms diplomacy). This was evident in his attempts to refocus U.S. diplomacy on the resolution of the Palestinian problem and persuade Israel to trade territory for a full peace with its neighbors. Similarly, his attempts to reinvolve the Soviet Union, through reconvening of the Geneva conference, were inspired in the hope of achieving a comprehensive peace. In other words, Carter had tried to move away from the more aggressive goals implicit in the Kissinger policy of exclusion, but such efforts proved abortive. His restraint was mistaken for weakness.

The reason for this was the rise of the right in the United States. A whole phalanx of conservatives and neo-conservative groups had been attempting since the mid-1970s to reinstate Cold War axioms in U.S. foreign policy and fiscal conservativism in domestic management. The Committee on Present Danger, supported by several grass roots organizations, such as the Moral Majority and defense-minded arms lobbies, as well as political action committees, finally succeeded in shifting the ideological balance decisively in their favor. The setbacks and the humiliations of 1979 were at hand to give further credence to their claims and to convince the public of growing U.S. vulnerability and the Soviet Union's aggressive designs.

The past four years' perspective has only further reinforced the conclusion that domestic perceptions of the international position of the United States were colored by this shift to conservativism and to the Cold War view of the world more than by objective features of the region. Indeed, this was part of a pattern that has held true since U.S. ascendancy to world leadership. One can see a certain lack of correspondence between objective balance of power in the world and the rhythm of domestic politics in the United States. Thus, just as Kissinger had achieved diplomatic preeminence in 1976 in Southwest Asia, and Reagan had achieved military preeminence in the aftermath of the Israeli invasion of Lebanon, domestic support for their policies had begun to ebb. Kissinger's *realpolitik* approach was attacked by both the doves and the hawks on U.S. policy, while President Reagan had to ward off fierce criticism for committing U.S. Marines to the quagmire of Lebanon.

Carter's policies were undone to some extent by the Soviet reaction to his predecessor's policies, for the USSR had also moved toward increased militarization, use of military proxies, and acquisition of bases. This was evident in its support of the Angolan FNLA, arms airlifts into Ethiopia, and commitment of Cuban forces in Africa. But what undid Carter was not the Soviet Union in the final anaylsis, but domestic developments in U.S. proxies—Iran and Saudi Arabia in 1979 and Ethiopia in 1974. The USSR could not have chosen a worse moment for invading Afghanistan, for it enabled blame in the United States to be focused on it for all the above reverses, and diverted blame from the real culprit, which was the excessive reliance on proxies for achieving what was essentially an aggressive goal, i.e., the exclusion of the Soviet Union. This is the danger Reagan's policy faces in the future.

To say this is not to exonerate the USSR in Afghanistan: It changed the rules of the game that had held since 1945, and suddenly increased the level of uncertainty in the international system. As was argued earlier, this increase virtually made certain a militarization of U.S.

response in this region, particularly because of the oil dependence, highlighted in the same year by the second rise in oil prices. Between the rising clamor for tougher action from the Cold War advocates, and the Soviet invasion, Carter had little choice but to move speedily into making a military response. The declaration of the Carter doctrine and the creation of the Rapid Deployment Force were a result of this. But the difference between Carter and what followed was the extent of shift from diplomacy to force. Carter's was a reluctant, limited shift, designed to leave the door of negotiations open; Reagan's was emphatically military.

Under President Reagan, diplomacy took a back seat. This was evident in his proposed defense budget, as in the upgrading of the RDJTF to a fully empowered central command, and the acquisition and strengthening of U.S. military facilities in Egypt, Oman, Diego Garcia, Berbera, and Kenya. It was also evident in strategic cooperation agreements with Israel and Egypt and in conscious efforts to subordinate local disputes to global U.S. objectives. The Reagan administration did not discourage Israel from using force to destroy the political base of the PLO, defeat Syria, or occupy southern Lebanon. It stepped up arms deliveries to Pakistan, Saudi Arabia, and other Persian Gulf states, routinely supplied arms to the Afghan Mujahadeens, and displayed its tough posture by shooting down two Libyan planes over the Gulf of Sidra in 1983 and ordering heavy naval bombardment of Syrian as well as Druse and Shiite positions in Lebanon.

Nor did the Reagan administration achieve a single agreement during its first term in office that could lay the foundation of peace in Southwest Asia. The Lebanon-Israel agreement of 17 May proved abortive; indeed, it resulted in undermining Amin Gemayel (who was Reagan's principal hope in Lebanon) and strengthening Syria. Although the administration improved ties with India during 1982, its arms aid to Pakistan and its refusal to negotiate the Afghan situation despite urgings from the United Nations did little to inspire confidence in its peaceful intent. In the Gulf War, the administration focused on a policy of military containment of Islamic fundamentalism and of Iran, and made no visible effort to end that conflict, although admittedly its leverage there is limited.

Herein lies the biggest weakness of Reagan's policies. Coercive diplomacy and use of force may tilt the balance in favor of the United States, but to preserve this advantage for any length of time will require greater and greater militarization and more frequent resort to force. In other words, preeminent influence, which the United States undeniably had in Southwest Asia in the 1980s, can be maintained only by raising the costs and hence the dangers for the United States in the region. There is no guarantee, however, that such militarization will bring stability. This was evident in the collapse of the Shah of Iran and in the U.S. Marine presence in Lebanon during 1982.

There is, then, a lack of direct connection between military power and political advantage: The means do not produce the desired ends. The main reason for this dissonance between policy and results is to be found in the objective conditions of multipolarity in the world and in the growing ability of even militarily weak states to secure a better bargain than is due them if measured in terms of their real power. It is equally difficult to deny forever expression to popular nationalist sentiments, however formidable an arsenal of arms the United States or its allies in Southwest Asia may possess. Nationalism, economic frustration, and resentment of external domination may all converge to undo any political advantage the United States may have gained. One cannot avoid the conclusion that power will have to be shared not only with the Soviet Union, but also with regional states, if the United States is to build a structure of enduring peace in Southwest Asia.

In this regard, the weakness of U.S. policy under President Reagan remains what it has always been. The objective has not changed: excluding the USSR. The method also has not changed: use of proxies. What has changed is the shift from diplomacy to military force. But the proxies' problems have not changed either: limited convergence with U.S. interests, instability, and domestic resistance to increased involvement with the United States. At the heart of this dilemma is the central question about the purpose of U.S. power and the conduct of policy toward the Third World. In the three and a half decades since the Second World War, the United States has failed to evolve a coherent policy toward nationalist aspirations in the Third World that is at once satisfactory to its ideals and to its imperial ambitions. Nor has it developed an effective mix of coercion and diplomacy.

As one looks at the situation in Southwest Asia in the 1980s, the drift is most certainly toward greater uncertainty, not less. The popularity of Islamic fundamentalism and the growing Islamization of Southwest Asian nations, whether out of hope or fear, still underscore the fact that these are societies in a state of crisis. Therefore, military containment of these forces may be neither possible nor wise. The conventional logic of coercion did not work during the revolution in Iran; it may not work against Islamic populism elsewhere. What is required, then, is an effort to sympathetically understand and gain intimate knowledge of the ideology and perceptions of the opposing forces in the region, for it is this that will ultimately guide the United States in designing a proper mix of coercion and diplomacy.

In the final analysis, preeminence cannot be reduced to a balance sheet of Soviet and U.S. gains. Such calculations may be misleading. Real power and influence have increasingly come to reside in the ability to structure regional relationships and shape interaction, to determine the distribution of payoffs among regional states, and to reward cooperation and punish contrary actions. Judging in this light, it is the United States, not the USSR, that has remained preponderant in Southwest Asia over the past decade. Only history will tell if the United States is content to remain so or whether it will use its not inconsiderable power to build a stable peace in Southwest Asia.

Postscript

The first year of President Reagan's second term in office witnessed a marked relaxation in the U.S. administration's attitude toward Southwest Asia.

U.S. goals in the region had not changed: It still sought to establish a structure of relationships and a heirarchy of military power that assured its continued dominance. But its strategy for doing so had undergone substantial changes, most notably a leaning toward the use of diplomacy versus force. The United States was now interested in bringing about a lasting settlement of the Arab-Israeli dispute—and stability in the rest of the region—by formalizing the gains it had made at the conference table.

In West Asia the shift toward diplomacy was precipitated as much by the profound changes that had taken place in the years following the Lebanon War as by the learning process that the Reagan administration had undergone. Principal changes included a major shift in the stance of the PLO; Israel's increasing weariness with incessant conflict, born as much out of its military losses in the war of attrition as by the growing weakness of its economy; and the rise of Shiite fundamentalism.

Lessons of the Lebanon War

After the collapse of the 17 May 1983 pact, the United States had withdrawn from Lebanon and disengaged itself from an active role in mediating the Arab-Israeli dispute. The end of President Reagan's first term saw no progress on the peace front and erosion of the few political

239

advantages resulting from the Israeli invasion of Lebanon. Indeed, even prior to the Israeli withdrawal, Lebanon had begun to divide internally, as various factions stepped up violence and waged war on each other. It was clear that two fundamental struggles were taking place in Lebanon. The first centered around the future course of Palestinian policy and the Arab orientation toward Israel. As Yasir Arafat showed signs of moving toward the "Jordanian option," the conflict between Syrian-supported Palestinians and Arafat loyalists intensified. The second struggle involved the domination of Lebanon. The brutal attacks by the Amal Shia and the Lebanese Sixth Brigade on the Palestinian camps at Sabra, Shattila, and Burj-al-Barajneh throughout April and May of 1985 was a primary example, as was the violent conflict between the Muslims and Christians in Lebanon. In an interview with Austrian television on 2 July 1985, Nabih Berri reasserted the Amal resolve to rid Lebanon of the Palestinian as well as the Israeli presence. In 1982, the Shias of Lebanon had openly welcomed the arrival of the Israelis in Southern Lebanon; but by 1984, the Israeli occupation army had rapidly run out of goodwill. Resistance and violent opposition mounted against its forces in Southern Lebanon. Israel in fact decided to withdraw from Lebanon, and by the end of the summer of 1985 its forces pulled out. Israel could not afford a war of attrition. Nor could it justify at home the war it was forced to wage against the civilian population. The Shias in Lebanon had in a sense showed the world that the strategy of armed civilian resistance could be effectively applied against an occupying Israeli army. These developments were fraught with grave consequences for the course of the Palestinian struggle, and for the chances of a U.S. mediated settlement in the Middle East.

Shift in PLO's Strategy

The year 1985 also saw a profound shift in the perceptions and the goals of the PLO, or at least of its acknowledged leader, Arafat. The war of the camps, the expulsion from Lebanon—indeed the entire sequence of events leading to the 1982 war and the obvious impotence of the Arab states—brought home with vivid clarity the fact that in 1985 the Palestinian movement faced a very different reality. In the mid-1970s there was still a belief that the PLO could ride on an Arab "tide," which had gathered great momentum in wake of the oil embargo. After the 1982 war however, the tide had turned and was in fact running against the PLO, to the point where none was prepared to permit an independent Palestinian movement to operate against Israel from its soil. The open conflict between Syria and the PLO was the most obvious indicator of this new turn of events, as was the now only token diplomatic and political support the PLO was receiving from the rest of the Arab states. It was also clear that the PLO no longer had a military bargaining chip in Southern Lebanon which could be used to force the United States and Israel to make concessions in the West Bank.

The recognition of these new and painful realities led to a growing conviction among a majority in the Palestinian community that the "Jordanian option" was the only alternative remaining. The Jordanian option required (1) that the United States and Israel formally recognize the PLO as the sole representative of the Palestinian people with the right to an independent national existence, i.e., a state, either in confederation with Jordan or in other form; and (2) that these arrangements be guaranteed not only by both the superpowers but by Israel and Syria as well. The latter, the PLO believed, could be accomplished only through an international conference with all parties to the dispute represented. This adoption of the "Jordanian option" thus underlined a fundamental shift in the PLO's strategy.

Prior to the 1982 war, the main constituency of the PLO consisted of the Palestinian population living in the refugee camps and cities of Lebanon and Syria. After the war, however, the PLO was forced to abandon Lebanon-Syria as a primary base and to move to the occupied territories proper. This brought the PLO politically and emotionally closer to the one million Palestinians living in Jordan, and the half a million in the Gulf. In keeping with the shift toward what Rashidi Khalidi called "less outspoken sectors of the Palestinian policy," the PLO had reoriented its strategy in the direction of diplomacy.

As a logical outcome of these two shifts in perspective, Arafat moved closer to Egypt and Jordan and their position on the preconditions for the discussion of the Palestinian question. The Syrian-supported radical Palestinian groups opposed this shift, however, and left the PLO to establish the Palestinian National Salvation Front (PNSF). The Front argued that the Jordanian option was a dead-end solution; that Arafat represented the reactionary forces in the Palestinian movement; and that he was forcing the PLO to surrender to combined pressures from Egypt and Jordan and make unacceptable concessions to Israel and the United States. The Front further maintained that instead of seeking a reconciliation with Jordan and the United States, what the PLO should do was to coordinate its strategies with Syria and Syrian-supported Lebanese forces. This was necessary, they believed, because Syria, and not Jordan, was capable of countering U.S. designs in the region. The Front pointed to the Shia success in driving Israel out of Southern

Lebanon, claiming that a dramatic increase in acts of resistance would reinforce Israel's fear of the "arc of violence" spreading to the West Bank and persuade it to concede the Palestinian demand. Israel's growing economic crisis and internal political divisions lent further credibility to this point of view. Nevertheless the left, pro-Syrian perspective remained a significant, albeit minority, viewpoint, whose proponents could not be easily assuaged.

These dissident views however did not inhibit Arafat's pursuit of the Jordanian option. In November 1984, he called the seventeenth meeting of the Palestinian National Council (PNC) in Amman. This meeting was significant not only for the resolutions passed but the venue chosen. It signified that the PLO and King Hussein had decided to bury the hatchet. On 11 February 1985, following the Amman meeting, Arafat and Hussein signed an accord enabling Hussein to explore the possibility of a settlement with the United States. In March, Hussein visited Egypt and won Egyptian support for this new diplomatic initiative. In the same month, Hosni Mubarak and Prime Minister Shimon Peres met in Cairo, where Peres restated the Israeli position, calling for an American mediated agreement and direct negotiations between Israel and a Palestinian-Jordanian delegation without representatives of the PLO. It was thus clear that Peres would consider exchanging territory for peace. It now seemed as if the peace efforts were gathering momentum although, with the exception of the PLO, no other party had made a fundamental change in its position. Even the PLO wavered in its acceptance of UN Resolutions 242 and 338, which required the Arab countries and the PLO to recognize the state of Israel.

The reasons for this reluctance were not difficult to understand. The February 1985 Amman accords between Arafat and Hussein had been based on three conditions. First, that the PLO would categorically accept UN Resolutions 242 and 338 which required the PLO to recognize the state of Israel but did not require (at this stage) a reciprocal recognition of the PLO's right to self-determination by Israel. Second, the accords required that the PLO categorically renounce terrorism, which meant it would have to forego the option of armed resistance against Israel although no such renunciation was required of Israel. Lastly, the PLO would be required to declare its willingness to negotiate with Israel, which meant abandoning the very cause that bound the Palestinian community together in its struggle for a homeland. All this the PLO would have to do in return for an invitation to an international conference where its role would remain ambiguous and where it would receive no advance commitments regarding recognition, representation, or self-determination. As far as the PLO was concerned, Israel would gain what it wanted most—diplomatic recognition by the neighboring Arab states. In contrast, the PLO would gain an irrevocable and certain split in its ranks. In the PLO's view, this was an unfair bargain.

It was not surprising then that Arafat sought refuge in ambiguity and hesitation. But his position within the PLO was shaky at best. The fact that Arafat had acceded to Hussein's demands in Amman showed how desperate he had become. Thus on the one hand, the PLO's willingness to go along with Hussein's initiative spurred on the peace effort. In the final analysis, however, its success depended on the extent to which the PLO was willing to compromise its quest for a homeland by conceding to Jordan domination over its future. These considerations had prevented progress in the past and, though pushed back momentarily in 1985, were likely to threaten the chances of a negotiated settlement in the future.

Even so, in June various names were suggested for the joint Jordanian-Palestinian delegation. Israel continued to object to any member of the PLO on the joint delegation and, following the Israeli positions, the United States refused to negotiate directly with the PLO. King Hussein had been insisting on an international conference, with the Soviet Union and Syria present at the talks. The United States and Israel initially objected to this also, but later both the Peres and the Reagan administrations agreed to pursue negotiations under an international umbrella, provided such a forum would lead to direct talks between the disputing parties.

The dissident groups within the PLO had been active as well. The hijacking of the TWA flight 478 and the Italian cruise ship Achille Lauro and the terrorist attacks in Vienna and Rome were intended to derail the ongoing negotiations. But negotiations survived the acts of sabotage. Indeed, the attacks may have had the opposite effect, for there was now a distinct sense of urgency in Washington, Tel Aviv, and Amman and a growing feeling that the time was ripe for a breakthrough in the Middle East. In December 1985, King Hussein met President Assad of Syria to normalize their strained relations. This further boosted hopes of a negotiated settlement. Throughout January 1986, U.S. negotiator Richard Murphy held a series of meetings with Hussein and Peres, hoping to persuade Hussein to constitute a delegation acceptable to the Israelis, and urging Peres to accept the idea of an international forum where it would talk directly with Syria. The United States insisted, however, that such a conference not have the power to modify or overrule any decisions that might be reached in the direct talks.

A New Urgency

Several developments were responsible for the renewed search for a durable peace in 1985. In Israel, Labor Party leader Shimon Peres had become prime minister at the head of a national unity government in August 1984. Peres favored the Reagan Plan concept and was anxious to work out a bilateral arrangement with Jordan along the lines of an Egyptian-Israeli agreement. In addition, Israel's domestic situation had created compelling reasons for Peres to go along with U.S. peace efforts. The Israeli economy was in shambles, with runaway inflation, rising unemployment, and a growing emigration of young Israelis to America in search of a better life. The country's economic woes, and its total dependence on the United States in the wake of the 1982 war brought Peres to power, but he faced the awesome task of repairing consequences that were close to disasterous. What was worse, he was working against a deadline. According to the terms of the coalition agreement, Peres was scheduled to hand over his office to Yitzhak Shamir of the Likud bloc in October 1986. Whereas Labor favored exchanging territory for peace on the West Bank, the Likud had rejected such a compromise. If negotiations began to look like a serious possibility, and Peres agreed to talks, it was very likely that the Likud bloc would walk out of the coalition government. In this event, Peres could call for early elections and consolidate his position. Various opinion polls showed that during 1985, the Labor Party enjoyed a slight edge over its rival in national popularity. Apart from these immediate political considerations, however, the Labor Party was of the opinion that Israel could not afford a state of permanent war with its neighboring Arab states and that the weakening of the PLO had provided Israel with a historic opportunity that should not be frittered away.

The Palestinians also felt that time was not on their side. The loss of Lebanon as a base had meant that they must now rethink their political and military options. There was also the remorseless logic of the expanding Jewish settlement on the West Bank. The Likud was committed to the annexation of the occupied territories. If it came to power and carried out its resolve, no future Israeli government would be willing or able to withdraw from them.

For Jordan too, the victory of Likud posed a grave threat. The Likud program envisaged the partition of Jordan into an Arab and a Palestinian state. In this event, Hussein would have no choice but to either accept this solution or face the prospect of frustrated Palestinians seeking to turn Jordan into the next military base for their continuing crusade. A PLO, weakened by having been driven out of Lebanon and split by the secession of pro–Syrian-Palestinian forces was easier for Jordan to influence and perhaps even to control. By getting Arafat to agree to a joint Jordanian-Palestinian negotiating delegation, Hussein hoped to initiate a series of talks with the United States, leading to negotiations with Israel. Hussein hoped that such negotiations would produce mutual recognition between the Arabs and Israel and create a Jordan-West Bank confederation in which Jordan would act as the senior partner.

There was yet another reason why Hussein was anxious to accelerate the peace talks. Throughout 1985, the Reagan administration's proposed sale of arms worth $1.5 billion to Jordan remained bogged down in an aggressively pro-Israeli U.S. Congress. Persuaded by the pro-Israeli lobby, the Congress forced the administration to freeze all Mideast arms sales pending a review. In October 1985, the Reagan administration notified Congress to proceed with its long-delayed proposal, but once again the package was shelved on the grounds that Jordan hold direct talks with Israel. This Hussein could not do without dealing himself out of the peace process altogether.

The U.S. Strategic Response

The question still remained as to why the United States had nurtured these peace moves and gone so far as to underwrite them with a mixture of promised rewards and threats. There was a growing realization in Washington that the policies of the early 1980s had produced grave dangers in the Middle East without altering the situation in ways that would ensure the United States and Israel's dominance.

Though Israel was the unquestioned military superpower in the region, it had paid a heavy price for this status. The 1982 war had nearly destroyed the Israeli economy and seriously divided the country. Operation "peace for Galilee" had failed in most of its objectives. Israel had won the war itself, but still faced a Soviet-backed Syria that was far more influential and powerful than before. In the same way, the war had forced yet another diaspora on the Palestinians but had not put an end to Palestinian nationalism. Israel had to deal with a million **Palestinians** within its territory and two million on the West Bank. The **split in the PLO** had produced a more amenable Arafat but also a more **intransigent Habash**. Finally, terrorism had gained a new lease on life. As if all this were not enough, the war had spawned a formidable and unpredictable new force in Lebanon—Shia fundamentalism—whose success in pushing the Israeli army out of Southern Lebanon could be viewed as a harbinger of things to come. The U.S. desire for a negotiated peace was thus essentially a belated attempt to establish control over the military-strategic balance in Southwest Asia.

Declining Importance of Oil

Further east, the sharp drop in oil prices has blunted the edge of U.S. concern over safeguarding its own vital interests, and enabled it to take a more discriminating approach to the member states of the region. In February 1983, Secretary of State George Shultz spoke to the House Foreign Affairs Committee of the vital importance of the Persian Gulf to "the economic and political security of the free world." Three years later, in his opening presentation to the same body on 5 February 1986, Shultz did not mention the Persian Gulf or the Middle East except in the context of international terrorism. This was only one of many signs of the declining importance of the oil question in U.S. global strategy. Nevertheless, the staying power of the Islamic Republic in Iran and the growing attraction of Sunni fundamentalism in Egypt could hardly be comforting to the United States. Khomeini's militant Islam remained the one element over which the United States had absolutely no control. Indeed, the drop of oil prices from $29 a barrel to under $20 a barrel had proved a mixed blessing, for it has greatly weakened the pro-American moderate Arab states in the Gulf and made them increasingly vulnerable to the revolutionary Islam being exported in Teheran.

According to a 1985 study by the U.S. Central Intelligence Agency, the return of thousands of unemployed workers to their home countries posed a grave threat to the stability of Egypt, Jordan, Sudan, and Yemen. The study estimated that by the end of 1986, one million to one-and-a-half million migrant workers were likely to return to their home countries. This, it believed, was likely to result in a sharp decline in remittances. According to one estimate, Egypt accounted for 43 percent of all Arab migrant labor. Over the next 2 years, 2 million Egyptians were expected to return. Some scholars called this a demographic time bomb, but the situation was equally dismal for even leading oil-producing states such as Saudi Arabia and Kuwait. According to industry figures, Saudi income from oil had plummeted from $120 billion in 1980 to $43 billion in 1984 and was estimated to drop to $25 billion in 1985. This had produced large-scale dislocation in the Saudi economy, halted important projects, and forced the Saudis to drastically cut back their planned investment.

During 1985 Kuwait expelled some 6,000 people—almost all of them Shiite Moslems of Iranian or Lebanese descent—following suicide truck-bomb attacks on the American and French embassies and an attempted assassination of the country's ruler. This was another danger facing all the pro-U.S. traditional monarchies or sheikdoms in the region. As the CIA study indicated, Washington was fully aware of its implications for U.S. interests. The most dangerous future for the United States would be the emergence of a growing, economically discontented majority turning to Islamic militancy in desperation and anger. The United States is likely to do all it can to prevent this, whether these efforts called for strengthening traditional regimes or keeping the peace initiative alive and on track.

The 1985 shifts in Soviet policy toward the Middle East also acted as a spur to the U.S. peace effort. The Soviet Union's policies had remained in tandem with those of Syria, but Moscow had shown a growing interest in an international conference on the Middle East, not ruling out the possibility of recognizing the state of Israel, provided Israel adhered to UN Resolutions 242 and 338.

Last but not least, the Reagan administration was probably tempted to equal, if not better, the achievements of the Carter administration at Camp David. It had become increasingly sensitive to the fact that the administration's place in history was more likely to be secured by diplomacy than force, though true to its original design the administration had not decreased the level of its military support in Southwest Asia. On the contrary, strategic agreements with Israel were strengthened enormously. Israel remained unaffected by the "freeze" imposed on all Middle East states during the summer of 1985. According to one estimate, the administration was proposing to raise the 1987 military aid to Israel by $90 million, bringing the total to a whopping $3.09 billion. Similarly, Washington had quietly and without much fanfare expanded military facilities in Oman. Egypt and Jordan also received particular attention, both believed to be of key importance in the defense of U.S. interest and objectives.

Early on in the second term of the Reagan administration, several directions were then apparent. First the United States, like Israel, had realized that however modified by the 1982 war, the Palestinian problem remained and had to be addressed. Delay was likely to weaken the moderate coalition of Arab states and strengthen the radical dissident elements and even increase the likelihood of a reentry of the Soviet Union and other rejectionist states into Middle East politics. Second, the administration had moved away from using arms assistance to secure declarations of anti-Soviet sentiment from its Arab allies. In Reagan's second term, the United States was more anxious to use this assistance to bring the regional states more in line with its own diplomatic goals. Third, the administration had finally accepted the argument that any real peace would have to be endorsed by the Soviet Union and Syria, though it was firm in denying both of them a direct veto power over the negotiation process. This new approach represented a definite departure from its earlier policy of denying Moscow any role whatsoever in the region and Syria any influence in Lebanon. Fourth, in an important shift of perspective, the administration sought to isolate the problems of terrorism from its efforts to draw disputing parties to the conference table. Similarly, it had tried to limit the spread of Islamic fundamentalism, particularly Khomeini's, thereby preventing it from destabilizing the region or derailing the negotiations. At the November 1985 summit in Geneva, both Moscow and Washington agreed to refrain from interfering in the Iran-Iraq War. Lastly, while the administration turned to diplomacy, it had not abandoned its strategic design nor Israel and Egypt's special role in this design. Nor had the administration abandoned the idea of bringing as many Arab states as it could within a framework of U.S. mediated agreement.

Thus, what distinguished the U.S. approach in Reagan's second term from the first was a willingness to press forward with serious effort if the potential for successful negotiations were apparent. This approach was markedly different from the one that had characterized the administration's policy during 1981–1982. The Reagan administration had also shifted tactics in allowing the regional actors Jordan, Egypt, and the PLO bear the burden of negotiations and the onus of success or failure associated with it. The administration thus appeared far more conscious than before of the basic dilemmas facing the states in the region and their precarious political stability. Indeed, this shift in emphasis from force to diplomacy was tacit acknowledgement of the weakness of the "military first" approach initially adopted by the administration. The one important conclusion at the end of the first Reagan term was that the Arab-Israeli conflict would not yield advantage, let alone be settled, unless the United States became more responsive to the diverse sensitivities in the region, particularly those of its opponents. As the developments of 1985 showed, diplomacy and compromise enhanced U.S. influence in the region as much as, if not more than, that resulting from the use of force.

Despite the inevitable uncertainties, throughout 1985 the overall strategic and political situation in the Middle East remained favorable to the United States. The disruptions caused by Islamic fundamentalism, the rising incidence of terrorism, and the continuing civil war in Lebanon did not affect the fundamental fact that in the first half of the 1980s the U.S. was the preeminent external power in the region. In contrast, Soviet influence remained extremely limited. It had few allies, and even these were none too firmly wedded to the cause of advancing Soviet objectives in the region.

The United States and Afghanistan

The administration's growing sensitivity to regional developments were not confined to the Middle East alone. During 1984 and 1985 there was a marked tilt toward a regional approach in U.S. dealings with India and Pakistan, though on Afghanistan the administration's perceptions and the main thrust of its policies remained unchanged. The United States in fact stepped up its assistance to the Afghan *Mujahadeens*. According to press reports, by 1985 the U.S. assistance program was a substantial $250 million a year—the largest CIA-funded secret operation since the Vietnam War. On the diplomatic front, the Geneva talks on Afghanistan produced no tangible progress. Tiring of the diplomatic impasse, and anxious not to appear weak, Moscow had been escalating its military operations in Afghanistan since 1983. Local cease-fires were not renewed, and the bombings and search-and-destroy missions in Afghanistan were stepped up. *Pravda* warned the Reagan administration that every U.S. escalation would be met with equal force on the Soviet side. By early 1985, the Soviet operations had moved much closer to the Pakistani border and Soviet planes had begun to exercise the right of hot pursuit into Pakistani air space with growing frequency. At Konstantin Chernenko's funeral, General Secretary Mikhail Gorbachov warned Pakistan's President Mohammad Zia, that although Moscow was ready to pursue a diplomatic option, it was equally prepared to step up military operations if the situation so required, but under no circumstances would the Kremlin countenance a prolonged stalemate in Afghanistan. The 1985 round of Geneva talks on Afghanistan must be viewed against this background.

At the end of these talks in December 1985, Pakistan's Foreign Minister Yaqub Khan reported that the first three "instruments," dealing with agreement on mutual noninterference, international guarantees, and the return of the refugees had been finalized. The talks had, however, stalled on the text of the fourth instrument concerning the timetable for Soviet troop withdrawals, which Moscow insisted could only take place after the refugees had returned to Afghanistan. In contrast, the United States and Pakistan demanded a reverse order, insisting that troop withdrawals should precede the return of the refugees. The one hopeful change in this situation was that in December 1985, the United States announced its willingness to extend guarantees of noninterference, provided the rest of the agreement worked out in line with its own and Pakistan's position. While the United States continued to see an advantage in keeping the issue of Afghanistan on the front burner, the regional context of its Afghan policy had undergone a significant change.

India-Pakistan Relations: A Change of Perceptions

The hardening of the Soviet position in Afghanistan had grave implications for Pakistan. It meant that Pakistan must continually risk more for its continued inflexibility at Geneva and for its role as a conduit for U.S. arms to the Afghan *Mujahadeens*. Zia's awareness of these dangers was evidenced in his attempts to reduce tensions on Pakistan's eastern border. At the Delhi meeting in December 1985, both Zia and India's Prime Minister Rajiv Gandhi agreed to refrain from attacking each other's nuclear facilities; step up trade, travel, and cultural exchange; and resume immediate discussions on merging Pakistan's no war pact proposal with India's counterproposal for a treaty of friendship and peace. The India-Pakistan normalization paralleled a growing warmth in ties between India and the United States. The first of two of the new Prime Minister Rajiv Gandhi's visits to the United States in 1985 resulted in a major agreement to transfer U.S. technology to India.

Indeed, the many and varied events of 1984–1986 ensured that India would remain very much in the public eye in the United States throughout the mid-1980s. The assassination of Indira Gandhi and the smooth transfer of power to her son in December 1984; the reassertion of Indian democracy in free elections (notwithstanding the harrowing traumas of the previous two years); the signing of the Assam and Punjab accords soon after the accession of the Prime Minister; and the statesmanship and strength displayed by Indian leaders in dealing with internal and external challenges strongly impressed the Reagan administration. It reconfirmed what had been evident ever since the 1971 war in Bangladesh—that India had gained "subcontinental preeminence" and "great power status" and that Pakistan could "no longer obtain strategic superiority on the subcontinent."

In the mid-1980s, the widening gap between India and Pakistan in terms of military and economic strength had become even more pronounced. The recognition of this fundamental reality was clearly apparent in the contradictory trends in Pakistan's policies. Throughout the 1980s, Pakistan had sought to achieve a technology feat by pouring all available resources into efforts to outstrip India in the nuclear weapons field.

It had sought the guarantee of Pakistan's security and large weapons assistance from the United States. Pakistan was expected to be less accommodating on this score when the present program ended and a new weapons package, beginning 1987, was under discussion. While its expanding military ties with Washington created serious tensions with India, Pakistan had sought to neutralize this. It had at no time allowed the diplomacy of India-Pakistan normalization to lapse for too long. Indeed, in pursuing both tracks, Pakistan underscored the fact that it had the choice between accommodating the Soviet Union (thereby reducing the risk of retaliation across the Durand Line) and India (in which case it would not need massive U.S. assistance), and continuing in the strategic role assigned to it by the United States. Accommodating Moscow clearly held appeal for those who believed that Pakistan, in serving American interests, was placing its own in unnecessary jeopardy. Others, distrusting India and fearing Soviet expansionism, opposed it vehemently. The increasingly fierce, although suppressed, internal debate over Pakistan's foreign policy had become embroiled with growing domestic opposition to Zia's dictatorial regime. By painting Zia as a lackey of a foreign state willing to jeopardize the security of his nation to keep himself in power, the opposition had succeeded to some extent in undermining Zia's position.

Pakistan's internal weakness had serious implications for U.S. policy in Southwest Asia. It was now clear to the Reagan administration that its massive weapons assistance could not stabilize the Zia regime. Although the administration was now more or less convinced that Soviet and Indian collusion to dismember Pakistan was unlikely, it was aware that Pakistan had to nevertheless deal with the Soviet Union on the west and India on the east. The United States was aware that, faced with growing domestic instability, even the Zia regime could find accommodation with the Soviet Union and India an attractive option. In other words, the changed circumstances in South Asia had forced the United States to question Pakistan's commitment to U.S. objectives in the future.

At the same time, impressed with India, many in and out of the administration had argued that the United States erred by selecting the weaker state in South Asia as the major vehicle of its policy. What was required, according to this line of reasoning, was an aggressive effort to compete with Moscow for influence in India. The problem with this argument was that India's perceptions of the Soviet Union were radically different from those of Washington.

The fact remained, however, that as far as the Reagan administration was concerned there was no great advantage to be had from settling the Afghan crisis so long as it did not spill over into Pakistan. Thus strengthening Pakistan with arms and economic assistance remained an important element of U.S. policy. The United States thus faced a dilemma: India was theoretically a better bet to contain Soviet influence in Southwest Asia, but India would not play the role the United States wanted it to play. By contrast, Pakistani President Zia was eager to play such a role, but there was no guarantee that Pakistan would either want or be able to do so in the future.

Thus during President Reagan's second term, the paradox of power had begun to sink into the administration and to affect perceptions and policies. The United States was learning, albeit after inflicting great cost on the nations of the region, that at best war was an extension of diplomacy; it could never be a substitute for it.

February 1986

Maps

I: The Region: Southwest Asia/Middle East

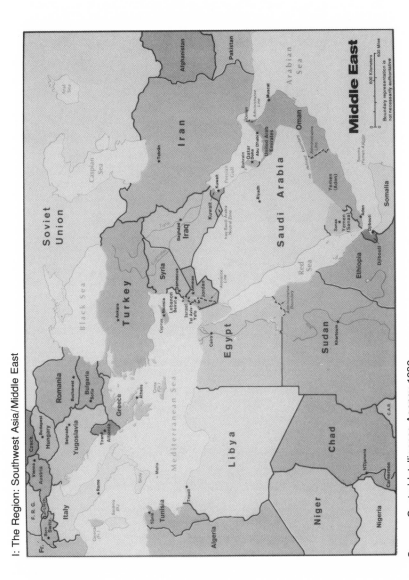

Source: Central Intelligence Agency 1982

II: Areas of Concern: Middle East/Southwest Asia

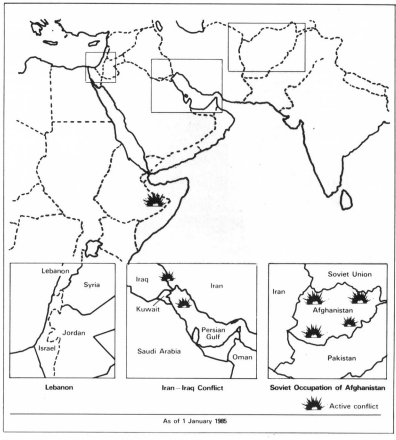

Source: Department of Defense, Annual Report FY 1982

III: Area of Concern for U.S. Rapid Deployment Forces in Southwest Asia

Source: U.S. Department of Defense, Annual Report FY 1982

Selected Bibliography

This bibliography lists only those books, articles, and documents that were of value in the preparation of this book. While not including every work or source I have consulted, it represents the range of material upon which I have drawn in formulating and supporting my ideas, and suggestions of the complex interactions between the United States and the nations of Southwest Asia.

BOOKS

Amirsadeghi, Hossein, ed. *The Security of the Persian Gulf.* London: Croom Helm; New York: St. Martin's Press, 1981.

Anderson, Jack. *The Anderson Papers.* New York: Random House, 1973.

Ball, George. *United States Policy in the Middle East.* Washington, DC: Center for Contemporary Arab Studies, April 1984.

Bhargava, G. S. *South Asian Security after Afghanistan.* Lexingon, MA: Lexington Books, 1983.

Bligh, Alexander. "Opposition Activities and Recent Trends." In *The Arabian Peninsula: Zone of Ferment,* ed. Robert Stooky. Stanford, CA: Hoover Institution Press, 1984.

Bonine, M. E., and Nikki Keddie, eds. *Modern Iran: The Dialectics of Continuity and Change.* Albany, NY: State University of New York Press, 1981.

Bowman, Larry W., and Jan Clark, eds. *The Indian Ocean in Global Politics.* Boulder, CO: Westview Press, 1981.

Brown, Harold. "U.S. Security Policy in Southwest Asia: A Case Study in Complexity." Occasional Paper, School of Advanced International Studies, Foreign Policy Institute, Johns Hopkins University, 1981.

Brzezinski, Zbigniew. *Power and Principle: Memoirs 1977–1981.* New York: Farrar, Straus and Giroux, 1983.

Carter, Jimmy. *Keeping Faith: Memoirs of a President.* New York: Bantam Books, 1982.

Chawla, Sudershan. *The Foreign Relations of India.* Encino, CA: Dickenson, 1976.

_____ , and D. R. Sardesai. *Changing Pattern of Security and Stability in Asia.* New York: Praeger, 1980.

Collins, John M., and Clyde R. Mark. "Petroleum Imports from the Persian Gulf: Use of U.S. Armed Force to Ensure Supplies." Washington, DC: Library of Congress, Congressional Research Service, 1979.

Cudsi, Alexander, and E. H. Dessouki, eds. *Islam and Power.* Baltimore: Johns Hopkins University Press, 1981.

Dawisha, Adeed. *Saudi Arabia's Search for Security.* Adelphi Papers, no. 158. London: International Institute for Strategic Studies, 1979–1980.

Deese, David A., and Joseph Nye, eds. *Energy and Security.* Cambridge, MA: Ballinger, 1981.

Dunn, Keith. *Soviet Constraints on Southwest Asia: A Military Analysis.* Strategic Studies Institute, U.S. Army War College, 7 December 1981.

Falk, Richard. *What Is Wrong with Henry Kissinger's Foreign Policy?* Princeton, NJ: Center for International Studies Policy, Memorandum 59, July 1974.

Farer, Tom. *War Clouds on the Horn of Africa.* Washington, DC: Carnegie Endowment for International Peace, 1976.

Freedman, Robert. *Soviet Policy towards the Middle East since 1970.* New York: Praeger, 1978.

George, Alexander, ed. *Managing U.S.-Soviet Rivalry.* Boulder, CO: Westview Press, 1983.

Glassman, Jon. *Arms for the Arabs.* Baltimore: Johns Hopkins University Press, 1975.

Grummon, Stephen. *The Iraq-Iran War.* The Washington Papers 10, no. 92, 1982.

Heikal, Mohamed. *Autumn of Fury.* London: Andre Deutsch, 1983.

Hoffman, Stanley. *Primacy of World Order.* New York: McGraw-Hill, 1978.

Hudson, Michael, ed. *Alternative Approaches to the Arab-Israeli Conflict.* Washington, DC: Center for Contemporary Arab Studies, Georgetown University, 1984.

Jansen, G. H. *Militant Islam.* New York: Harper & Row, 1979.

Keddie, Nikki, and Eric Hooglund, eds. *The Iranian Revolution and the Islamic Republic.* Washington, DC: Conference Proceedings, Middle East Institute, 1982.

Kedourie, Elie. *Islam in the Modern World.* New York: Holt, Rinehart and Winston, 1980.

Kerr, Malcolm, and Yassin El Sayeed, eds. *Rich and Poor States in the Middle East.* Boulder, CO: Westview Press, 1982.

Kissinger, Henry. *White House Years.* Boston: Little, Brown and Co., 1979.

Ledeen, Michael, and William Lewis. *Debacle: The American Failure in Iran.* New York: Alfred A. Knopf, 1981.

Lenczowski, George. *The Middle East in World Affairs,* 4th ed. Ithaca, NY: Cornell University Press, 1980.

Litwark, Robert. *Security in the Persian Gulf: Sources of Inter-State Conflict.* London: International Institute for Strategic Studies; Montclair, NJ: Allanheld, Osmun, and Co., 1981.

Malik, Hafeez, ed. *International Security in Southwest Asia.* New York: Praeger, 1984.

Martin, Lenore. *The Unstable Gulf.* Lexington, MA: Lexington Books, 1984.

McLaurian, R. D. *The Political Role of Minority Groups in the Middle East.* New York: Praeger, 1979.

Morris, Roger. *Uncertain Greatness.* New York: Harper & Row, 1977.

Nakhleh, Emile. *The Persian Gulf and American Policy.* New York: Praeger, 1982.

Niblock, Tim, ed. *State, Society and Economy in Saudi Arabia.* New York: St. Martin's Press, 1982.

Nutter, Warren. *Kissinger's Grand Design.* Washington, DC: American Enterprise Institute, 1980.

Oil Diplomacy: The Atlantic Nations in the Oil Crisis of 1978–79. Philadelphia: Foreign Policy Research Institute, 1980. Originally published as *Orbis* 23:4 (1980).

Pakravan, Karim. *Oil Supply Disruptions in 1980.* Stanford, CA: Stanford University Press, Hoover Institution Press, 1984.

Peterson, J. E. *Conflict in the Yemens and Superpower Involvement.* Occasional Paper, Center for Contemporary Arab Studies, Georgetown University, 1981.

Quandt, William. *Decade of Decisions.* Berkeley: University of California Press, 1977.

————. *Saudi Arabia in the 1980's.* Washington, DC: Brookings Institute, 1981.

Ramzani, R. K. *The United States and Iran: The Patterns of Influence.* New York: Praeger, 1982.

Record, Jeffrey. *The Rapid Deployment Force and U.S. Military Intervention in the Persian Gulf.* Cambridge, MA, and Washington, DC: Institute for Foreign Policy Analysis, February 1981.

Reich, Bernard. *The United States and Israel: Influence in the Special Relationship*. New York: Praeger, 1984.

Ricks, Thomas M. "The Iranian People's Revolution: Its Nature and Implications for the Gulf States." Center for Contemporary Arab Studies Reports. Washington, DC: Georgetown University, April 1979.

Rubin, Barry. *Paved with Good Intentions: The American Experience and Iran*. London: Oxford University Press, 1980.

Rubinstein, Alvin. *Red Star on the Nile*. Princeton, NJ: Princeton University Press, 1977.

Rustow, Dankwart. *Oil and Turmoil: America Faces OPEC and the Middle East*. New York: W. W. Norton, 1982.

Schiff, Ze'ev, and Ehud Ya'ari. *Israel's Lebanon War*. New York: Simon and Schuster, 1984.

Sheehan, Edward R. F. *The Arabs, Israelis, and Kissinger*. New York: Reader's Digest Press, 1976.

Steinfels, Peter. *Neo-Conservatives: The Men Who Are Changing America's Politics*. New York: Simon and Schuster, 1979.

Stempel, John. *Inside the Iranian Revolution*. Bloomington: Indiana University Press, 1981.

Stossinger, John. *Kissinger: The Anguish of Power*. New York: W. W. Norton, 1976.

Sullivan, William. *Mission to Iran*. New York: W. W. Norton, 1981.

Tahir-Kheli, Shirin, *The United States and Pakistan*. New York: Praeger, 1982.

Tario, Ali. *Can Pakistan Survive? The Death of a State*. Harmondsworth, England: Penguin Books, 1983.

Tillman, Seth. *The United States in the Middle East*. Bloomington: Indiana University Press, 1984.

Wolfe, Ronald, ed. *The United States, Arabia, and the Gulf*. Washington, DC: Georgetown University Center for Contemporary Arab Studies, 1980.

Yergin, Daniel. *Shattered Peace*. Boston: Houghton Mifflin Co., 1978.

Ziring, Lawrence. *Iran, Turkey and Afghanistan: A Political Chronology*. New York: Praeger, 1981.

ARTICLES

Arjomand said Amir. "Shi'ite Islam and the Revolution in Iran." *Government and Opposition* 16:3 (1981), 293–316.

Ayoob Mohammed. "The Superpowers and Regional Stability: Parallel Responses to the Gulf and the Horn." *The World Today* 35:5 (1979), 197–205.

Banerjee, Jyotirmoy. "Hot and Cold Diplomacy in Indo-Pakistani Relations." *Asian Survey* 23 (March 1983), 280–301.

Bayat, Mangol. "The Iranian Revolution of 1978–79: Fundamentalist or Modern?" *Middle East Journal* 37:1 (1983), 30–42.

Bergstern, Fred. "The Threat from the Third World." *Foreign Policy* (Summer 1973), 102–124.

Chadda, Maya. "Reagan's Strategy in South Asia." *India Quarterly* 38 (July–December 1982), 317–334.

————. "Superpower Rivalry in Southwest Asia." *India Quarterly* 37 (October–December 1981), 501–521.

Chubin, Shahra. "The Soviet Union and Iran." *Foreign Affairs* 61 (Spring 1983), 921–949.

Cooper, Richard, "A New International Order for Mutual Gain." *Foreign Policy* 26 (Spring 1977), 65–119.

Dawisha Adeed. "The Motives of Syria's Involvement in Lebanon." *Middle East Journal* 38 (Spring 1984), 228–237.

————. "Internal Values and External Threats: The Making of Saudi Foreign Policy." *Orbis* 23:1 (1979), 129–143.

Harrison, Selig. "Dateline Afghanistan." *Foreign Policy* 41 (Winter 1980–1981), 163–187.

Khalidi, Rashid. "The Palestinians in Lebanon: Social Repercussions of Israeli's Invasion." *Middle East Journal* 38 (Spring 1984), 255–267.

Levy, Walter J. "Oil: An Agenda for the 1980's." *Foreign Affairs* 59 (Summer 1981), 1079–1101.

Menashri, David. "The Shah and Khomeini: Conflicting Nationalisms." *Crossroads*, no. 8 (1982), 53–79.

Mottahedeh, Roy. "Iran's Foreign Devils." *Foreign Policy*, no. 38 (1980), 19–34.

Paul, Jim. "Insurrection at Mecca." *MERIP Reports* 10:91 (October 1980), 3–4.

Peterson, J. E. "Guerrilla Warfare and Ideological Confrontation in the Arabian Peninsula: The Rebellion in Dhufar." *World Affairs* 139:4 (1977), 278–295.

Petrossian, Vahe. "Dilemmas of Iranian Revolution." *The World Today* 36:1 (January 1980), 19–25.

Peterzell, Jay. "Reagan's Covert Action Policy III." *First Principles* 7:5 (March 1982), 1–7.

Pranger, Robert J., and Dale R. Tahtinen. "American Policy Options in Iran and the Persian Gulf." *AEI Foreign Policy and Defense Review* 1:2 (1979), entire issue.

Quandt, William. "Reagan's Lebanon Policy." *Middle East Journal* 38 (Spring 1984), 237–255.

_____ . "Riyadh between the Superpowers." *Foreign Policy* 44 (1981), 37–56.

Rosenfeld, Stephen. "Dateline Washington: Anti-Semitism and U.S. Foreign Policy." *Foreign Policy* 12 (Summer 1982), 172–183.

Rubin, Barry. "Iran's Year of Turmoil." *Current History* 82:480 (January 1983), 28–31, 42.

Sale, Richard. "Carter and Iran: From Idealism to Disaster." *Washington Quarterly* 3:4 (1980), 75–87.

Sciolino, Elaine. "Iran's Durable Revolution." *Foreign Affairs* 61 (Spring 1983), 893–921.

Shankar, N. "Pakistan and U.S. Congress." *Strategic Analysis* 10 (January 1982), 503–513.

Smolansky, Oles M. "Soviet Policy in Iran and Afghanistan." *Current History* 80:468 (October 1981), 321–324, 339.

Spiegel, Steven. "Does the United States Have Options in the Middle East?" *Orbis* 24 (Summer 1980), 395–413.

Thompson, W. Scott. "The Persian Gulf and the Correlation of Forces." *International Security* 7:1 (1982), 157–180.

Tucker, Robert. "American Power and the Persian Gulf." *Commentary* 70:5 (1980), 25–41.

Weinbaum, M. G., and Gantam Sen. "Pakistan Enters the Middle East." *Orbis* 22:3 (1978), 595–612.

DOCUMENTS

Nixon, Richard. *U.S. Foreign Policy for the 1970's I: A Report to the Congress by Richard Nixon, President of the United States.* Washington, DC: U.S. Government Printing Office, February 1970.

Tahir-Kheli, Shirin, and Col. William O. Staudenmeir. *Saudi-Pakistani Military Relationship and Its Implications for U.S. Strategy in Southwest Asia,* ACN 81026. Carlisle Barracks, PA: 1 October 1981.

U.S. Central Intelligence Agency. *The International Energy Situation: Outlook to 1985.* Washington, DC: U.S. Government Printing Office, April 1977.

U.S. Congress. *U.S. Security Interests in the Persian Gulf; Report of a Staff Study Mission to the Persian Gulf, Middle East, and Horn of Africa, October 21*–November 13, 1980. Washington, DC: U.S. Government Printing Office, 1981.

U.S. Congress, Committee on the Budget. *Military Readiness and the Rapid Deployment Joint Task Force (RDJTF)* Hearings 30 September and 1 October 1980. Washington, DC: U.S. Government Printing Office, 1980.

U.S. Congress, Congressional Budget Office. *The Marine Corps in the 1980's: Prestocking Proposals, The Rapid Deployment Force, and other issues.* Washington, DC: U.S. Government Printing Office, 1980.

U.S. Congress, House Committee on Foreign Affairs, Subcommittee on Europe and the Middle East. *Proposed Arms Transfers to the Yemen Arab Republic.* Hearing, 12 March 1979. Washington, DC: U.S. Government Printing Office, 1979.

U.S. Congress, Joint Economic Committee. *Economic Consequences of the Revolution in Iran: Compendium of Papers.* Washington, DC: U.S. Government Printing Office, 1980.

U.S. Congress, Senate Committee on Foreign Relations. *Situation in Afghanistan.* Hearing before the 97th Congress, 2d session. Washington, DC: U.S. Government Printing Office, 8 March 1982.

U.S. Congress, Senate Committee on Foreign Relations. *U.S. Security Interests and Policies in Southwest Asia.* Hearing before the 96th Congress, 2d session. Washington, DC: U.S. Government Printing Office, March 1980.

U.S. Department of Defense. *Soviet Military Power.* Washington, DC: U.S. Government Printing Office, 1981.

U.S. Department of Energy, Energy Information Administration Office of Oil and Gas. *The Petroleum Resources of the Middle East.* Washington, DC: U.S. Government Printing Office, May 1983.

U.S. Department of State, Bureau of Public Affairs. *Middle East Regional Security.* Washington, DC: March 1981.

Index

coup by, 82
demand for arms, 23, 83, 85–86
durability of regime, 218
economic policy of, 220
refusal of bases in Pakistan, 181
and nuclear capability, 22
opposition to, 221, 225

and "period of peril," 177
postponement of elections by, 83
request for treaty, 176
and threat from Afghanistan, 140
Ziring, Lawrence, 2–3
Zumwalt, Elmo, 115

About the Author

Maya Chadda is currently Professor of Political Science at William Paterson College, NJ. She has taught in the past at both Brooklyn College and New York University. Chadda holds a B.A. in Economics from Bombay University, an M.A. in Government from New York University, and a Ph.D. in Political Science from the Graduate Faculty, The New School of Social Research. Her publications include *Indo Soviet Relations* (Vora & Co.); several articles in *Asian Survey, India Quarterly, Institute of Defense Studies and Analysis Journal;* chapters to compendiums on peace studies; and frequent contributions to *The Time of India* and the *Indian Express* on foreign policy and world affairs. Dr. Chadda has worked with the United Nations Development Program as an economic affairs officer and, later, as a consultant.